DATE			

© THE BAKER & TAYLOR CO.

THE ARMS RACE

THE ARMS RACE

The Political Economy
of Military Growth

Miroslav Nincic

PRAEGER SPECIAL STUDIES • PRAEGER SCIENTIFIC

Library of Congress Cataloging in Publication Data

Nincic, Miroslav.
    The arms race.

    Includes indexes.
    1. Armaments—Economic aspects—United States.
2. Armaments—Political aspects—United States.
3. Defense contracts—United States. 4. United
States—Military policy. 5. World politics—
1945- .1. Title.
HC110.D4N54   338.4'76234   81-13808
ISBN 0-03-060332-3   AACR2

Published in 1982 by Praeger Publishers
CBS Educational and Professional Publishing
a Division of CBS Inc.
521 Fifth Avenue, New York, New York 10017 U.S.A.

© 1982 by Praeger Publishers

23456789 145 987654321

Printed in the United States of America

To the memory of my father

PREFACE

After a decade of declining scholarly concern with military matters, particularly those with a strong East-West component, political reality is once again forcing us to redefine our conception of what is most immediately relevant in world affairs. The more recently discovered interest in the relations between developing and developed nations, international stratification, and transnational actors should not be encouraged to wane. Nevertheless, the main current danger stems from the possibility of a nuclear confrontation between the two giants; the human, economic, and ecological costs of this might well overshadow anything humanity has previously experienced. This threat will be substantially shaped by the course of the arms race and, even it does not produce the ultimate catastrophe, the enormous drain that it imposes on our resources impairs our ability to address other needs and challenges. I have attempted in this book to provide a comprehensive analysis of the major causes and consequences of the superpower military competition. Although my own sympathies are, understandably, on the United States side of the overall rivalry, every effort was made to present as balanced and objective a picture as possible.

Several colleagues have been good enough to comment on portions of the manuscript and I have invariably profited from their suggestions. Bruce Russett from Yale University, David Singer from the University of Michigan, and Peter Wallensteen of Uppsala University have been particularly generous with their time and advice. It is a pleasure to record my indebtedness to these friends. My wife, Jacqueline, and son, David, did more than put up with the reclusiveness and occasional grumpiness that accompanied my writing; they provided the warmth, encouragement, and cheer without which I would not have completed the task.

Miroslav Nincic
Ann Arbor, Michigan
June, 1981

CONTENTS

LIST OF FIGURES AND TABLES

Tables   **Page**

THE ARMS RACE

1

INTRODUCTION

It has become commonplace to point to examples of rapid expansion in such crucial quantities as global population, energy consumption, inflation, and so forth. Surging growth is widely recognized as part of the fabric of contemporary life, yet there is usually an awareness that this may ultimately threaten our ability to deal with the conditions of our physical and socioeconomic existence; consequently this awareness often translates into active steps to resist tides of unwelcome growth. One trend, however, to which we seem passively inured is the accelerating, and apparently ineluctable, increase in the capacity for mass destruction and in the resources that this is claiming. Whether or not we recognize and appreciate the nature of this development, its implications are considerable and may represent one of the most oppressive burdens that international society will have to shoulder.

The global community, at the time of this writing, spends the equivalent of over $500 billion annually for military purposes, which is more than the GNP of Africa and the Near East taken together and approximately 500 times the regular budget of the United Nations. These are disturbing figures. Of this, some $350 billion, or about 70 percent of the total, are accounted for by the defense budgets of the United States and the Soviet Union. During the next several years, U.S. military spending seems destined to rise more rapidly than at any time during its postwar history, and the Soviet Union should not be expected to lag too far behind. While each side often laments the enormous outlays that its security claims, neither country has expended more than token efforts at controlling (much less reversing) the trend.

1

If the sums that the two nations devote to expanding their destructive capacities appear immense, the attained capacities are even more disconcerting, both in absolute terms and when placed in historical perspective. Throughout most of history, man's ability to destroy life and property has progressed in a basically incremental manner. It did experience occasional surges such as the first effective military use of gunpowder in the sixteenth century,[1] but these appear to have been comparatively manageable. The first truly momentous discontinuity occured in 1945 with the development and wartime use of the atomic bomb, whose nature altered the parameters of warfare and significantly influenced the conduct of international affairs. Unlike chemical bombs, whose power results from the rearranging of atoms within a molecule, the power of atomic explosives comes from the energy released by the shattering (fission) of uranium or plutonium nuclei.[2] The fission of a single nucleus can release several million times as much energy as the explosion of a molecule of TNT, and the bomb dropped on Nagasaki produced 2,000 times the yield of the largest conventional explosive employed during World War II. Notwithstanding this disquieting feat, barely seven years elapsed before the next quantum leap in destructive potential was taken. The discovery that the energy released from the fission of heavy atoms was in fact paltry compared to that produced by the combining of light atoms of hydrogen, led to the development of the even more awesome thermonuclear (fusion) bomb. Whereas the power of classical explosives was measured in tons (their yield being approximately equal to their weight) and that of atomic bombs in kilotons (each representing the equivalent of 1,000 tons of TNT) the power of thermonuclear bombs called for the use of units representing millions of tons (megatons).

Megatonnage has been unsparingly amassed on both sides as have the warheads designed to deliver them. At present the United States possesses some 10,000 long-range nuclear weapons, while the Soviet Union's arsenals contain over 6,000; these numbers will, moreover, almost certainly be dwarfed by those of the next decade. We seem to apprehend very dimly what the possession of such amounts of nuclear weaponry implies; future generations, one way or another, are likely to have a far better understanding.

Nor has the magnitude of military growth been reflected only in money spent and megatons acquired. Missiles are achieving pinpoint accuracies (thus possibly encouraging preemptive strikes), conventional arms have experienced an insufficiently acknowledged revolution of their own, and weapons placed in the seas, on land, and in the atmosphere may soon be complemented by space-based systems such as laser-beam platforms and armed satellites. Elaborate strategic doctrines have been developed to justify the newest acquisitions, explaining why they are so ideally suited to the cause of national security. (The fact that the doctrines' assumptions often directly contradict those that had been confidently espoused at other stages is rarely considered a problem.) Appropriate belief systems flow from these developments—indeed, it is considered morally wanting in many quarters not to embrace new military systems and unpatriotic not to view the rival superpower with sufficient distrust and revulsion. Moreover, there is little evidence to presage a reversal of these trends.

It is likely that for each manhour of effort directed toward controlling the arms rivalry, at least several thousand are devoted to perpetuating the race and magnifying its proportions. If manhours are translated into dollars or rubles, a similar conclusion is apparent. For example, it is instructive to note that the budget of the U.S. Arms Control and Disarmament Agency represents less than half of what is spent on military bands in the United States.[3] Similarly revealing statistics could undoubtedly be found for the Soviet Union as well.

Arms limitation and arms control seem to be perpetually receding targets. Negotiations occasionally take place and agreements are sometimes reached, but these achievements are easily overshadowed by parallel military developments. For each agreement that seems to portend future moderation, the arms race takes several giant steps forward—crushing the hopes that may have been fleetingly entertained. It is rather clear, moreover, that agreements have been reached mainly where the issues were least contentious and are, thus, of rather modest significance. The ABM treaty of 1972 was born of the general realization that the state of the art did not allow for reliable interception and destruction of incoming missiles. (As the requisite technology is being developed, the commitment to the treaty is being reexamined.)[4] Three treaties were signed to prevent the militarization and nuclearization of the Antarctic, outer space, and the seabed.[5] Significantly, none of the three locations were considered particularly attractive as basing areas for weapons of mass destruction. In 1963, after lengthy efforts, Washington and Moscow signed the Limited Nuclear Test Ban Treaty barring nuclear weapons tests in the atmosphere, under water, and in outer space. Underground tests, which sufficed for most military purposes, were not barred. The agreement was supplemented in 1974, by the Threshold Test Ban Treaty limiting underground nuclear tests to 150 kilotons—a virtually meaningless accomplishment since this exceeded the yield typically required for the new, and increasingly accurate, missiles procured by the superpowers. Both the Vladivostok Accord of 1974 and that portion of the SALT I agreements that concerned delivery vehicles set ceilings on missile and bomber numbers significantly in excess of those characterizing existing arsenals. SALT II, the only treaty that would have set meaningful limits on nuclear arms, was considered unacceptable to the U.S. Senate and withdrawn from ratification. The Comprehensive Test Ban talks, which were initiated in 1977, have sought to prohibit *all* nuclear tests by the Soviet Union, Great Britain, and the United States; as yet, they have produced no tangible result. Nor, for that matter, have the Mutual Force Reduction talks, designed to limit conventional force deployments in Europe, and which have been underway since 1973. Not only have past efforts failed to produce meaningful constraints, but some, it can be argued, may actually have further stimulated the arms race. As the parties rush to acquire bargaining chips (weapons meant to strengthen their leverage in negotiations) the development of new systems is accelerated. Ultimately, it appears, these systems tend to be accommodated within the agreement rather than negotiated away.

What, one may ask, are the consequences of all this? I do not believe that many scholars or statesmen would seriously argue that the superpowers enjoy more security now than when they possessed considerably less numerous and less powerful weapons. As I shall argue at some length, the most plausible assessment is that military rivalry has increased the costs entailed by a *permanently dubious* level of security. It will also be argued that, while cyclical effects sometimes obscure the fact in the United States, long-term economic problems may be partly attributable to the military burden. In the Soviet Union, the economic consequences are even less ambiguous.

It may also be asked whether arms races do not actually threaten security by increasing the likelihood of warfare? Our understanding of the causal connection between the two phenomena is as yet inconclusive, but what evidence we do have is by no means heartening. One recent study (covering the period from 1816 to 1965) found that disputes preceded by an arms race escalated to war 82 percent of the time, whereas those that were not eventuated in war only 8 percent of the time.[6] Another piece of research showed that serious disputes in the twentieth century tended to lead to warfare in only 2 percent of the cases when neither side was experiencing rapid increases in its military spending, but in 33 percent of the cases when both protagonists were expanding their military outlays at a very fast rate.[7] These are not reassuring findings.

Finally, it bears stressing that the consequences of superpower military activity transcend the two countries' borders. Quite apart from the fact that the effects of a nuclear duel (should this be the ultimate outcome) will not be confined to the territories of the belligerents, the lack of Soviet and U.S. restraint encourages military growth on a broad international scale. The anticipated race in European-based theater nuclear forces is a direct extension of the superpowers' competition and it may mean that the brunt of destruction will be borne by others than themselves. Nuclear proliferation is another consequence that the international system must suffer. The number of nations possessing nuclear weapons seems to be doubling approximately every 11 years: at that rate there may be about 30 such states by the year 2000. Clearly, this is a trend that suggests many disturbing scenarios. The Non-Proliferation Treaty of 1970, sponsored principally by the superpowers, has been the only substantial attempt to arrest the process. Signatories that did not possess nuclear devices agreed not to seek to acquire them, and the United States and the Soviet Union undertook to "pursue negotiations in good faith on measures relating to cessation of the nuclear arms race at an early date and to nuclear disarmament" (Article 6). Their utter failure (and lackluster efforts) has deprived Soviet and U.S. efforts to restrain nuclear proliferation of any semblance of moral authority and has seriously weakened the treaty's foundations. Furthermore, superpower military activity does not create international ramifications exclusively by the damaging example it sets. The willingness of both sides to export sophisticated conventional arms, often to the nations that are most likely to use them, induces regional arms races where they might not otherwise exist and increases the costs of conflicts when they do occur (see Chapter 6).

This is an inglorious record and it may seem surprising that it generates so little adverse reaction within the United States and, to all appearances, within the Soviet Union. While the authoritarian nature of the polity and the lack of objective information may account for this in the Soviet Union, one is more mystified at the low level of public concern in the United States. Most people, when pressed, would probably deplore the situation but, plainly, it does not command the attention and affect that, say, the current problems of the U.S. automobile industry do. An astonishingly low level of political awareness is part of this apparent apathy. In a Roper poll of December 1978, only 34 percent of the respondents could identify the two nations involved in the SALT negotiations. (When this was done for them, only 58 percent showed that they knew the talks involved long-range weapons, 27 percent simply had no idea, and the rest were fairly evenly divided between those who thought the negotiations concerned troop reductions in Europe, Soviet-U.S. trade, and halting arms transfers to developing nations.)[8] Nor do people seem measurably more concerned about the ultimate ends to which the most destructive weapons could be put. This may be because of the sheer magnitude of the disaster that nuclear warfare would entail, something for which there are no adequate standards of historical reference.[9] Perhaps it is difficult to feel concern about something that one has so much trouble envisaging.[10] Partly, also, unconcern may be the result of the amount of time we have lived with the danger (people seemed more disturbed about the prospect of nuclear war in the 1950s) and of the likelihood that we shall never again enjoy a world that is free from the threat of nuclear annihilation. "Impending disaster has become an every-day concern, so commonplace and familiar that nobody any longer gives much thought to how disaster might be averted."[11]

Statesmen and military leaders have not contributed much to public enlightment on the nature and causes of the problem; nor is it reasonable to expect that they should. More often than not, they are quite comfortable with the notion that, lamentable though this no doubt is, it is the inevitable outcome of the other side's ambitions, aggressiveness, and baseness. Even when they do rise above this level of discourse and understanding, their position usually involves only a partial perception of the overall problem. Also, the temporal horizon of political leaders (and others as well) is such that, while proximate consequences might be adequately understood, implications are rarely traced down a sufficiently long causal chain.

Under these circumstances, what is the role of social scientists, particularly those who spend a significant portion of their profes-sional efforts grappling with these issues? One suggestion may be that their main responsibility in this regard is to sensitize as large an audience as possible to the nature of the predicament. Perhaps, but this should not be pushed too far, and if the preceding pages suggested that this book was to be an exercise in consciousness raising then they were misleading. Academics should certainly be charged with identifying problems, and they do bear some respon-sibility for bringing them to the public's attention. Others, however, may be considerably better at sounding the clarion, while the social scientists' academic insight should induce them to concentrate on providing the descriptive and analytical foundations needed to penetrate the problem. Important issues should certainly be selected and their contours traced, but the main task should be to discern relevant patterns of causation, to indicate how undesirable causal developments might be diverted or reversed, and to suggest how those that are beneficial might be reinforced.

Explicit and systematic knowledge, articulated by those with adequate training in the area, is not the only basis on which good policy can proceed. For example, it has recently been pointed out that "ordinary knowledge," based on common sense and casual observation, is often better suited to social problem solving.[12] I do not entirely disagree. The layman frequently has the right answers where the academic does not, and intimate knowledge and everyday wisdom are sometimes more useful than formal analysis. The point, however, is that ordinary knowledge may be best suited to coping with ordinary problems—those that we deal with recurringly, most often successfully, and that are not of particularly momentous import. If a problem is conspicuous by its tenacity, this suggests that casual empiricism and common sense are not serving us well. If the unresolved problem is of manifest significance, we should certainly feel compelled to try harder by mustering whatever capacity for disciplined analysis we possess. Social science should never aim to be abstruse, but it should aim to systematically dissect the structure in which the problem is imbedded and to demonstrate "the range of possible alternatives and the potentiality for effective action."[13]

As far as the arms race goes, this will require much work by many people, and this book has a limited goal: to interpret pertinent beliefs and knowledge, to place various claims in better perspective, and to suggest some first steps on policy that, in my opinion, seem particularly promising. The principal causes of military growth in the United States and the Soviet Union will be probed and compared, and an effort will be made to fathom its short-term and long-term consequences. The economic dimension of these questions will be emphasized more than is usually done in works of this sort. An attempt will be made to link trends in weaponry to strategic doctrine and to see in which direction the causal arrow points more strongly. The arms trade will be discussed and considerable attention will be devoted to the concept of security itself. Finally, a significant portion of the book will address strategies (most of which remain untried) for curbing a process over which control is rapidly being lost.

There are several focuses through which these questions might be examined. One could view military growth through the prism of some index of overall destructive power, or through that of specific types of weapons; one might focus on the quantitative aspect of the process or on its qualitative side, and so forth. In this study, two indicators will be used to define and to trace the arms race: military budgets and the development of strategic weaponry.

To a certain extent, a nation's spending for any purpose provides an idea of the human and material resources that it applies toward achieving a certain end—it thus says something about the capacity to attain assigned goals. It also taps degree of commitment, that is, the costs that will be accepted in the pursuit of these goals. For these reasons, military budgets do provide a useful and inclusive indicator of military activity. Strategic weapons are usually defined as nuclear weapons that can be used against the rival superpower's homeland. These are the deadliest weapons that the United States and the Soviet Union possess, and they define the frontiers of extant destructive power. While there are other aspects of arms race behavior that could be discussed (e.g., conventional weapons), these two facets should provide the handle needed to address the relevant questions.

Throughout, there will be no attempt to pretend that the odds favor arms limitation rather than the perpetuation (perhaps even acceleration) of past trends. They do not and few things are as unprofitable as facile optimism. Under the circumstances, efforts to understand the problem must be extremely vigorous, and policies must be adequately informed. The first question should concern the causes and consequences of Soviet and U.S. military growth. Let us begin with the United States.

NOTES

1. Gunpowder (or its predecessors) had been used even earlier on occasion. Rockets, for example, were used for diversion by the Chinese in the twelfth century.
2. Typically uranium 235 or plutonium 239.
3. According to Nigel Calder, *Nuclear Nightmares: An Investigation Into Possible Wars* (New York: Viking Press, 1979), p. 158.
4. See, for example, Richard Burt, "After Almost a Decade, the ABM Argument Is Resumed," *New York Times*, August 30, 1980.
5. These are the Antarctic Treaty of 1959, the Outer Space Treaty of 1967, and the Seabeds Arms Control Treaty, which entered into force in 1972.
6. Michael D. Wallace, "Arms Races and Escalation," *Journal of Conflict Resolution* 23 (1979):3-16.
7. J. David Singer, "The Management of Serious International Disputes: Historical Patterns Since the Congress of Vienna." Paper delivered at the Eleventh World Congress of the International Political Science Association, Moscow, August 1979.

8. Reported in David W. Moore, "The Public Is Uncertain," *Foreign Policy* 35 (Summer 1979):70-71.
9. There have, nevertheless, been a few recent attempts to depict its likely consequences and initiation. See Calder, op.cit., and Louis René Beres, *Apocalypse: Nuclear Catastrophe in World Politics* (Chicago: University of Chicago Press, 1980).
10. This is discussed in Robert J. Lifton, *The Broken Connection* (New York: Simon and Schuster, 1979).
11. Christopher Lasch, *The Culture of Narcissism: American Life in an Age of Diminished Expectations* (New York: W. W. Norton, 1979).
12. Charles E. Lindblom and David K. Cohen, *Usable Knowledge: Social Science and Social Problem Solving* (New Haven, Conn.: Yale University Press, 1962)
13. Barrington Moore, Jr., *Political Power and Social Theory* (New York: Harper, 1962), p. 159.

2

ACCOUNTING FOR
U.S. MILITARY GROWTH

While certain groups within each superpower may claim that their own nation's strength is inadequate relative to that of their adversary, few would deny the fact of mushrooming defense programs and swelling military budgets. To the extent that a debate exists among scholars, it usually centers on whether this pattern of seemingly inexorable growth represents a race (in the classical sense of a contest fueled by the dynamics of competitive rivalry) or a response to forces originating within the superpowers' own societies. The debate is rarely cast in binary, "either-or," terms but typically seeks to compare and to rank the causal impact of endogenous and exogenous drives—a pertinent matter both from a purely theoretical standpoint and in terms of arms-control and disarmament policy. The dust has by no means settled on the controversy and, while it will not be resolved in this book, several significant issues bearing on the U.S. military effort should at least be clarified.

If the arms race is ever to be curbed, a better understanding of the dynamics that underly it must be acquired. This chapter will begin by examining the evidence for and against the notion of a reciprocally stimulated arms race. Following this, the likely domestic determinants of both growth and fluctuations in U.S. military programs and outlays will be surveyed and discussed. As suggested in the previous chapter, the focus will be on the acquisition of strategic weapons as well as, more generally, on levels of overall defense spending.

IS THERE A COMPETITIVE ARMS RACE?

The intuitively compelling and generally accepted notion is that, just as nations fight one another in wartime, so do they have one another in mind when arming in peacetime. The notion of an interactive and competitive arms race is, indeed, central to the theory of international conflict, the study of superpower inter-action, and the current debate on arms policy. The idea is simply the following: observing changes in one's rival's capabilities, the reaction is to do better or at least to match these changes; this, in turn, leads the rival to take another large step forward, which generates another cycle of response and counterresponse, and so on. Thus is born an arms race on the model of, say, the British-German naval race or the French-German land-army race, both preceding World War I.

The basic assumption, of course, is that defense policy is interactive, that what each side does is a response to a previous or current activity of an opponent's. If the other side were to cease all activity of a given sort so presumably would the first. These are, indeed, the conceptual lenses through which most of the U.S. public views the arms race and on which the military's spokesmen rely when justifying their desired programs as necessary and prudent responses to parallel Soviet initiatives. The notion of a continuous pattern of action and reaction has also enjoyed con-siderable academic acceptance. Much of this has rested on the pioneering work of Lewis Fry Richardson[1] who first provided a formal model of competitive arms races—in fact, the pattern itself is often termed a Richardsonian process in recognition of his contribution. Nevertheless, and despite its compelling simplicity, the "action-reaction" model has never claimed total adherence, and several critics have either placed interactive dynamics low on their list of significant causal influences or else, like defense analyst Albert Wohlstetter,[2] dismissed the concept altogether as a valid explanation of U.S. defense efforts. Debates, when cast in purely conceptual terms, can become interminable, and the most useful thing at this point might be to examine some relevant data in order to gain a first grip on the merits of the hypothesis. While data on entire weapons systems are understandably hard to come by, particularly in the Soviet case, fluctuations in overall levels of military *spending* can be estimated for both nations. Yearly changes in both U.S. and Soviet defense budgets are plotted in Figure 2.1 for the period spanned by the available data. If the Richardsonian hypothesis does indeed have some foundation, increases on the

U.S. side should follow on the heels of a USSR shift in the same direction; the same rule should, furthermore, apply to decreases.

A simple visual inspection of the graph does not suggest an evident lock-step pattern to fluctuations in superpower military budgets. At times they do seem to move in tandem, at times they appear to progress along independent paths and, occasionally, they seem to be driven in opposite directions. The eye is, nevertheless, an imperfect instrument of empirical analysis, and a more rigorous view of the process can be obtained by presenting the data in the form of a simple two-by-two matrix. This is provided in Figure 2.2 where instances of both increases and decreases in U.S. military spending in each year t (in 1972 dollars) are associated with either growth or decline on the USSR side during the preceding year.

A number of unexpected observations emerge from this table. While Soviet spending increased during 21 of the 28 years covered here, only 8 of these instances were matched by subsequent U.S. increases; approximately 62 percent of the time (on 13 occasions) the U.S. response was to let its real level of spending *fall*. At times, Soviet decreases were met by U.S. increases and, slightly less frequently, by an U.S. decline. The ϕ^2 measure of association (0.03) is hardly indicative of a compelling correlation. The picture changes slightly if U.S. spending is viewed in *current*, rather than

FIGURE 2.1
Yearly Changes in Superpower Defense Spending

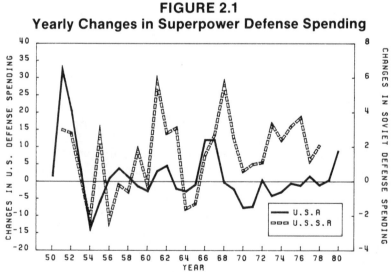

Note: Data on the United States are in billions of 1972 dollars as reported in the *Economic Report of the President, 1981*, Washington, D.C. (The fact that 1972 dollars are used implies that the nominal value of 1979 spending, for example, would be more than 60 percent higher.) Data for the Soviet Union are explained in Figure 4.2.

constant, dollars. The major difference is that 19 rather than 13 instances of growth appear and that in only 38 percent (rather than 62 percent) of the cases did an U.S. spending decrease follow a Soviet increase. Nevertheless, the association between the two nations' trajectories is extremely modest in this case as well (ϕ^2 = 0.05).

This appears damaging to the hypothesis, but it need not be critically so; it may simply be that to expect a continuous and yearly pattern of response is to place an overly heavy burden on the model. Although the dynamics may not always operate in a continuous fashion, it is possible that *major* discontinuities and changes will follow this pattern in a more obvious manner. It seems conceivable, for instance, that abrupt reversals in U.S. defense spending or the development and deployment of new strategic weapons are usually responses to comparable Soviet actions. In other words, competitive dynamics may be most obviously operative *beyond a certain threshold* of defense activity. To investigate this possibility, three instances of major discontinuities on the U.S. side will be examined, each of which has frequently been explained precisely as a reaction to some major USSR initiative. These are: (1) the accumulation of a massive ICBM force in the

FIGURE 2.2
U.S. Responses to Changes in Soviet Military Budgets: 1952–79

| | | Soviet Union t-1 | | |
		Increases	Decreases	Sum
United States	Increases	8	4	13
	Decreases	13	3	15
	Sum	21	7	N = 28

Note: $\phi^2 = 0.03$
Source: Same as for Figure 2.1.

early 1960s; (2) the deployment, a decade later, of a system of MIRVed missiles; and, (3) the reversal, around 1975, of the post-Vietnam decline in real levels of U.S. defense spending. While this does not provide a fully comprehensive survey, it does incorporate some of the most momentous changes—each of which was of an apparently reactive nature—in the nation's postwar military posture.

Bridging the Missile Gap?

Although the development of certain light missiles such as the air-breathing Snark and the Navajo proceeded soon after World War II, serious work on long-range missiles seems not to have been undertaken before the early days of the Eisenhower administration.[3] Even then the efforts seemed rather lethargic and, by the summer of 1957, the United States had not flight tested any ICBMs. One major reason for the absence of a strong sense of urgency was the Soviet Union's perceived technological inferiority. The notion of USSR backwardness was, in fact, so widely accepted that the first test flight of a long-range Soviet missile in August 1957 came as an unwelcome, and very jarring, revelation, which was surpassed in impact only by the launching of Sputnik just two months later. The adversary's intercontinental delivery capability was unambiguously demonstrated and dire predictions were made of its consequences for U.S. security. Senator John Kennedy made the issue of a "missile gap" a central part of his presidential campaign and warned of an even greater Soviet lead in the 1960s. The Department of Defense was similarly concerned, congressional committees were charged with examining the situation, new scientific talent was mobilized, and a crash program to overtake the Soviet Union's ICBM force was initiated. The results were predictable: the first U.S. intercontinental missile was successfully flight tested in December of 1958 and the first Minuteman squadron became operational in 1962. By 1964 the United States had over 400 ICBMs (as opposed to 90 for the Soviet Union) and two years later the number had swelled to over 90.[4]

Here we have the appearance of a clear action-reaction sequence—initial Soviet achievements were met by major and successful U.S. efforts to match them. The notion of an interactive arms race thus seems vindicated in this first instance of an important U.S. strategic program. One apparent illustration does not, however, constitute definitive evidence. Furthermore, there is nothing in the paradigm that dictates that a response must always be made with a functionally equivalent weapon. Strategic logic may in fact require something rather different; such was the case with the decision to develop the MIRV system, for example.

The Decision to MIRV

Since the discovery, in the early 1960s, of a string of radars along the "Tallinn line" on the western edge of the Soviet Union, U.S. intelligence sources speculated that the Soviets were well on their way toward developing an ABM system designed to track and destroy incoming U.S. missiles. In November 1964 a huge cannister, dubbed the "Galosh," deemed to contain an interceptor missile was displayed at the Moscow military parade. In 1966, to the consternation of defense analysts, the Soviets began deploying a ring of these missiles around Moscow and the resulting threat to the United States was interpreted in terms of deterrent logic: if an ABM system protecting Soviet cities from an U.S. retaliatory strike was successfully deployed, a major constraint on a USSR first strike would be removed and, therefore, the very essence of deterrence would thus be jeopardized. Pentagon hardliners and their supporters argued that the nation's security required an ability to penetrate Soviet defenses and that this could best be acquired by placing several warheads on U.S. missiles. By thus MIRVing the missiles, it would be possible to outnumber and to overwhelm Soviet ABMs and a functioning system of deterrence would be preserved. The reasoning prevailed and, in 1970, the first United States MIRVed missiles became operational.

Again we have the apparent ingredients of a Richardsonian process: the Soviet Union developed an ABM system capable of threatening U.S. retaliatory capacity, and the U.S. reacted with the logical counterweapon. The image of a lock-step movement is reinforced and we seem to be moving closer to a confirmation of our initial suspicions. While this second example illustrates the existence of nonequivalent strategic responses, neither of the two instances concerned the more obviously quantitative race involved in reciprocal upward adjustments of *spending levels* for military purposes. It is to this that we will now turn.

Military Budgets in the 1970s

Following the peak of U.S. military involvement in Vietnam, trends in the nation's defense spending were reversed and began to decline. While outlays reached $73.5 billion in 1970, the figure three years later was unchanged, which represented an actual fall in real terms. In 1975, however, a sharp shift in this downward trend became apparent and, by 1977, military spending rose to $94.3 billion, which, even in real terms, amounted to a 28 percent climb. At the time of this writing, the increase shows no sign of abating. Can this dramatic change be explained as a response to a corresponding leap in Soviet defense budgets? A seemingly strong case can be made in support of this statement. In 1975 the Department of Defense vigorously challenged existing CIA estimates of Soviet military spending and soon an eight-page document was published by the Agency in which the previous estimates of the former's military outlays were substantially revised.[5] By the new estimates, the outlays amounted to $114 billion dollars, which meant that, instead of the previously assumed rough parity, the Soviet Union were actually outspending the United States by a full 40 percent; it also meant that their defense budget accounted for 13 percent of their GNP—more than twice the U.S. figure. This new estimate, which was prominently advertised in the media and enthusiastically pounced on by hardliners, alarmed much of the public and many policy makers within the nation—that same year marked a substantial increase in the U.S. military budget, which has been growing rapidly ever since.

Again the notion of a closed system of interlocking decisions seems vindicated: a reversal of previous trends apparently followed a realization that the other side had been investing much more heavily in its own military activities than had been previously assumed.

What should we conclude? Three major decisions in U.S. military procurement have just been reviewed, and each suggested that abrupt and significant changes on the U.S. side were prompted by previous Soviet initiatives of a comparable sort. Nevertheless, there remains some ambiguity about the model and additional discussion and probing is necessary. In the first place, the concept of an action-reaction pattern is still somewhat fuzzy; it may, for example, be viewed as much in terms of *responses* to preexisting threats as from the perspective of *anticipatory* reactions to subjectively perceived challenges. This distinction is crucial to the examples at hand, since it can be argued that, in none of these instances, were the U.S. decisions taken in response to preexisting and real Soviet threats. This seems like a strong and unexpected statement and some additional explanation is called for. Let us begin by taking a closer look at each of the three cases.

Despite the political impact of the "missile-gap" theme in the late 1950s and early 1960s, there is very little indication that there ever was such a gap to the United State's disadvantage. While it is generally accepted that a "space gap" may have existed at the time, in retrospect, it is doubtful that this translated into a corresponding military disparity, since the early USSR missiles, while appropriate for launching artificial satellites, were too large and heavy to provide a weapon that could be manufactured and deployed in threatening numbers at the time. The fact that the first hard data that became available on missile numbers showed the United States well ahead of its rival supports what is now a general realization. Former Defense Secretary Robert McNamara, one of the major architects of the ICBM program, subsequently recognized that,

> in the course of hedging against what was only a theoretically possible Soviet build-up, we took decisions which have resulted in our current superiority in numbers of warheads and deliverable megatons.[6]

Herbert York, director of Defense Research and Development under the Eisenhower and early Kennedy administrations remarked that,

> As we now know, by the time the numbers of deployed ICBMs became a significant factor in the strategic balance between the two superpowers, the United States was well ahead of the USSR.[7]

The situation seems to have been rather similar with respect to the MIRV program. Although the Soviets did begin deploying a ring of Galosh missiles around Moscow in 1966, construction slowed down the following year and, by 1969, a mere 67 missiles were deployed. By the late 1960s, CIA experts seem to have concluded that the Tallinn system was an air defense system against attack by strategic bombers[8] that could not be used against strategic missiles. Nevertheless, deployment of MIRVed Minuteman III missiles was undertaken in 1970 and, as a result, the number of U.S. warheads reached 4,000 that year—an effort that is logically hard to relate to any conceivable ABM deployment by the Soviet Union.

What this suggests of course is that objective threats do not provide a totally compelling explanation for the U.S. decisions and that, to the extent that competitive interactions were at all relevant, subjective anticipations rather than current threats were the overriding factor. This, by itself, is not a major problem since it only requires a consensus on an extended definition of an action-reaction process. The fact, however, that the predictions that formed the basis of the anticipatory responses were often wrong is more problematic and further beclouds the theory. Are we to redefine the concept to include cases in which preemptory action is taken for anticipated threats that ultimately do not eventuate? The obvious problem is that, by accepting false estimates, one runs the risk of accepting predictions that even their authors may not really have believed but are used as a public rationale for decisions taken in response to other drives. For example, a service of the armed forces desiring a new weapon or a larger slice of the military budget can usually make some more or less plausible claim about future USSR plans to justify its request and, in a situation of imperfect information and intelligence, it may be years before the claim can be adequately assessed and possibly dismissed. Should this be considered evidence of a Richardsonian process?

What about our third example? The increase in U.S. defense spending after the mid 1970s was not based on the uncertain logic of preemptive responses, since it was explained in terms of reestimated values of past and current Soviet levels of spending on military activities. Yet here too we encounter a problem. Despite the association that the U.S. public and many policy makers drew, the increased estimate did not include a revised assessment of that nation's military *strength*. All that had changed was the estimate of how much their military programs *cost*. The CIA's director explained that the upward revision "does not indicate that the Soviets have any more weapons or manpower than previously estimated but rather than the cost of these defense programs is greater than we originally had estimated."[9] Nevertheless, the effect was the same as if actual USSR military output, rather than merely the assessment of its price, had suddenly soared.

The dilemma is obvious here: whether we are dealing with real or perceived threats, the notion of an arms race that is presumably relevant concerns changes in the rival's strength. Had the Soviet Union's strength been reflected in the revised calculations there would have been no real problem; but should one also assume that the concept involves a desire to sacrifice as much or more financially as one's competitor?

It now appears that, even with respect to the big decisions, the historical record does not unambiguously support the action-reaction paradigm. Although it is always easy to set up tendentious examples, the informed reader will recognize that the three cases that have been examined here have frequently been invoked in *support* of the model and, indeed, the prima facie case did seem quite compelling. On the other hand, clear counterexamples could have been suggested as well. For example, how could the model explain the massive U.S. deployment of MIRVs in the 1970s at a time when the ABM treaty had removed even the public rationale for this weapon? How could the Pershing II be explained as a direct response to the Soviet SS 20, since the former "began as an evolutionary improvement to an existing short-range (400 nautical mile) system long before the Pentagon had ever heard of the SS-20."[10] This is not to say that the paradigm is not occasionally relevant: nevertheless, it would constitute a rather fragile foundation on which to build a comprehensive theory of ever-increasing defense establishments and military material.

If there is ample cause for dissatisfaction with the notion of strong exogenous stimulation as the reason for arms race behavior, then where are we to seek an explanation? Perhaps we should turn our gaze *within* the nation. As indicated at the beginning of this chapter, there is some support for the idea that the major push stems from endogenous sources and that interactive dynamics are, at best, of secondary importance.[11] This would be both theoretically interesting and of obvious significance to any discussion of arms-limitation policies. It is, nevertheless, difficult to probe very deeply into the foundations of the hypothesis, since the issues are even more complex and blurred than for the action-reaction model. There, the basic logic was, on the whole, simple and straightforward. This is not the case where internal dynamics are involved, as the nature of the relevant actors is ambiguous and the rules of the game they play are elusive to the observer. Notwithstanding the difficulties, some work has been done on the subject, and there is at least a sense of where the more promising avenues of inquiry lie.

DOMESTIC POLITICS, INTEREST GROUPS, AND THE ARMS RACE

An appropriate way to approach the matter of the domestic determinants of U.S. military growth is to inquire who the pertinent domestic actors are, that is, who is concerned with defense programs and can, at the same time, muster enough clout to make a difference? Those groups that are most frequently invoked are the various bureaucracies and organizations that make up a large part of the entity loosely referred to as the "government." If we tentatively recognize their relevance, the main task is to discern what it is about their constitution and functioning that affects defense activities in peacetime.

One often mentioned attribute of governmental institutions is associated with their method of dealing with a complicated and fluctuating environment. The amount of information that these bureaucracies must process and the staggering complexity that they confront could often make it difficult for them to act in a consistent and predictable manner. To make things more manageable, highly structured modes of behavior, ranging from unofficial routines to codified operating procedures, must be developed and adopted. As behavior is routinized, dealing with its environment becomes more tractable for the organization. Furthermore, it is on the very basis of this routinized predictability that policy can, according to certain scholars, be accounted for. As one eminent foreign policy analyst points out:

> Major lines of organizational behavior are straight, i.e., behavior at one time is marginally different from that behavior at $t - 1$. Simpleminded predictions work best: Behavior at $t + 1$ will be marginally different from behavior at the present time.[12]

This would mean that military growth is principally the result of organizational inertia, a suggestion that endows it with a rather ineluctable quality. Nevertheless, most authors associated with this line of thought would probably also counsel its selective use. Perhaps the most natural application of the hypothesis is to levels of military spending and to changes in these levels rather than to the development of specific weapons; as one frequently quoted source explains:

> Participants in budgeting deal with the overwhelming burdens by adopting aids to calculation. By far the most important aid to calculation is the incremental method. Budgets are almost never actively reviewed as a whole in the sense of considering at once the value of all existing programs as compared to all possible alternatives. Instead, this year's budget is based on last year's budget, with special attention given to a narrow range of increases or decreases.[13]

While this reasoning may provide a partial explanation of trends in U.S. defense budgets there is, even here, some scope for improvement. Most obviously, the fact that the model predicts a smooth, "bit-by-bit" growth in levels of military spending is inconsistent with the jagged trajectory that these movements have actually displayed. It accounts well for changes of a progressive nature but it is flawed in portraying as incremental that which has followed a discontinous path with temporary plateaus surrounded by steep slopes, sharp peaks, and even occasional dips. To depict the point visually, it is useful to plot jointly levels of military spending across time and the yearly differences (increases or decreases) in these levels (see Figure 2.3).

The pronounced volatility of the second series clearly demonstrates how misleading it would be to maintain that smooth and incremental growth is the essence of the trend while the leaps, bounds, and dips are merely occasional and mutually compensating, aberrations. Despite this obvious shortcoming, we have not yet exhausted the explanatory utility of bureaucratic dynamics by focusing on the notion of bureaucratic momentum. Additional insights can be gained by considering the nature of *inter*bureaucratic relations, particularly within the defense establishment itself. It has actually been suggested that such dynamics may be the principal driving force behind U.S. military programs and that its most important manifestation is the competitive rivalry between the Army, Navy, and Air Force.[14] By seeking to match or to outdo each other, they are said to account for some of the most pronounced surges in defense procurement.

For example, the sudden increase in missile capability, and the corresponding acceleration in strategic spending, can be partly explained in terms of interservice competition for a role in long-range missile programs. After the successful launchings of Sputnik I and Sputnik II, the Air Force was in a position to substantially

FIGURE 2.3
U.S. Defense Spending, 1950–80

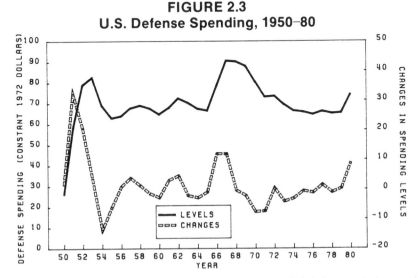

Note: Data are the same as for Figure 2.1. Note that 1972 dollars are being used again.

increase the volume of its space-related activity which, in addition to the Atlas program, came to include the Skybolt missile system, the series of Discoverer satellites, and even a project on controlled thermonuclear propulsion. Largely in reaction to these acquisitions of a rival service, the Navy added to its Polaris program the development of a satellite known as Transit, which was designed to aid navigation. Not to be totally outdone, the Army lobbied for and acquired the Juno I Intermediate Range Ballistic Missile system.

It would seem that as soon as the possibility of adding a function, weapons system, or new slice of funds to the national military effort looms on the horizon, each service strives to garner as big an addition to its previous resources and roles as possible. The logical result is a particularly large pressure for expansion, which leads to an even greater military surge than had initially been anticipated.

This view of interbureaucratic dynamics provides the analyst with additional explanatory leverage. Substantial surges, as well as incremental progressions, can now be accounted for. Yet, even thus equipped, we still cannot explain enough. Military services are not the only influential actors with a vested interest in matters of defense. Furthermore, while intramural military competition may account for abrupt increases when possibilities of new acquisitions and expanded functions appear, it does not explain where these possibilities *originate*.

Perhaps we should, at this point, go beyond the military and search for the origins of the impetus to interservice jockeying. A good place to begin may be with the initial, and often little noticed, advances in military research and development which, according to certain observers, provide the foundation on which much of the subsequent dynamics build.[15] Although the nature of this research is often too esoteric to grasp the attention of all but a very restricted group of people, it proceeds along its own paths and occasionally yields discoveries of considerable novelty and practical appeal. As significant ideas and discoveries are produced, specialized coteries of individuals and groups coalesce around the innovation and develop—even in the early phases of the process—a vested interest in its ultimate adoption. These are the scientists responsible for the original discovery, private interests that anticipate lucrative contracts as producers of the new weapon or equipment, and the agencies and institutions that sponsored the original research. Independent even of the actual military at this stage, they may begin to develop a strategic or tactical rationale for the innovation. It is claimed that it is not only useful but absolutely essential to national security, or that it is the answer to something that the Soviets might possess or be capable of someday possessing. Very soon, the coalition swells to include the military (within which internal rivalry tends to further stimulate demand for the new product) as well as, eventually, their hardline political supporters and some segment of public opinion. By this time, the arguments for actual deployment have been developed and refined and the burden of disproving the need, in the face of imperfect information on what the other side might be contemplating (currently or in the future), falls on the putative, and probably less well organized, opponents of further military growth.

Occasionally this process seems to provide a more satisfactory explanation of major armament decisions than does the assumption of U.S. reaction to Soviet initiatives. For example, it is likely that the decision to develop and deploy MIRVs was at least as a much a response to the push of technological innovation as it was a reaction to the anticipated development of a Soviet ABM system. A brief review of the nature of the push in this particular instance may be instructive.[16]

The capacity to independently target several warheads from the same delivery vehicle reposes on the ability of the offensive missile to undertake a series of rather complicated maneuvers. Following the initial boost, and after the final rocket stage drops off, a "bus" carrying several warheads must coast along a planned trajectory and eject, at the appropriate moment, a warhead at a chosen target. It must then adjust its trajectory and actually accelerate its pace toward a second target at which it delivers another warhead, and the process is repeated until the supply of warheads carried by the "bus" is exhausted.

Though complex and integrated, the capability to execute this set of maneuvers was developed as the result of several previous, and more or less unrelated, projects none of which had a MIRV system as its final goal. The first such project involved the development, in 1960, of a missile named the Able-Star with a propulsion rocket that incorporated a restart and guidance capability. The purpose of this missile, however, was to launch satellites rather than to deliver nuclear warheads. Three years later, a rocket (the Agena) capable of placing a pair of satellites in different orbits was created. Finally, an advanced postboost control system (Transtage) was created for use with the Titan III booster rocket. Like the Able-Star and the Agena, it was capable of coasting and restarting, but could effectuate even more complex and extensive maneuvers (as well as carry a larger payload); its initial mission was to launch a series of defense satellites in different orbits. All the properties of the MIRV weapon were thus assembled from a series of diffuse programs that were unrelated to the objective of overwhelming an adversary's missile defenses.

Although these early developments did not attract much public attention, a movement devoted to ensuring eventual application and adoption gathered momentum as the technology was developed. Soon, since a stronger rationale than the mere multiple launching of satellites seemed necessary for this purpose, the notion and strategic justification for MIRV weaponry was articulated. In its early phases this effort involved mainly the participants in the relevant research and development process, such as the Advanced Research Projects Agency, the Space Technology Laboratory, and the Air Force Space and Missile System Office. Very rapidly it incorporated a number of private industrial and consultant companies such as Lockheed, the Aerospace Corporation, and the Thompson Ramo Wooldridge Corporation. To these were soon added the powerful voices of the Air Force and Navy leadership and even of the Army. The total impact of this coalition was predictably effective and, in 1970, the first MIRVs were deployed and their expansion has, despite the subsequent agreements on ABM limitation, continued steadily since.

On the whole, the process appears to have had an ineluctable quality about it since the outset: as soon as the means were developed the pressures toward practical adoption became overwhelming. As a very close observer of the process has remarked, "Once the technology was developed MIRV assumed a momentum of its own; the chances of halting it were by then slim."[17] Although he recognized the concern that many felt about a possible Soviet antimissile system, he concluded that "even without the stimulus of ABM, however, MIRVs would probably have been devised and probably at about the same time."[18]

The point is that the research and development phase in the development of a new weapon system is marked by low "visibility"; therefore, it does not attract much attention nor generate much opposition. This is the consequence of the relatively modest expenditures involved at this stage, the highly technical nature of the work involved, and the frequent initial vagueness regarding the military purpose to which the innovation will be put. While it does not generate much political challenge, it may well produce the increasingly committed support of groups and organizations with some vested interest in ultimate development, procurement, and deployment. The spectacular current surge in U.S. arms-race behavior is at least partly due to the fact that a number of major technological innovations have emerged in recent years, involving an extremely powerful aggregate of interests.

While the picture is progressively becoming more complete, the notions of bureaucratic and technological drives must, nevertheless, be placed in proper perspective. Despite their obvious importance, none of the actors involved make final decisions on matters of military programs and expenditure. Nor does everything that has strong technical appeal or military and industrial backing necessarily survive beyond the research and development stage. The nuclear-powered airplane and the B-70 and B-1 bombers provide examples of weapons around which powerful bureaucratic, technocratic, military, and corporate constituencies had formed yet did not enter the stage of actual deployment.[19] It is obvious that none of the factors described can account for instances such as these and, perhaps, the most useful explanations should incorporate a higher level of political authority as well. It is not merely a matter of determining how certain vested interests coalesce around new military projects; it is, just as importantly, a matter of understanding what determines the behavior of elected power holders and those who wield final decision power over matters of peacetime defense procurement and spending. The stage of final decision is, furthermore, characterized by high visibility, close scrutiny by the media, and a modicum of public interest. Open challenges must be faced and more than just the preferences of specialized interest groups will have to be taken into account.

Each time their interests become involved, these groups can be assumed to exert considerable pressure on political authorities, and the crucial question will then concern the degree of *responsiveness* that the latter will exhibit toward these pressures. While various groups might press their interests with varying amounts of intensity, it seems unlikely that even identical amounts of pressure would be equally effective at all times and under all circumstances. Certain conditions might make the ultimate decision makers particularly vulnerable so that even slight pressure should produce the desired effect; at other times, they may have reason to display considerable resistance and even the most intense and concerted efforts of such groups will be ineffective. Therefore, it is to the level of political authorities with final decisional power on issues of defense that we will now turn.

POLITICIANS AND DEFENSE ACTIVITIES

It is obvious that ideological differences may determine the general orientation of politicians to the issue of defense, and conservatives in the United States are particularly willing to view foreign policy issues in military terms, as has recently become amply evident. Nevertheless, different forms and levels of military activity will affect the goals and values of incumbents in various ways; to understand their susceptibility to interest group influence, the nature of the interests that incumbents pursue must be understood. Three broad categories of objectives, which are salient to incumbents and affected by military programs, are (not necessarily in this order of significance): (a) national security, (b) economic prosperity, and (c) continued incumbency. As the relevance of the arms race to the second set of goals may be less apparent than that of the other two, most of this section will deal with the economic dimension of defense. Let us begin, however, with the more obvious categories.

Security, the Arms Race, and Domestic Politics

An important concern of virtually every political decision maker is to decrease national vulnerability to external coercive threats. This would probably rank near the pinnacle of most hierarchies of political values and any evidence, albeit dubious, of a growing external threat can be expected to increase the vulnerability of politicians to demands for expanded military activity. This is all the more true given the context of uncertainty within which many defense-related decisions must be taken. Robert McNamara, for example, has justified the massive U.S. deployment of long-range missiles in just these terms; observing that the Soviet Union had demonstrated possession of considerable technological and industrial capacity in the late 1950s, he explained that,

> We had no evidence that the Soviets did plan, in fact, fully to use that capability. But, as I have pointed out, a strategic planner must be conservative in his calculations; that is, he must prepare for the *worst plausible* case and not be content to hope and prepare merely for the *most probable*. . . . Since we could not be certain of Soviet intentions, since we could not be sure that they would not undertake a massive build-up, we had to ensure against such an eventuality by undertaking a major build-up of our own Minuteman and Polaris forces. . . . But the blunt fact remains that if we had more accurate information about planned Soviet strategic forces, we simply would not have needed to build as large a nuclear arsenal as we have today. (emphases added)[20]

The effect of imperfect knowledge is compounded, at least as far as the acquisition of new strategic systems is concerned, by the extent of the lead time that is necessary to produce a major new weapon. A period of 10, 15, or more years is the rule rather than the exception, and to delay new projects pending a definitive clarification of the other side's plans may appear rather irresponsible.

Furthermore, the issue of national security is related to another goal that was attributed to political decision makers: retaining their incumbency. U.S. security from foreign threats is a matter with considerable emotive content and is well suited to political rhetoric and debate—particularly at election time. From the point of view of both the public and the political opposition, incumbents can err in either of two ways: by overreacting or by underreacting to perceived external challenges, but the punishment meted out is likely to be much harsher for the second type of error than for the first. At worst, overresponding may induce mild criticism, and even the charge of stimulating the arms race unnecessarily is salient to only a restricted part of the electorate. On the other hand, to be considered guilty of slighting the claims of national security in the face of a Soviet threat is a far more serious matter, and the costs to an incumbent of such a charge, as well as the benefits to political opponents, are likely to be substantial. As Colin Gray has pointed out, "in all significant respects, the raising of defense as an electoral political issue would seem to have resulted in accelerated arms race efforts."[21]

Thus, the vulnerability of incumbent decision makers to interest-group pressures tends to increase with any information or rumor concerning mounting Soviet capabilities; the difficulty of gauging the adversary's true intentions and the domestic political context account for this. The fact that these interest groups are well situated to produce or interpret such information probably goes a long way toward explaining why both pressures and vulnerability should typically increase at the same time. Indeed, the direst warnings of Soviet threats frequently coincide with the desired introduction of major new weapons—whether it is the original Minuteman missile or the MX system.

All of this would seem to suggest the existence of yet other factors promoting permanent military growth. Nevertheless, when these pressures result from erroneous claims, they may eventually, and for a short time at least, yield counterproductive effects. If the ill-founded nature of a warning is widely recognized, the credibility of alarmist information may be reduced, and irresponsiveness to demands for more spending and new acquisitions is a politically less risky attitude for incumbents to assume. An illustration of this reverse effect is provided by the fate of the B-70 bomber.

A program to develop a supersonic strategic bomber, designated the B-70, was initiated in the mid 1950s. Interests that were mustered in its support included a multitier network of contractors, subcontractors, suppliers, high-ranking military personnel, and so forth. The campaign for the bomber gathered momentum and its support by the administration peaked in the fall of 1960 (at the height of a presidential election campaign often dominated by the missile-gap issue). Yet the bomber was ultimately not deployed despite its enthusiastic support by concerned interest groups and their hardline supporters. While several considerations may have militated against the B-70, one strong reason for its abandonment was that the truth concerning the alleged Soviet lead became generally known and the credibility of shrill warnings on the dangers of inaction and the need for new weapons were treated with some scepticism. Despite the continued clamor by vested interests, presidential support for the airplane plummeted and sufficient congressional succor was not forthcoming. Thus there is some reason to believe that the same vector of forces that drives increased defense activities may, on occasion at least, encourage subsequent curbs on military growth.

The manner in which the domestic political context conditions the link between national security and military expansion is tolerably well understood. An appreciation of the link has reduced the appeal of the concept of a closed and automatic system of responses and counterresponses in superpower defense programs. Though less well understood, another objective of political authorities also affects U.S. arms-race behavior: the perceived claims of the economy.

Economic Needs and the Arms Race

There is a vague public awareness that military needs occasionally serve an economic function as well and that disarmament, while desirable from many points of view, may cause dislocations of a more material nature. The relation between economics and defense is usually not explicitly articulated, but it is generally not disputed either, and good theoretical grounds can be invoked to explain this association. Although the issue has traditionally been more central to radical political and economic thought than to mainstream writings, there are a number of points of potential convergence on this issue.

The lack of long-term viability that many radicals impute to capitalist economies is usually based on their assumed tendency to generate unabsorbable "surpluses." Baran and Sweezy, possibly the most influential authors within this school, define such surplus as "the difference between what an economy produces and the costs of producing it."[22] They maintain that, as capitalism progresses from a competitive to an oligopolistic market structure, the surplus will necessarily rise as a proportion of total output. Neither private consumption nor business investment will, according to these authors, be in a position to adequately absorb it, which, in turn, will lead to inventory accumulation and sluggish or negative growth. Barring periods of "epoch-making innovations" (such as the automobile) an increasing reliance will be placed on the absorptive effects of militarism in an attempt to salvage growth. In the view of most radical authors, however, this can constitute only a temporary panacea to ultimate economic stagnation.[23]

Similar, though less pessimistic, statements can also be made on the basis of the more conventional Keynesian doctrine. While the phenomenon of stagflation has recently led to some reexamination of orthodox economics, the Keynesian legacy still constitutes the basis of economic theory and policy in the West. As is well known, this body of thought rejected the "classical" notions of the automatic adjustment of employment and investment (the former through wages, the latter through interest rates) to levels consistent with healthy economic activity. Rather, due to an inability of savings to smoothly translate into equivalent investment, private demand would fall short of the economy's productive capacity and recession, or even depression, might be the outcome. Government spending should, therefore, supplement private demand to effectuate the necessary adjustment. Since military spending can perform this function on a large scale, it might appear to have an economically useful role as a tool of countercyclical macroeconomic policy— particularly in economies where both public spending in general, and military outlays in particular, represent a significant part of the economy. As John Kenneth Galbraith has pointed out with reference to the United States,

If a large sector of the economy, supported by personal and corporate income taxation is the fulcrum for the regulation of demand, plainly military expenditures are the pivot on which the fulcrum rests.[24]

Obviously, military spending is not a *necessary* tool of economic stabilization, nor should exclusive primacy be accorded to fiscal policy. Monetary policy (manipulating the money supply to affect interest rates and hence investment activity) is another option. Strategies other than public spending are also available, as in the policy of boosting private consumption via tax cuts (as was done during the Kennedy administration).[25] Yet the first strategy may be ineffective in times of severe depression (when interest rates are already so low that an expanded money supply is unlikely to produce much additional impact) and the second may be less potent than direct government spending (since some portion of the money returned to the consumer will be saved rather than spent).

It may, additionally, be argued that public expenditure can assume many forms other than defense spending and that the economic role of military outlays should not be overestimated. There is obviously some truth to this, and exaggerated claims should certainly be avoided; nevertheless, it has been suggested that defense spending is particularly expandable, and often politically more acceptable than public spending for civilian needs. These are important issues and I will return to them but, before proceeding much further, it may be a good idea to examine the recent historical record in the United States.

If military outlays can serve as a tool of countercyclical economic policy, and if political authorities are aware of the fact, one would expect to find an inverse correlation between the more controllable portions of defense expenditure and short-term economic performance. While it is difficult to engage in short-term manipulation of such things as military salaries or the cost of day-to-day operations and maintenance, the government can affect, even on a quarterly basis, the timing and magnitude of prime contracts awarded for equipment, supplies, research and development, and so forth. This provides political authorities with one instrument of "fine tuning" and furnishes the observer with a possible basis for explaining defense activities that are not attributable to the factors previously discussed.

A survey of recent trends and fluctuations is revealing in this respect. For example, as the economy was expanding in late 1956 and early 1957 to reach a peak in August of the latter year, military contracts experienced a decline—dropping from $5.4 billion in the third quarter of 1956 to $4.2 billion for the second quarter of 1957[26] (presumably with the aim of combating the associated inflation). Yet, as the nation descended into the trough of a recession in the second quarter of 1958, contracts increased to $7.4 billion. The recovery that followed peaked in April 1960 and defense contracts fell again, reaching $5.9 billion by the second quarter of that year. As the economy slid into a new trough in

February 1961, contracts increased again as they jumped from $5.2 billion in the last quarter of 1960 to $6.2 billion during the very next quarter. Economic activity experienced a remarkably long expansion in the mid-to-late 1960s reaching a peak in late 1969 and generating substantial inflation in the process—between 1969 and 1970, contracts dropped from $35.5 billion to $33.4 billion. A mild trough occurred in November 1970 and the decline was halted that year. When the economy troughed again in 1975, a new and major phase of military growth was initiated.

The record is not perfect, but the contours of the process are amply discernible, and it is difficult to doubt that fluctuations in military contracts and short-term movements in the economy are, ceteris paribus, inversely associated as a result of a consciously pursued policy. While not entirely unexpected, this is certainly significant, especially from the point of view of arms-control strategies. An interesting issue in this context concerns the manner in which this association is affected by the desire of elected officials to retain their incumbency. The following question is particularly relevant: to what extent do the economic consequences of military procurement influence the electoral fortunes of political office holders? The answer is clearly not simple, since it involves a causal chain that subsumes three specific questions:

1. Does economic performance affect incumbents' chances for reelection?
2. If so, do incumbents attempt to manipulate the economy to their electoral advantage?
3. If so, is military spending also used for electoral/economic ends?

We are not treading on virgin territory here; the third question has been dealt with previously by this author in a collaborative piece of research, and the first two have been competently addressed within the appropriate branches of political science. The results of this work have been revealing. It has been convincingly demonstrated, first of all, that economic conditions do affect electoral outcomes in the United States. Fluctuations in per-capita income and real disposable income have been shown to be particularly reliable predictors of the outcome of congressional and presidential elections, with increases in election and preelection years helping incumbents and declines benefitting the opposition.[27] There is also evidence that indicates that incumbents attempt to manipulate the timing of economic fluctuations to increase the likelihood that upswings will appear at electorally opportune moments, thus giving rise to what has been termed the "political business cycle."[28]

All of this leads to the third question: given their economic impact, can fluctuations in military spending be accounted for in terms of electoral considerations? Though the whole idea may seem a little farfetched at first, some evidence supports its validity. Richard Nixon, for example, recalls in *Six Crises* that Arthur Burns visited him in March of 1960 and

> expressed great concern about the way the economy was then acting. . . . Burns' conclusion was that unless some decisive governmental action were taken, and taken soon, we were heading for another dip, which would hit its low in October, just before the elections. He urged strongly that everything be done to avert this development. He urgently recommended that two steps be taken immediately: by loosening up credit and, where justifiable, by increasing spending for national security.
>
> The next time I saw the President I discussed Burns' proposals with him and he in turn put the subject on the agenda for the next Cabinet meeting.[29]

Although Nixon supported Burns' suggestions, they did not prevail apparently because the economic situation was not considered serious enough. Yet the potential payoffs of such methods were clearly perceived, even in an administration noted for its conservative approach to matters of economic policy.

The idea no longer seems altogether implausible and, if it is indeed correct, we would predict that, other things remaining equal, military spending should increase in the period preceding on-year elections, as incumbents strive to accelerate income growth and to reduce unemployment levels. In the period following the elections, a slowdown in military growth would be anticipated since political needs would no longer be as acute and since efforts would be made to dampen the inflationary pressures that had been generated (to prepare the ground for a new spurt of real growth in the next preelectoral period).

Thus, alongside the previous military/economic cycle dictated by objective economic fluctuations, we also expect to find an associated military/electoral cycle based on the economic link. This hypothesized association has been statistically tested in a piece of research jointly undertaken with Thomas Cusack.[30] An econometric model was designed to account for rates of U.S. military spending that included, among its predictor variables, fluctuations in private aggregate demand (consumption and investment) as well as a variable that indicated the period in the electoral cycle associated with a given year (that is, whether it preceded or followed an on-year election). Linear regression analysis clearly confirmed the predictions. First of all, military spending does accelerate when private demand dips and it slows down when this demand rises. Even more apparent is the tendency for accelerations to coincide with electoral periods and for slowdowns to characterize post-electoral years. Not only does military spending seem to perform an economic function but a related electoral function as well.

The implications of this may be considerable since it may mean that U.S. military growth is imbedded in fundamental national properties: competitive politics and an economy subjected to cyclical fluctuations in an era when political authorities are increasingly being held accountable for economic performance. It is not being claimed that defense procurement must inevitably perform a function in domestic politics and the national economy; it can however be very conveniently used for such purposes.

CONCLUSIONS

This chapter has attempted to cover considerable ground by examining a variety of explanations for the U.S. side of the arms race. The first explanation attributed changes in U.S. force posture or spending levels to previous Soviet initiatives in the context of an escalating spiral of actions and reactions. Overall, the evidence did not seem supportive of this view and, to the extent that a case can be made for it, it would involve only a convoluted process of anticipatory responses to professed beliefs concerning future Soviet undertakings (many of which ultimately did not occur). Nevertheless, this does not imply that Richardsonian dynamics would not materialize under the proper circumstances; the point here is simply that the Soviet Union has rarely managed to precede the United States in major innovations. The United States would almost surely have reacted had this been the case and would have expanded its defense capacity even sooner, faster, and possibly in different directions. Indeed, while Soviet initiatives would probably always constitute a *sufficient* condition for intensified U.S. efforts, they are by no means a *necessary* condition.

We then turned to the currently popular hypothesis that places most of the explanatory burden for military expansion on the momentum of bureaucracies and on the dynamics of inter-service competition for new weapons, extended functions, and increased budgetary resources. When complemented by the notions of the drive of technology and associated vested interests, it was possible to account for both incremental growth and sudden surges in levels of defense activity. Yet we still could not satisfactorily account for plateaus, slowdowns, and occasional reversals of direction. What seemed to be lacking most in all of these explanations was a sense for the broader national conditions and an appreciation of the role and interests of the incumbent political authorities who are responsible for ultimate decisions on matters of military procurement. By slighting the role of the domestic political milieu, we were left with an unnecessarily emaciated theoretical structure and could produce only partial explanations of a complex process. We did observe, however, that the nature of internal political processes may tend to produce military over-reactions due to the political punishments that might otherwise be meted out.

Another suggestion that strongly emerged from a more comprehensive perspective was that the domestic political and economic context could condition the arms race in a fashion bearing little relation to the objective claims of national security. The implications of this are somewhat disconcerting; it implies, in particular, that disarmament and effective arms control may be partially a hostage to electoral concerns and economic fluctuations and, if so, that more conventional considerations (such as the reduction of international tensions) may be of less relevance. If U.S. military procurement and defense programs serve domestic functions for political incumbents, in addition to or despite the international political context and the activities of the adversary, traditional solutions may seem somewhat inapposite. Once again, this does not mean that they must inevitably serve these functions, merely that it may be very expedient to have them do so. The attractions of expedience and convenience must, however, be recognized for it is precisely this that is the stuff of much policy.

Chapter 7 will deal with some of the associated problems in some detail but, for the moment, it may be useful to deal with another aspect of U.S. defense activity: its domestic *costs*.

NOTES

1. Lewis Fry Richardson, *Arms and Insecurity* (Chicago: Quadrangle Books, 1960).
2. Albert Wohlstetter, "Is There a Strategic Arms Race?" *Foreign Policy* (Summer 1974):3-21; and Albert Wohlstetter, "Rivals But No Race," *Foreign Policy* (Fall 1974):48-81.
3. For a description of early U.S. missile and rocket programs, see Edmund Beard, *Developing the ICBM: A Study in Bureaucratic Politics* (New York: Columbia University Press, 1976).

4. For data on trends in comparative numbers of missiles, see Bruce M. Russett and Bruce G. Blair, eds., *Progress in Arms Control?* (San Francisco: Freeman, 1979), p. 6. A classic source of information on these matters are the various annual issues of *The Military Balance* (London: The International Institute for Strategic Studies).

5. *A Dollar Cost Comparison of Soviet and US Defense Activities*, Washington, D.C., SR-78-10002, January 1978.

6. Robert McNamara, *The Essence of Security* (New York: Harper & Row, 1968), p. 58.

7. Herbert York, *Race to Oblivion* (New York: Simon and Schuster, 1970), p. 109.

8. Also see below, p. 414.

9. George Bush as quoted in "CIA Says It Has Underestimated Soviet Defense Costs," *New York Times*, May 19, 1975.

10. Christopher Paine, "Pershing II: The Army's Strategic Weapon," *The Bulletin of the Atomic Scientists* 36 (1980):26.

11. See, for example, Nancy Lipton and Leonard S. Rodberg, "The Missile Race—The Contest with Ourselves," in Leonard S. Rodberg and Derek Shearer, eds., *The Pentagon Watchers* (New York: Doubleday, 1970). For some statistical research on this issue, see A.F.K. Organski and Jacek Kugler, *The War Ledger* (Chicago: University of Chicago Press, 1980), chap. 4.

12. Graham T. Allison, "Conceptual Models and the Cuban Missile Crisis," in William D. Copley and Charles W. Kegley, eds., *Analyzing International Relations: A Multimethod Introduction* (New York: Praeger, 1975), p. 58.

13. Otto A. Davis, M. A. H. Dempster, and Aaron Wildavsky, "A Theory of the Budgetary Process," *The American Political Science Review* 60 (1966): 529.

14. A relevant author is Samuel Huntington, *The Common Defense* (New York: Columbia University Press, 1961). See also Warner Schilling, "Scientists, Foreign Policy and Politics," *The American Political Science Review* 66 (1962): 287-300.

15. See Ralph E. Lapp, *Arms Beyond Doubt: The Tyranny of Weapons Technology* (New York: Cowles Book Co., 1970); and Ernest Yarnarella, *The Missile Defense Controversy: Strategy, Technology and Politics, 1955-1972* (Lexington: University Press of Kentucky, 1977).

16. The standard work on this subject is Ted Greenwood, *Making the MIRV: A Study of Defense Decision Making* (Cambridge, Mass.: Ballinger, 1975). Also see Herbert York, "Multiple Warhead Missiles," in Russett and Blair, op. cit., pp. 122-31.

17. York, op.cit., p. 124.

18. Ibid., p. 131.

19. The B-1 program, at the time of this writing, seems likely to be reactivated by the Republican administration and Senate.

20. McNamara, op.cit., p. 58.

21. *The Soviet-American Arms Race* (Westmead, England: Saxon House, 1976), p. 34.

22. Paul Baran and Paul Sweezy, *Monopoly Capital* (New York: Monthly Review Press, 1966), p. 9.

23. Victor Perlo, *The Unstable Economy: Booms and Recessions in the United States Since 1945* (London: Lawrence and Wishart, 1973); and Ernest Mandel, *Marxist Economic Theory*, vol. 2 (New York: Monthly Review Press, 1970).

24. John Kenneth Galbraith, *The New Industrial State* (New York: Penguin,

1967), p. 235.

25. Discussion of these strategies can be found in any good textbook on macro-economic theory and stabilization policy.

26. Data on military contracts are from U.S. Department of Commerce, *Handbook of Cyclical Indicators, 1978*, p. 121. Economic cycles are as reported in U.S. Department of Commerce, Business Conditions Digest, June 1978, p. 103.

27. Gerald Kramer, "Short Term Fluctuations in US Voting Behavior, 1896-1964," *The American Political Science Review* 65 (1971): 131-43; and Edward Tufte, "The Determinants of the Outcome of Mid-Term Congressional Elections," *The American Political Science Review* 69 (1975): 812-26

28. William D. Nordhaus, "The Political Business Cycle," *Review of Economic Studies* 42 (1975): 169-90. The matter is comprehensively addressed in Edward Tufte, *The Political Control of the Economy* (Princeton, N.J.: Princeton University Press, 1978).

29. Richard Nixon, *Six Crises* (New York: Doubleday, 1962), p. 309.

30. "The Political Economy of U.S. Military Spending," *Journal of Peace Research* 10 (1979): 101-15.

3

MILITARY GROWTH AND
THE U.S. ECONOMY

If the *causes* of U.S. military procurement are to a large extent endogenous, it is appropriate to ask what its major internal *effects* are. Despite their special nature, few public "goods" are free and military power certainly does not belong to the restricted category of those that are. A capacity for mass destruction cannot be acquired without bearing substantial costs and accepting various sacrifices. Since it was suggested in the previous chapter that fluctuations in levels of U.S. defense activities are partly conditioned by the desire to produce politically beneficial economic effects, this chapter will focus on the economic consequences of military programs. How do they affect unemployment, the private sector, and national productivity? While the desired, and often obtained, economic benefits are of a cyclical and easily perceptible nature, the most consequential effects are probably those that are felt in the long run and are diffused throughout the economic system. Such effects are not immediately apparent, yet it is likely that the long-term costs may outweigh the immediate gains.

How should one assess such costs? The simplest method would probably be to adopt the accountant's notion of cost, which is based on the monetary value of an outlay. Using this definition, one would say that the cost of defense to the United States was $49 billion in 1964 and, perhaps, $138 billion in 1980. This is, however, not the most useful approach and it may be more fruitful to rely on the economist's concept of *"opportunity costs"* rather than on the former, more restrictive, notion. The opportunity costs of some activity are given, quite simply, by the value of the alternative goods and pursuits foregone by the decision to embark on the chosen course. It might, for example, be misleading to claim that defense efforts cost U.S. society $138 billion in 1980 if no useful alternative applications were available for these funds. On the other hand, if different uses of this money would have enriched the nation by some multiple of the original outlay, one would obviously underestimate the true costs of defense by adopting the accountant's perspective. The more comprehensive definition will therefore be used in this chapter and, since military programs most obviously concern the public sector, I will begin by asking what alternative uses of public monies, if any, must be sacrificed to the arms race.

DEFENSE AND THE PUBLIC SECTOR

It is frequently maintained that spending for social purposes has put an unjustifiable squeeze on the legitimate needs of the military sector during the past decade or so. Less often, but equally emphatically, it is asserted that defense spending detracts from human needs that should have a prior claim on fiscal resources. While such statements involve important value judgements, they also repose on certain empirical assumptions. Whether or not "butter" has been outrunning "guns" depends, for example, on how these concepts are measured. In the figure for social expenditures by the government, should one include only those sums that are financed through general taxes and are subject, like defense, to annual congressional appropriations? Or should one also count those programs (like social security or highway construction) that are financed mainly by contributions from the direct beneficiaries and are merely administered as a trust fund by the federal government? In the second case, "butter" would seem to be doing considerably better than in the first case. Which base year should one select when comparing the trends in the two variables? If the height of the Vietnam involvement is chosen, as has sometimes been done, the military sector would seem to have lost much more ground than if the base year preceded the U.S. engagement altogether.

These are, however, matters with straightforward implications and the more difficult issue concerns the nature of the causal link between defense and other social needs. Does every dollar spent on tanks, missiles, or officers' salaries *necessarily* imply a corresponding reduction drop in spending for education or health? This assertion is frequently made and, intuitively, it appears evident to the point of tautology. The apparent tradeoff between military and civilian needs has also produced a predictable amount of controversy and political dispute. Conservatives, on the one hand, have adhered to a preference for tight spending at home coupled with a staunch support of military programs. On the other hand, such liberal groups as the congressional Black Caucus, organized labor, or Americans for Democratic Action, have pressed for ample spending on civilian programs either in preference to, or in addition to, expanded military budgets.

While conventional wisdom would tend to view guns and butter as necessarily incompatible, the issue is not entirely clearcut. Different assumptions can lead to different conclusions and, therefore, these should be stated as explicitly as possible.

At the simplest level, a "static" perspective could be adopted by considering a short period of time, during which revenues cannot be expanded and when the only choices involve the apportioning of a fixed sum among different needs through whatever discretionary power political authorities may have. Given this assumption, a tradeoff must obviously exist since, in anything with a fixed volume (and some elasticity), expansion at one end must be matched by retraction at the other. The only way to avoid the tradeoff would be to boost both civilian and military spending at the expense of a third and residual category of expenditure, for example, by reducing the operating budget of the federal bureaucracy. While theoretically conceivable, such solutions are rather implausible as a practical matter and, from the "static" perspective that is appropriate to the very short run, military programs involve clear opportunity costs in terms of public spending for civilian purposes.

In the longer run, the tradeoff may be more debatable. If we consider a length of time spanning at least one full budgetary cycle, it becomes possible to increase public revenues and hence to boost spending for both categories—the problems of the short run thus no longer seem altogether evident. Yet the possibility of opportunity costs does not necessarily vanish, as can be seen by recasting the issue in terms of the respective *rates of increase* in civilian and military expenditure. For example, if both were increasing but at different rates, it could still be claimed that the better performance of one was due to the less impressive performance of the other. In fact, unless government revenues could grow in a completely unconstrained fashion, or if they were bounded only by needs, guns and butter may somehow compete. Whether indeed they do, and to what extent, would depend on additional considerations.

If it were demonstrated that the only reason why one category of spending should not grow as rapidly as desired was that another had laid a prior and stronger claim to available resources, the opportunity costs would be evident; if each gain for one implied a corresponding loss for the other, the substitutibility would be of a "one-to-one" sort. On the other hand, it might be that additions to guns would not affect butter one way or the other. If it were shown that fluctuations in one type of spending were related to additional, and perhaps more salient, considerations, the tradeoff would be far less evident.

As this second possibility needs more explaining, we will pursue the issue by asking what should be the central question: would public revenues in the United States increase as much as in the first place whether they are appropriated for civilian *or* military purposes? If not, the tradeoff might be illusory—guns could not be displacing butter in the competition for a larger share of an expanding pie if the only way of justifying additional revenues is to invoke military needs. In other words, the opportunity costs to the civilian sector should be nonexistent if it could be shown that it would not be more amply funded *whether or not* military spending were simultaneously to increase. The argument may be quite appropriate in the United States where, for a very substantial part of the public, a distaste for governmental presence in social and economic life coexists easily with support for a high level of military preparedness. A strong military posture has typically received more bipartisan support and public approval than have, for example, health, antipoverty, and education programs. Specific pressure groups do lobby for the interests of their constituents, and the Department of Defense does sometimes differ with other parts of the executive branch (and various sectors differ among themselves). However, once a military budget is submitted to Congress, it is rarely seriously challenged, major items are typically not deleted, and the military is occasionally granted even more than it had requested. Such acquiescence has admittedly been somewhat less pronounced in the wake of the Vietnam war. However, a combination of congressional log-rolling in the quest for defense contracts and the traditional priority accorded to national security concerns has meant that the Pentagon is usually spared the routine, and frequently successful, challenges that civilian programs must face.

For this reason, it might be argued that there is no perfect substitutibility between guns and butter in the growing federal budget and that, therefore, every dollar spent for national defense does not necessarily detract a dollar from nonmilitary ends. Nevertheless, the points should not be overstated. An absence of perfect substitutibility does not imply that there is no tradeoff at all, merely that it is of less than one-to-one nature. Thus, while an increase in military spending may not imply an *equivalent* decrease in civilian outlays, it certainly will place *some* limit on its size and growth. There are several reasons why this should be so.

In the first place, the high rates of taxation needed to finance expensive defense programs further lower the tolerance of a public that feels fiscally overburdened to additional levies for whatever purpose. Also the inflation generated by runaway military budgets reduces the willingness of many U.S. citizens to support additional governmental outlays. Thus, while military expenditures are often more acceptable at the outset than spending for civilian needs, they may *further* limit the expansion of nondefense spending. This, in any case, seems to be the opinion of those well placed to know. A principal economic adviser to President Kennedy has explained that,

Since defense makes government budgets frighteningly large and taxes unpleasantly high, political instincts and pressures work to restrain the growth of other government activities and of revenues to finance them.[1]

In a similar vein, Lyndon Johnson's chairman of the Council of Economic Advisers has remarked that, as a direct result of the swelling military expenditures occasioned by the involvement in Vietnam,

The federal civilian program in the January 1966 budget and every budget thereafter was a good deal lower than would have been desirable and possible had it not been for the military emergency.[2]

While there is a dearth of serious empirical investigations on this subject, it seems likely that, while the opportunity costs of the arms race in terms of civilian needs are less than the full value of the defense expenditures, they are nevertheless real and that the military's gains are in some part society's losses. Currently, this is being illustrated in a very obvious manner.

Nor is the tradeoff exclusively reflected at the federal level, since one consequence of the pursuit of military power may also be the reduction of the real revenues of state and local governments. In the first place, the curbs on disposable income occasioned by the fiscal claims of military programs naturally affect the ability of governments of any administrative level to extract resources for their particular needs. In addition, resistance to state and municipal taxes will be aggravated by inflation attributable to defense spending, which may, in fact, produce two additional effects. In the first place, as the price of the goods and services that these governments must purchase increases, the real value of their revenues will fall unless their nominal value (and thus taxes) grows at a more rapid rate than inflation. Since resistance to such growth is likely to be strong, the governments will be able to provide less. Secondly, and less obviously, state and local governments often meet a substantial portion of their needs by borrowing on financial markets. Inflation, however, drives up the interest rates that they face, and more revenue must consequently be devoted to debt servicing. This, in turn, means that the share of the revenues that can be devoted to the needs of the government's constituents must shrink.[3] The losses to civilian programs may, therefore, actually exceed those that can be identified at the federal level.

If we are to base our conclusions on the defense budget's impact partially on inflation, we must ask precisely how military spending contributes to rising price levels. While economists have done little to enlighten us on this score, at least one statement should seem evident: all inflation is not "made in Washington" and culprits other than government spending should be recognized. To the extent that a substantial part of modern inflation is of the "cost push" rather than of the "demand pull" variety, it is the result of such factors as noncompetitive market structures, the power of organized labor, and the scope of collective bargaining. Furthermore, some of it is attributable to entirely exogenous circumstances, such as an increase in the price of major imports or a surge in foreign demand for U.S. grain.[4] Nevertheless, some of the onus must be borne by massive government spending as well, particularly that part of it that is not matched by corresponding taxation. To the extent that military spending accounts for a large portion of the total, and is at least partly financed by deficit spending, it too must bear a share of the blame for the persistent and serious inflation that the United States seems destined to live with in the foreseeable future. By injecting additional purchasing power into the economy without simultaneously increasing the amount of goods and services available to the civilian consumer, the military budget helps drive up the price of what is available. In fact, it may well be that the military dollar is *more* inflationary than the public dollar appropriated for civilian ends. Empirical research is still scanty and economists have taught us little on this issue, yet it is a fact that spending for such things as roads will contribute, at least indirectly, to the sum of goods and services available to the consumer; military outlays will not.

A glance at the time plot of fluctuations in defense spending and inflation during three recent decades (see Figure 3.1) supports the view that, while the two variables are not linked by a perfect association, military growth is not irrelevant to price levels. The series moved in virtual tandem in the very late 1940s and early 1950s and, although defense spending has been more volatile, along generally similar paths until the late 1960s. Since then, "cost-push" inflation appears to have taken over although a joint upward surge has been registered since 1975. It is being claimed, with increasing frequency, that inflation is the most threatening current economic problem for the United States; if this is indeed so, and a strong case can be made for the proposition, any successful deflationary policies would have to acknowledge the influence that expanding military programs are likely to have on price levels.

The focus so far has been rather narrow. The opportunity costs of defense are not felt solely in the public sector and it is necessary to expand the scope of our inquiry if a comprehensive view of these costs is to be acquired.

JOBS AND THE ARMS RACE

If the expansion of military power does involve sacrifices in terms of civilian needs (though perhaps less than is sometimes

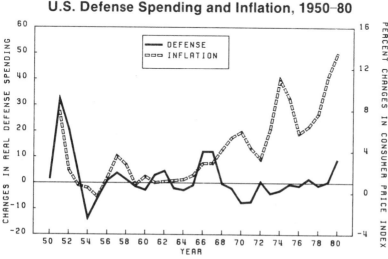

FIGURE 3.1
U.S. Defense Spending and Inflation, 1950–80

Note: Data on both defense spending and inflation are from the *Economic Report of the President, 1981* (Washington D.C.).

claimed) its most helpful role seems to result from an ability to generate a large number of jobs. Since the reduction of unemployment is a major goal of macroeconomic policy and an important concern to the electorate, this point deserves close attention.

The issue of jobs lies just beneath the surface of many debates on appropriate levels of military spending and, while the link is not explicitly stated as a rule, it does occasionally surface in the heat of political debates. During the 1972 presidential campaign, Spiro Agnew denounced George McGovern in the following terms:

> While he [McGovern] has gone around the country deploring present rates of unemployment, he is apparently oblivious to the fact that his defense proposals would throw an estimated 1.8 million Americans out of work. But I'm sure the people of St. Louis and the employees of McDonnel-Douglas are not unaware of the fact, especially since the Senator has specifically stated that he would cancel the F-15 as part of his defense cutbacks.[5]

When the Pentagon decided to close a number of apparently unnecessary bases in New England in 1973, a member of the Massachusetts congressional delegation reportedly told Defense Secretary Richardson: "As I've always said, Elliot, you used to have a great political future in Massachusetts."[6] The issue of jobs was an explicitly stated presidential consideration when the advisability of producing the B-1 bomber was being debated.

The question of the Pentagon's ability to create significant employment is thus of obvious political and economic import; it also suggests a number of questions. In the first place, how many jobs are actually created by military programs? Secondly, and more importantly, how does the defense dollar perform at job creation when compared with alternative sorts of expenditure?

Figure 3.2 indicates that periods of high military spending have also been times of relatively low unemployment. Dips in joblessness were particularly pronounced during the involvements in Korea and Vietnam, while the moderate military outlays of the late 1950s and very early 1960s were associated with surges in unemployment. Although there are exceptions to this inverse correlation, most notably in the mid 1970s, the general message is rather clear. Let us then begin with our first question. Estimates of the number of people whose employment is somehow related to the military effort vary, and no consensus exists on a specific figure. On the one hand, there is no great difficulty in agreeing on the employment *directly* attributable to defense spending. Counting the civilian and military personnel on the payroll of the Department of Defense is a

FIGURE 3.2
U.S. Defense Spending and Unemployment: 1950–80

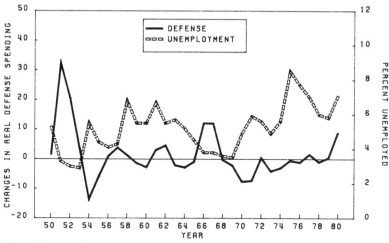

Note: Same as for Figure 3.1.

fairly simple matter; likewise, computing the number of jobs defense procurement provides to principal contractors is not a Herculean task. Things become more complicated, however, when one attempts to estimate how many jobs are *indirectly* related to the military enterprise via the various supporting industries and services—the food producers, the petroleum refiners, the bankers, miners, lawyers, and construction workers whose services and products feed into defense activities, although they may be totally unaware of the military relevance of their work. The task is then to determine the magnitude of the defense employment "multiplier", that is, the number of additional jobs indirectly created for each job that is directly related to defense.

According to one estimate for 1970, with 2.9 million people engaged in the armed forces, 1.2 million civilian employees in the Department of Defense, and 3 million employees in defense industries (principal contractors), a total of 7.1 million people were directly employed in military related activity.[7] Furthermore, the authors of this estimate argue that for each job directly created by defense spending (in both the public and the private sectors) one additional job will be created in related private endeavours. The total level of defense related employment would thus have been about 14 million or 26 percent of the labor force. In 1970, however, the Vietnam involvement was at its height; it might also be unreasonable to assume a multiplier as large as unity. If one were to choose 1976, for example, and assume a multiplier of one half rather than one, the full number of jobs attributable to defense would be roughly 7.2 million—a more likely, but nevertheless quite substantial, figure. Even if we take the latter figure as approximately representative of the magnitudes involved, a number of caveats would have to be made. It would be inappropriate, for example, to assume that the number of unemployed in the United States would have increased by that amount had there been no military spending. Some fraction of the released labor would surely be absorbed by the *private* sector, but just how large a fraction would depend on how well the civilian economy could do without the arms race (a matter to be dealt with in the next section). A certain number could also be employed in the civilian *public* sector, but again, precise estimates would depend on how much of the reduction in military spending could be translated into an increase in nondefense government spending (an issue that has already been discussed). Whatever the ultimately correct answers may be, the more important issue is contained in our second question, that is, does military expenditure make a significantly *greater* contribution to employment than would other, more socially useful, types of spending? In particular, what effect would the same dollar produce were it allocated to some other federal program (e.g., education), or were it, for example, channeled down to state and local governments? Two studies, one conducted by the Public Interest Research Group in Michigan (PIRGIM),[8] the other by the Center for Defense Information,[9] have recently addressed this matter. Both conclude that military spending is not a particularly effective method of creating jobs. PIRGIM compared the number of jobs created by $1 billion of public expenditures for various nondefense purposes (see Table 3.1); it concluded that roughly

TABLE 3.1
Number of Jobs Created by $1 Billion of Public Expenditure

	Number of Jobs
Job Corps	145,000
Teachers	76,000
Nurses	85,000
Police	73,000
Fire	70,000
Defense (military personnel)	58,000

Source: Public Interest Research Group in Michigan (PIRGIM), *The Empty Pork Barrel* (Lansing, Michigan: PIRGIM, 1974).

2.5 times as much employment could be generated via the job corps as through military outlays, while about 50 percent more jobs could be created by other categories of crucial social services.

The results provided by the Center for Defense Information present a similar picture (see Table 3.2) and indicate that several obvious alternative types of spending might perform the employment-generating function better. Public service employment, for example, would create nearly twice as many jobs as would the military dollar, while antirecession aid to state and local governments would do fifty percent better. Although neither study takes multiplier effects explicitly into account, these would have to be quite substantial to mitigate the impression of feeble job-creating abilities.

Yet another study[10] compared the employment impact of expenditures for a specific weapon—the MX—with a set of socially beneficial alternatives. The conclusion, as illustrated in Table 3.3, was that each of the other possibilities would do better at creating jobs.

The appropriate conclusion seems to be that unemployment might, at least in the short run, be aggravated were there no arms race as long as alternative forms of public spending were not available. If the political will needed to fund civilian programs in preference to military needs could be mustered (a dubious prospect at the time of writing), the problem of joblessness could, however, be less acute than it normally is (barring some major downfall in national economic activity). The unimpressive impact of the military dollar is probably due to the fact that the sum of salaries, equipment, and other associated costs tends to be higher in the area of defense (particularly without the draft) than in the other spheres of activity represented in the tables. The equipment used is often very sophisticated and the labor highly skilled. The point

TABLE 3.2
Number of Jobs Created by $1 Billion of Expenditure

	Number of Jobs
Public service employment	98,000
Antirecession aid to state and local governments	71,000
Civilian production	53,000
Defense spending	45,800

Source: Center for Defense Information, "Jobs and the Pentagon: Is Military Spending Good for the Economy?," The Defense Monitor, Sept.-Oct. 1977, p. 3.

TABLE 3.3
Number of Jobs Directly and Indirectly Created by $1 Billion
of Public Expenditure

	Direct Plus Indirect Employment
MX Missile	53,248
Solid waste treatment	65,859
Railroad construction	54,220
Day care	120,496
Solar energy/ energy conservation	65,079
Solar energy	57,235
Mass transit	79,300

Source: David Gold, "MX and the American Economy," Arms Control Today, Feb. 1980, p.4.

for the latter is that it may involve precisely the people who would have the least trouble in finding employment in the civilian sector. Therefore, if military spending is at all guided by considerations of full employment, as seems likely, the policy seems based on misapprehensions. Even so, two caveats are in order. In the first place, one may point out, as was done in the previous section, that public funds may simply not be forthcoming for nonmilitary programs. It may, for example, be much more difficult to raise money for assistance to some depressed area than to boost income levels in the region through a few Department of Defense contracts to local firms. Secondly, there is the matter of the capacity of the private sector to absorb labor released from military activities and this, as has been already suggested, will depend on how healthy this sector would be without military spending. It is to this issue that I will now turn.

DEFENSE AND THE PRIVATE SECTOR

When the intended economic role of military outlays was discussed in the previous chapter, it was suggested that they might be used as countercyclical tools of macroeconomic policy designed to maintain desired levels of growth despite occasionally insufficient levels of aggregate private demand. Can it be said that, in this context, the arms race performs a useful function for the economy?

People of different ideological persuasions will have different ideas on this score. True radicals, assuming that an unabsorbable surplus is a necessary property of capitalist economies, may recognize the short-run utility of defense spending while considering it irrelevant in the long run. Keynesian liberals may also view military outlays as an effective tool for countering temporary downswings; under conditions of normal growth, however, they might regard them as no more than unnecessary deflections from private consumption and investment. Finally, true economic conservatives would tend to view any form of government participation in the economy as inherently harmful, although they may feel that, in this case, the economic damage is mitigated by the gains to national security. There are thus a number of doctrinal orientations that may lead to different conclusions. How then should the true macroeconomic role of the military dollar be evaluated? In the first place, an adequate assessment would have to recognize that the U.S. economy, like virtually all market economies, tends to move through a sequence of clearly defined cyclical phases and that the effect of military expenditure may vary depending on whether the economy should happen to be in an expansionary or a recessionary phase. Secondly, the possibility that a desired short-term effect may produce unwelcome economic outcomes should also be addressed.

In a period of recession, private investment and consumption are typically insufficient to match the productive capacity of the economy and, consequently, labor is unemployed, capital is underutilized, and inventories pile up. In these circumstances, any additional form of spending, particularly one that is relatively easy to generate, can perform a useful absorptive function and dampen the effects of the downslide. Does this mean that military spending should be viewed as a useful tool of countercyclical macroeconomic policy? The answer, perhaps, is that this is an expedient short-run palliative, but that, in the longer run, it is more harmful than beneficial. To begin with, it is much easier to *expand* the military budget to counter temporary downswings than it is to *reduce* it in order to dampen an inflationary upswing—political resistance alone will usually preclude this. The associated problem is that, while increases may fill a void in effective demand during recessions, military spending can actually jeopardize subsequent recovery. By stimulating inflation and driving interest rates up, lavish outlays on military power may imperil the vigor of the upswing, for example by inducing tight monetary policies by the government. In addition, the fiscal claims of swelling Pentagon budgets will almost surely have the effect of curbing civilian investment and consumption, thus reducing levels of private demand and hurting the recovery in another manner. Military spending may thus lead, in two distinct ways, to the very situation that it is then called upon to remedy. The link with inflation has already been discussed and the effect of military expenditure on consumption and investment will now be examined.

Kenneth Boulding, one of the nation's foremost contemporary economists, has estimated that the greatest burden of military spending is borne by the U.S. consumer. By observing economic data for the 40-year period between 1929 and 1969, he noted that the defense budget increased roughly twelvefold as a percentage of gross capacity product—from 0.6 to 8.2 percent. During the same period, personal consumption's share experienced a substantial decline— dropping from 72.6 to 59.8 percent. Consequently, according to Boulding, military spending takes its largest bite out of the nation's consumers.[11] This conclusion is supported by Bruce Russett's research at Yale, which indicated that, for the period 1938 to 1969, each dollar spent on defense implied a loss of 42 cents from consumption.[12]

Without disputing the essence of this conclusion, it should be pointed out that it is relatively easy to overestimate the reductions in consumption occasioned by the arms race. First of all, it could be maintained that much of this consumption would, in any case, have been wasted in frivolous consumption.[13] Perhaps, but this is not so much an economic argument as it is a statement of specific social values. A stronger argument would point out that money returned to the consumer would not have been entirely devoted to consumption, since some fraction would presumably have been saved rather than spent.[14] The implication of this is that, in times of recession, a greater boost can be given aggregate demand by military spending than by relying on individual propensities to consume. In order to keep things in proper perspective, however, the following two points should also be made. By embarking on a military expansion that is very difficult to reverse (except, for example, upon the termination of overt hostilities) a slow but constant erosion is forced on personal consumption's share of national income; this weakens private demand for the goods and services that the economy is capable of producing. This, in turn, may perpetuate a reliance on defense spending as an alternative component of demand. Using the expedient of the arms race to counter cyclical downturns may thus lead to an economic dependence on a form of spending that is not only suboptimal in terms of job creation but, in addition, provides few goods or services capable of satisfying normal social and personal needs.

What effects does military spending produce for investment? By Boulding's estimates, the costs in terms of foregone investments are not momentous. In the same study he noted that, during the 40-year period, investments' share of gross capacity product dropped almost imperceptibly—from 15.2 to 14.5 percent. According to Russett,[15] the loss to investment from defense spending is 29 cents to the dollar. But here, even more than in the case of consumption, it would be misleading to equate the ultimate opportunity costs with the size of the relevant decrease. Investment, it should be remembered, produces a multiplier effect on income that is some multiple of the value of the actual outlay, which further reduces private demand's ability to drive sustained growth. In addition, the loss may not only be on the side of demand, since investment, undertaken at some specific time, enhances the nation's future productive capacity for a period that, while dependent on the depreciation rates of the plants and equipment involved, is usually sufficiently long to make the *cumulative* loss very great (a point that Russett also makes).

Despite apparent short-term benefits, it is therefore hard to escape the conclusion that, in the long run, the economy is ill-served by massive military expenditure. Nevertheless, at least one more, possibly exculpatory, effect must be discussed.

ARMS, SCIENCE, AND TECHNOLOGICAL PROGRESS

Among the benefits most frequently attributed to a substantial military effort are the scientific and technological advances it generates. Scientific discoveries, when given practical application by technology, are clearly crucial to the well-being of modern economies. By increasing the range of available goods and services and by driving productivity, they promote growth despite constraints on traditional factors of production. It may thus be considered fortunate that the defense effort has produced numerous and often dramatic discoveries, many of which have been relevant to nonmilitary activities and needs as well. Some of the most obvious and beneficial spillovers into the civilian sector have resulted from the discovery of atomic energy, the computer, and integrated circuits. Other, less momentous civilian products that have stemmed from military programs have included the helicopter, flameproof fabrics, and certain insecticides. Indeed, since Eli Whitney laid the foundations of modern manufacture with the immediate aim of producing more rifles, the link between military activities and civilian technological progress has been established and accepted.

While recognizing the link, one should bear certain considerations in mind. The fact that discernible benefits from spillovers have occurred should not be construed to mean that civilian needs and the economy in general derive a *net* benefit from the concentration of research and development within the defense establishment. There is, on the contrary, every reason to believe that goals are more efficiently and effectively achieved by *direct* efforts rather than by reliance on spillovers. Clearly, a dollar directly spent on research and development in the civilian sector would yield more pronounced and immediate effects in terms of human and economic needs than could be expected from secondary and incidental effects. Of course, what is theoretically desirable may be hard to achieve in practice. It could be pointed out, for example, that much of the research and development proper to the military sector is, because of the complexity and sophistication involved, very expensive; it is also, particularly in the early stage of many projects, quite risky since a useful application of the research may never eventuate. Under these circumstances, it may seen unlikely that the endeavour would be undertaken at all were it not for the lavish subsidies provided to the defense establishment. This is a plausible but not unassailable argument. On the other hand, much potentially important research and development may indeed be too costly and risky for all but the largest private firms to undertake on their own. On the other hand, public funds for such purposes could, in principle, be diverted from military pursuits. The latter solution would, of course, imply a propitious political climate since it assumes that massive amounts could be mustered, at the taxpayers expense, for nonmilitary purposes. We have thus moved back to square one and our previous discussion of the willingness of the U.S. public to support large outlays for civilian needs.

Another consideration should also be borne in mind. Independent of whether past spillovers strike one as impressive or not, such effects may be becoming less and less significant and frequent. This should come as no surprise since the functions that military discoveries and innovations are expected to perform are becoming connected to increasingly complex and specialized military needs.

Consequently, analogous or corresponding applications to the civilian economy tend to become increasingly implausible and scarce.[16] There were many civilian uses of integrated circuits or the helicopter, but nonmilitary applications of killer satellites may be very rare.

On the whole, it is unlikely that as many benefits will be appropriated by the civilian economy in the future as in the technologically less-specialized past. In fact, if the defense sector continues to represent the preferential focus of so much advanced research and development, the civilian sector may actually suffer as a result. Concern is already being expressed about the decline in rates of productivity growth in the United States compared to its principal economic competitors. To the extent that such a trend does indeed exist, some of the responsibility must recently lie with the military. Most obviously, the concentration of research and development efforts within the military establishment will often mean that civilian scientific and technological endeavours will be bereft of needed resources. As large and potentially innovative firms choose the security of the subsidized military market, it becomes increasingly difficult for the civilian economy to muster the available talent and resources for the technological advances needed to cope with complex challenges and external competition. This may in fact be one of the reasons for the United States' apparent movement from a productive industrial power toward an affluent service economy, a harbinger of a loss of economic vitality. Civilian production may also be hampered in other ways. A very high defense bill and associated high rates of taxation may put a considerable financial squeeze on private producers, which affects in turn, their willingness and ability to undertake innovative (and hence risky) behavior. Furthermore, many firms that engage in defense-related production also possess some consumer goods operation; they thus participate simultaneously in a subsidized and in a theoretically competitive line. To the extent that the former is lucrative (as it most often is), it will be able to carry the firm's consumer goods business, insulating it from the salutary effects of market pressures and stimuli. Again, the civilian economy suffers. To an extent, of course, this risk is inherent in any multiple-track, conglomerate-style activity; it may, nevertheless, be particularly acute when one of the tracks is associated with a low risk/ high-earning operation subsidized by public monies. On the whole, there are strong theoretical reasons to doubt that military spending has had a helpful effect on productivity in recent years. While the

FIGURE 3.3
U.S. Defense Spending and Productivity Growth: 1947–79

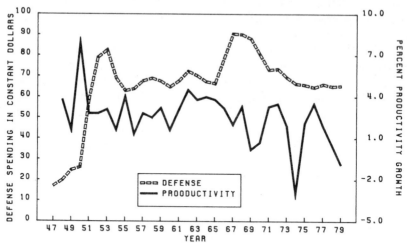

Note: Defense spending measured in constant 1972 dollars. Data are from the *Economic Report of the President: 1980* (Washington, D.C.).

growth of defense spending traces a very volatile trajectory, Figure 3.3 suggests that the current high defense outlays may be increasingly incompatible with healthy rates of productivity growth.

CONCLUSIONS

While any discussion of specific costs of the arms race must necessarily be qualified, it is difficult to escape the general conclusion that a highly militarized economy will also tend to be a structurally impaired, lethargic, and possibly a declining economy. Admittedly, it may be that by expanding military spending one can dampen the amplitude of recessionary downswings and avoid as low a trough as would otherwise have occurred. In fact, this seems to be a function with which political incumbents consciously endow the military budget. Nevertheless, in the long run, this is likely to be a misguided and even a counterproductive policy. The process is not symmetrical, since it is understandably difficult to reduce levels of spending on defense purposes during an upswing, although the burden of financing the increased outlays may actually eat into private demand. In turn, this may jeopardize the vigor and duration of the recovery and help to recreate the state of affairs that the increase was initially meant to redress. The remedy thus creates the conditions of its own application and is, albeit unintentionally, self-perpetuating. As the concentration on military research and development may be curbing productivity growth in civilian industry in an ever more evident manner, the situation is likely to become further aggravated in the future. To the extent that a specific aim of defense spending is to create jobs in an economy that chronically suffers from more unemployment than many of its industrialized partners, we face a particularly puzzling misconception about the effect of the military dollar. While governmental intervention is certainly necessary to reduce unemployment, the issue is simply that many other forms of public expenditure would achieve the goal more efficiently.

Nevertheless, adjustments to popular beliefs are needed at the other end as well. While the arms race is certainly not as good for jobs as is often maintained, it may not be quite as detrimental to public spending as could conceivably be thought. There would clearly be a one-to-one tradeoff with static resources, yet growing governmental revenues and increases in *both* guns and butter make the degree of substitutibility between the two categories contingent on additional assumptions: in particular, on how much one would expect butter to grow if guns were effectively held constant. On the whole, it seems that, due to the differential political acceptability of the two categories of expenditure in the United States, public spending for social ends would probably gain in response to a slower rate of military expansion though almost certainly not by the full amount of the foregone guns. Yet there is *some* loss to civilian spending, and the economy as a whole is subtly though effectively threatened in the long run.

These charges may, of course, make the reader pause. If they are indeed well founded, why should politicians seek to produce short-term economic gains via surges in military programs? Why should such ephemeral benefits not be sought outside of this context, through public spending for civilian needs? The most evident reason has already been alluded to and flows from the resistance of a substantial portion of the U.S. public to what has been termed "creeping socialism," a distaste that is apparent at various levels of political awareness, and more so now than at any time during the past several decades. Nevertheless, not all reasons are political and a number of additional, and perhaps equally cogent, explanations will be examined in our discussion of the problems of conversion from military to civilian activity in Chapter 7. At the moment, it is necessary to take a look at the other party to the superpower arms rivalry—the Soviet Union.

NOTES

1. James Tobin, *National Economic Policy* (New Haven, Conn.: Yale University Press, 1968) p. 71.
2. Arthur M. Okun, *The Political Economy of Prosperity* (New York: W. W. Norton, 1970), p. 78.
3. Such effects of Vietnam-related spending are detailed in John E. Petersen and Paul F. McGouldrick, "Monetary Restraint and Borrowing and Capital Spending by Large State and Local Governments in 1966," *Federal Reserve Bulletin*, July 1968; and "Monetary Restraint, Borrowing and Capital Spending by Small Local Governments and State Colleges in 1966," *Federal Reserve Bulletin*, December 1968.
4. An interesting theoretical overview of the causes and context of modern inflation is contained in Fred Hirsch, ed., *The Political Economy of Inflation* (Cambridge, Mass.: Harvard University Press, 1978).
5. Quoted in Seymour Melman, *The Permanent War Economy* (New York: Simon and Schuster, 1974), p. 130.
6. Reported in "Military Base Cuts Will Be Detailed Today: Job Losses Apt to Hit New England Hardest," Wall Street Journal, May 28, 1971.
7. Michael Best and William Connolly, *The Politicized Economy* (Lexington, Mass.: D. C. Heath, 1976), pp. 53-54.
8. Public Interest Research Group in Michigan, *The Empty Pork Barrel*, Lansing, 1974.
9. Center for Defense Information, "Jobs and the Pentagon: Is Military Spending Good for the Economy?," *The Defense Monitor*, Sept.-Oct. 1977.
10. David Gold, "MX and the American Economy," *Arms Control Today*, February 1980, pp. 3-5.
11. "The Impact of the Defense Industry on the Structure of the American Industry," in U.S. Arms Control and Disarmament Agency, ed., *Adjustments of the US Economy to Reductions in Military Spending*, 1970, pp. 401-2.
12. Bruce Russett, *What Price Vigilance? The Burdens of National Defense* (New Haven, Conn.: Yale University Press, 1970) pp. 140-41.
13. This argument is made with decreasing frequency.
14. See any good macroeconomic text for an elaboration of this point; for example, Paul Wonnacott, *Macroeconomics* (Homewood, Ill.: Richard D. Irwin, 1974), p. 68.
15. Russett, op. cit., pp. 143-44.
16. This is disucssed in Edwin Mansfield, "Contribution of R&D to Economic Growth in the United States," *Science* 175 (February 1972): 477-87. See also John Shaw and Don Leet, "Research and Development and Productivity Change, 1948-1968," *Journal of Industrial Economics* 22 (December 1973): 153-55.

4

THE ARMS-RACE
BEHAVIOR OF
THE SOVIET UNION

We know considerably less about the forces driving Soviet defense activities than we do about those behind U.S. arms-race behavior. Information is scantier, interpretations are even looser and, as a result, one is confronted with quite divergent statements and explanations that are often more reflective of the exponent's ideological predispositions than of the actual situation. This makes assessments of USSR military power and intentions potentially vulnerable to political manipulation and typically undermines efforts at rational arms control. Nevertheless, there is some good scholarship on Soviet domestic and foreign policy as well as a limited, but not negligible, body of data on trends in Soviet defense capabilities. Thus, while not as much can be confidently stated about the Soviet Union as about the United States, we are not forced to grope entirely in the dark.

The published work on the USSR side of the arms race, at least that which is not intended to serve an immediate political purpose, has been of predominantly two sorts. First of all, there have been elaborate efforts at reconstructing the framework within which defense-related decisions are made.[1] Much effort has gone into the detection and description of the organizations and institutional mechanisms that provide the context for such decisions (e.g., the Politburo, the Council of Ministers, and so forth) and some research has been directed at the actual behavior and power relations that are involved. The payoff has been that we are acquainted with the broad outlines, though usually not the details, of Soviet decision making on matters of defense policy and procurement. The second, and less vast, body of literature comprises efforts at evaluating contending explanations of the race in a data-based, statistical fashion.[2] The focus of such efforts has been on the simultaneous evaluation of the action-reaction and organizational-momentum explanations operationalized in a fairly simple manner. While rigorously quantitative research is certainly welcome, these particular studies have encountered a number of technical problems inherent in diachronic statistical analysis and multicollinearity and have, thus, been inconclusive to date.

There is therefore a paucity in our knowledge and understanding of the dynamics of Soviet military spending and weapons procurement, a paucity that can be only partly blamed on the closed nature of Soviet society. The aim of this book is to progress somewhat further in the comparative analysis of *both* sides of the arms race, and an important issue that must be addressed at the outset concerns the level of symmetry that may be assumed to characterize the behavior of the two superpowers. In other words, is it useful and legitimate to rely on similar sorts of hypotheses to explain the defense endeavours of both nations? While the statistical studies typically test perfectly symmetrical models, other writings have warned about the pitfalls of reasoning by analogy each time a gap in our knowledge of the other nation is encountered.

The issue would not be very relevant if action-reaction dynamics were all that propelled the arms race, but the recognition of any additional factors requires the analyst to explicitly deal with this question. While much in this chapter will address this issue, a preliminary statement should bring the following pages into proper focus.

The two superpowers are plainly characterized by sociopolitical and economic systems that are extremely different and, whatever merit there may be to theories of ultimately converging trends in their development, the differences at present are substantial and show no visible indication of narrowing. Nonetheless, there may be certain similarities that bear on our specific concerns. In the first place, no matter what their interests, composition, and stated values may be, the national security establishments of both superpowers have the form of large and complex organizations operating in intricate and fluid environments. It is reasonable to assume that the nature of organizational dynamics should be among the shared features of the two systems. A second observation may seem rather obvious: while it would be fruitless to seek analogous explanations at too great a degree of specificity, it should be perfectly feasible to do so at the more general level of analysis. For example, although there are no electoral constraints on Soviet defense behavior, decision makers may, nevertheless, be captive to certain political forces that should be taken into explicit consideration in the USSR case as well. Or, as a further example, while the problems on inadequate aggregate demand may be irrelevant in a centrally planned economy, *some* features of the Soviet economic system probably do influence military efforts in a significant way. Thus there are important differences but, also, a number of possible general similarities with a bearing on military activity. The aim of this chapter will then be to apply similar categories of theoretical explanation while assuming no necessary analogies with respect to the specific content of the categories.

A SOVIET REACTION PROCESS?

Let us begin by entertaining once more the notion of a Richardsonian process and examining it from the other side. Might it be that the Soviet Union's military programs are a response to previous U.S. decisions independent of whatever may have prompted the U.S. decisions? There is no reason to assume that the process must be symmetrical and it should be useful to begin (as was done for the United States) by observing some data on yearly fluctuations in military budgets. As in Figure 2.2, Figure 4.1 provides a two-by-two matrix in which increases and decreases in Soviet military spending in each year t (for the 1951-79 period) are associated with growth or decline on the U.S. side during the previous year. How does the behavior thus portrayed compare to that which we discern for the United States?

The situation for the Soviet Union is no more indicative of a Richardsonian pattern than it was in the U.S. case. In any given year, the Soviets were three times more likely to increase their spending than to decrease it, but the increases are quite evenly divided between instances of previous U.S. growth and instances of U.S. decline. Furthermore, drops in USSR military budgets seem unrelated to prior shifts by the United States, since they are virtually as likely to occur after a fall as after a rise. The main point is that a U.S. upward shift will almost always (here 85 percent of the time) be followed by a year of U.S. growth, but, almost as frequently (73 percent of the time in this period) a U.S. *drop* will precede a Soviet rise.

Apart from the greater frequency of Soviet increases (which is rather less striking, however, when U.S. outlays are measured in current dollars), a major difference between the two superpowers

FIGURE 4.1
Soviet Responses to Changes in U.S. Defense Budgets: 1951–79

United States
t-1

	Increases	Decreases	Sum
Increases	10	11	21
Decreases	3	4	7
	13	15	N = 28

Note: $\phi^2 = 0.002$

Source: Data on the United States are in billions of 1972 dollars as reported in the *Economic Report of the President, 1981*, Washington, D.C. (The fact that 1972 dollars are used implies that the nominal value of 1979 spending, for example, would be more than 60 percent higher.) Data for the Soviet Union are explained in Figure 4.2.

concerns the shape of the trajectories that they have followed. Their respective paths are visually depicted in Figure 4.2 and seem to indicate that U.S. military spending has followed a more *volatile* path than that of the Soviet Union. USSR surges have tended to be less pronounced than those of its rival and its drops have been slighter as well. The standard deviation in the size of changes in U.S. defense expenditure during this period was 8.4 units, while the same figure for the Soviets was but 2.1. In other words, while the Soviet Union grew in a comparatively steady fashion, the United States displayed a somewhat more jagged progression.

Let us begin with this difference and inquire whether it may not provide a first handle on the nature of Soviet arms race behavior.

A SYSTEM OF ENDOGENOUS DRIVES?

It was suggested in Chapter 2 that organizational and bureau-cratic inertia should predict relatively smooth and regular military growth, devoid of sharp discontinuities and dramatic reversals. It

FIGURE 4.2
Levels of Superpower Defense Spending

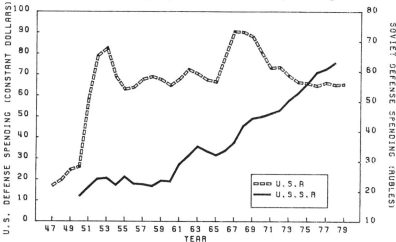

Note: U.S. spending is in constant (1972) dollars. Soviet spending for 1955-75 is measured in rubles as estimated by the CIA and reported in Robert Shishko, *Defense Budget Interactions Revisited*, The Rand Corporation, P-5882. For 1976 and 1977, this was supplemented by CIA, *Estimated Soviet Defense Spending: Trends and Prospects* (June 1978). For 1978 ruble values were estimated from adjustments from 1977 with CIA data on the percentage dollar change during that year. The decision to use ruble estimates rather than CIA dollar estimates was based on the apparently much exaggerated values that the latter yield.

was also maintained that, precisely because the U.S. pattern lacked such continuity, this sort of momentum could not account for a significant portion of U.S. arms race behavior. But what of the Soviet Union? Things may be very different here since the difference between the two nations' paths indicates that a focus on *bureaucratic momentum* may be more appropriate in the USSR case, a possibility that merits further investigation.

While the extent of USSR bureaucratization had been a concern to Trotsky and even to Lenin, the issue became really central to the conceptual baggage of U.S. Sovietologists in the post-Stalin era as an apparent consequence of two factors.[3] In the first place, the transition to the new political climate of the Khrushchev regime meant that Soviet rule could no longer be adequately accounted for in terms of the sole and massive application of terror. This required a new explanation for the directed nature of the regime; the concept of a powerful, all-encompassing, and rigidly hierarchical bureaucratic machine was provided whereby commands from the top could be effectively transmitted and implemented throughout society. It came to be thought that Soviet society was thoroughly administered rather than terrorized and that a mammoth organizational structure was erected for this purpose. A second reason for the new emphasis on bureaucracy was the realization that economic and technological development in *any* nation creates a need for rationality and predictability in collective endeavours— the very attributes that are supposedly embodied in bureaucratic institutions and practices. The implications of the two explanations are admittedly different: the first envisages bureaucracy as a vehicle of centralized political command, while the second suggests that it will actually inhibit the exercise of absolute power. Nevertheless, they both stem from a recognition that bureaucracy permeates Soviet society. An adequate understanding of that nation's policies must take this into account.

What does this imply for arms-race behavior? No matter what the origins of large-scale bureaucratic structures may be, there are good reasons to believe that decision making in such a context will eventually become incremental by aiming at producing no more than a modest amount of change. There are, of course, reasons why this should be so independent of the polity in which a bureaucracy may happen to have its roots. As has been suggested in Chapter 2, when intricate organizational structures cope with complex and unpredictable environments, they tend to adopt schematic and routinized modes of behavior that are typically inconsistent with dramatic change. Furthermore, as Jerry Hough observes, there is "a natural tendency for specialists to fear change that would make their specialized knowledge and experience out-moded."[4] Both are presumably factors that are as applicable to the United States as to the Soviet Union, yet there is cause to suspect that bureaucratic incrementalism operates more powerfully in the latter country.

In the first place, the *scope* of bureaucratic regulation seems to be greater in the Soviet Union. In the United States, substantial inputs into policy formation come from sources that are not associated with formal bureaucratic structures. The role played by the electorate, the media, political parties, and private interests either have no counterpart in the Soviet Union or have, at most, a vague and tenuous parallel. Therefore, there is simply less that remains outside the bureaucratic embrace in one nation than in the other.

In addition, *incrementalism* may be even more characteristic of Soviet than of U.S. governmental institutions. Arthur Alexander, in a study of decision making in the Soviet Union, considers that conservatism and flaccidity of initiative are prominent features of behavior in these organizations[5] and maintains that this is typical of military policy as well. One significant reason, according to Alexander, is the characteristic concern to neither anticipate one's superiors nor to do anything that would challenge the correctness of previous decisions—both are consequences of authoritarian rule. Furthermore, this is compounded by the secrecy that is endemic to Soviet society and by the narrow departmentalism that this promotes. The effect is a sluggish flow of information and a situation in which few people acquire a comprehensive view of an issue or are in a position to suggest more than partial solutions to overall problems.

If true, this would imply that substantial deviations from trends in military spending would be only the occasional result of major decisions originating at the very pinnacle of political authority and taken independently of (or contrary to) bureaucratic preferences. This reasoning should be as applicable to specific weapon systems as to overall movements in defense budgets. In fact, the visible continuity in the sort of weapons designed and produced by the Soviets has been explained in precisely these terms.[6]

What emerges thus far is a picture of a massive bureaucracy chugging along a steady course that progresses within a relatively narrow band centered on a rising trend. Furthermore, we seem to have come a longer way with a single-factor interpretation than would have been possible in the U.S. case. Nevertheless, bureaucratic dynamics should not be endowed with more explanatory power than the evidence warrants. While Soviet trends do manifest somewhat less volatility than do those of the United States, they are not altogether smooth either. Peaks and troughs in the Soviet Union appear less pronounced for the most part, but they are, nevertheless, quite discernible. While the trend dominates the trajectory, the most useful task should be to account precisely for the *deviations*.

Let us begin with the more pronounced increases and inquire whether they were caused by similar types of forces in the Soviet Union as in the United States. An intriguing possibility for the United States was that technological innovation (by prompting the formation of scientific, economic, and military coalitions devoted to translating the discoveries into new acquisitions for the armed forces) was an especially potent stimulant to the arms race. This, however, may be less apposite to the Soviet case due to structural differences between the two superpowers. In the United States, discoveries that are only tenuously connected to specific defense aims are often *made relevant* to such objectives by those whose interests are involved. An analogous reasoning may be inapplicable to the Soviet Union, where technological innovation is less likely to shape future defense postures than it is to be mobilized to serve political and military goals that have already been explicitly articulated. In the United States, the process can be partly explained by the relative autonomy of the scientific and economic establishments from political control and by the ability of pressure groups to translate their interests into effective policy. This would not be an accurate description of the Soviet situation where little initiative is left to the scientific community and where research, development, and production are undertaken in response to specific decisions transmitted downward and enforced through hierarchical structures of authority. Influence usually does not flow in the opposite direction. As one observer describes it, "the Soviets selectively screen out elitist pressures on policy, and thereby retain a stronger political dominance over technological inputs."[7] Another study noted that "the Soviet decision-making system is set up to insure the application of political judgement to technical decisions."[8]

An examination of the relevant institutional context confirms this view. Although the Ministry of Defense has some direct responsibility for military research and development, most work on weapons planning and design, on prototype development, and, generally, on improving technological processes in the sphere of military production is undertaken by research and development establishments that are directly incorporated into the eight major industrial ministries in the defense sector.[9] These are closely supervised by the Military Industrial Commission,[10] which represents an interface between central political authority (in this case the Politburo and probably its Defense Council) and the higher echelons of the Ministry of Defense on the one hand, and the ministerial bureaucracies that manage military production on the other hand. Defense-related research and development is thus directly incorporated into a political command structure where authority is concentrated at the pinnacle. As the eight major defense/industrial ministries are part of this structure, there is no direct equivalent to those segments of the American economy that lobby, as independent actors, for military programs that benefit them—whether or not their preferences coincide with those of incumbent political authorities.

This does not mean, of course, that the defense industries and their research and development branches do not have their vested interests and that they do not seek to promote them. They represent a favored sector of the economy with a priority claim to scarce resources and the best manufactured goods as well as exceptionally high pay rates and other facilities.[11] Obviously, they have a strong interest in preserving arrangements that have enabled them to attain a privileged position in the national economy; it is, however, worth stressing that it is by the faithful implementation of the demands of political elites rather than by attempting to impose their own ideas on force posture (assuming that they have them) that they seem most likely to promote their interests.

The search for domestic drives should not end here and, if one were searching for endogenous forces most likely to promote expanded defense activities, one would probably scrutinize the Soviet military establishment most closely. In the United States, the military has actively lobbied for larger defense budgets and new weapons and has sometimes managed to prevail over the apparent preferences of the administration by mustering a sufficiently strong coalition in its own support. Does something similar tend to occur in the Soviet Union?

Let us begin by inquiring into the nature of civil/military relations in the Soviet Union. Considerable speculation has surrounded this issue and Marshal Grechko's exceptional elevation to full Politburo membership in 1973 fueled suggestions of an ascending political role for the armed forces. Nevertheless, the dominant view is that the military services are firmly subordinated to the civilian party leadership.[12] The tendency in the Soviet Union, particularly since the ouster of Marshal Zhukov, has been to discourage the emergence of Bonapartist tendencies and to reinforce party primacy in matters of defense. This has been achieved by the resurgence of tight political controls, by the restricted access of military men to the highest echelons of the Communist Party of the Soviet Union (CPSU) hierarchy, and by the vigorous socialization of officers to norms of party supremacy in all spheres of collective activity. According to the *Communist of the Armed Forces*, the political organ of the military services:

Party leadership over the armed forces is carried out in all areas . . . determining the main direction for the development of types of armed forces, their organizational structure and equipping with modern technology and weapons, the training and indoctrination of military personnel, [and] the taking of specific measures related to further raising the level of Party political work. . . . Essentially, there is no area of military activity in which the leading role of the Communist Party, its Central Committee, and the Politburo of the CPSU Central Committee would not be manifested.[13]

Nevertheless, the military's influence is clearly more substantial with reference to the specific case of the arms race than it is in general matters of foreign and domestic policy, and here the fact that the armed forces can in no way *dictate* decisions does not signify an absence of influence. They certainly do make their preferences known to the political leadership and, at times no doubt, engage in some effective lobbying. Khrushchev, who once declared that "I do not trust the appraisal of generals on questions of strategic importance," also recalled a meeting with Eisenhower at Camp David during which the latter explained how

> My military leaders come to me and say, "Mr. President, we need such and such a sum for such and such a program." I say, "Sorry, we don't have the funds." They say, "We have reliable information that the Soviet Union has already allocated funds for their own such program. Therefore, if we don't get the funds we need, we'll fall behind the Soviet Union." So I give in. That's how they wring money out of me. They keep grabbing for more and I keep giving it to them. Now tell me, how is it with you?"
>
> It's just the same. Some people from our military department come and say, "Comrade Khrushchev, look at this! The Americans are developing such and such a system. We could develop the same system, but it would cost such and such." I tell them there's no money; it's all been allocated already. So they say, "If we don't get the money we need and if there's a war, then the enemy will have superiority over us." So we discuss it some more, and I end up by giving them the money they ask for."

Khrushchev, in the same text, complained that

> Every commander has all sorts of very convincing arguments why he should get more than anyone else. Unfortunately, there's a tendency for people who run the armed forces to be greedy and self-seeking. They're always ready to throw in your face the slogan "If you try to economize on the country's defenses today, you'll pay in blood when war breaks out tomorrow."[14]

Thus the Soviet armed forces seek to defend their corporate interests to the same extent as their U.S. counterparts; the issue, however, concerns the ultimate amount of leverage that both military forces can wield over the final decision makers. The conclusion that suggests itself to this author is that, while the military establishment may attempt to *persuade* political authorities of the legitimacy of its needs in the Soviet Union, it cannot force its own desires in the face of contrary preferences of the top political leadership. In this respect, the armed forces of the Soviet

Union may not be as effective promoters of their own interests as are their U.S. counterparts.

While the success of the U.S. military in affecting the course of the arms race has been mitigated by a variety of factors, those instances where it has successfully influenced policy must be largely attributed to the support of powerful allies. It has been able to enlist the support not only of concerned economic and professional interest groups but also of sympathetic legislators and large portions of public opinion. With several relatively independent sources of political power, a sufficiently potent coalition can often be formed to neutralize the potential opposition of those incumbents who have formal authority over final decisions. The situation is probably not analogous in the Soviet Union. Although earlier notions of monolithic political power exercised by the party elite have been dispelled more recently, it would be idle to suggest that the distribution of power characteristic of Western democracies has some parallel in the Soviet structure. Rather, contemporary understanding is that, while different constellations of interest arise on various policy issues, they are *articulated* within the political elite. For example, it has been suggested that heavy industry is typically supportive of a preferential emphasis on defense production, while agricultural groups and those associated with light industry within the elite would prefer to have scarce resources allocated for their own sectors.[15] The Politburo will usually attempt to strike some balance between these interests but will not have its policy dictated by any of them.

Yet the military does display a limited ability to influence the arms race, an ability that derives from two major sources. In the first place, the military often has exclusive access to specialized knowledge and information that is not independently available to the civilian leaders. In fact, the armed services seem quite aware of the advantage that this confers when they are making their desires known and appear careful to preserve their monopoly on expertise.[16] On the whole, however, it is unlikely that the armed services can cause significant deviations from behavior, which would otherwise be expected by selectively withholding or interpreting information. In other words, this ability may help account for the trend rather than for major deviations from it (our current task). A second, and perhaps more potent, source of influence may come from the fact that civilian authorities in the Soviet Union often empathize very closely with the values and goals of the armed forces. Many current political leaders have been active participants in World War II, and it can be expected that a history so strongly shaped by warfare and armed resistance would have had a secular socializing effect on civilian authority. What this seems to lead to is an easy division of labor between soldiers and civilians. As Thomas Wolfe of the RAND corporation describes it:

> Rather than a sharp dichotomy between the two groups, there seems to be what amounts to a division of labor between them, with the political leadership tending to leave the professional details of security planning, as Kosygin once put it, "to the Marshals," while reserving to itself the right of final decision, especially on matters involving large resources of war and peace.[17]

The point is, of course, that significant departures from trends in levels of defense spending are precisely matters of the latter sort. The most plausible inference may be that, while members of the professional defense establishment can ensure that these trends will not decline, and can probably also effectuate limited adjustments to major decisions, they do not have it in their power to cause major shifts in trends solely by dint of their own interests and efforts. Of course, their desires will frequently coincide with major policy changes, but it is doubtful that these are a sufficient condition for their occurrence.

The difference with the United States may thus be one of degree: political authorities in the Soviet Union may be more independent of bureaucratic, interest-group, and other political constraints than those of a nation characterized by pluralistic curbs on governmental autonomy. This impression of relatively unfettered power is reinforced by the apparent ability of the Soviet leadership to implement desired shifts in the face of bureaucratic inertia on those occasions (which may not be very frequent) when it does decide that substantial changes are called for.[18]

What may be concluded so far on the role and impact of endogenous drives on Soviet arms-race behavior? The general conclusion is that, while bureaucratic sluggishness may account for much of the progressive upward trend, technological momentum or military self-interest can affect changes only in directions that are not discordant with preferences at the pinnacle of the political power structure. Consequently, if major changes are to be explained, there must be some understanding of the nature of these preferences and it might be useful to inquire, as was done for the United States, which important goals and values of Soviet political elites are affected by defense programs and procurement.

Security of incumbency is an important goal of U.S. political authorities and it can certainly be assumed to be as much a concern of Soviet politicians. The principal difference is that the attainment of this objective may be less sensitive in the Soviet Union to levels of military spending or to the deployment of specific weapons. In the United States, an opposition can reap substantial benefits if incumbents can be plausibly charged with neglecting national security, but this is clearly less of a problem for Soviet office holders because of the very nature of the regime. It is true that Khrushchev's ouster of Georgi Malenkov was accompanied by criticism of the latter's laxness on defense; it is also true that Khrushchev's own removal was partly justified on grounds of irresponsibility in military matters. In both cases, however, these accusations were only part of a more general litany of grievances, which seemed as much a rationalization of the change in leadership as its explanation. Moreover, the practice of consensual decision making in the post-Khrushchev era has meant that divergences on matters of defense policy now tend to be worked out *before* definite determinations are made at the highest levels. Thus, while different or conflicting initial viewpoints may characterize authority at the top, the final decision is unlikely to be challenged from within. Furthermore, the concentration of power at the level of the political elite, especially the Politburo, implies that specific policies will not usually be challenged from outside either. This leads to the conclusion that, in the current Soviet political context, arms-race activity will not be the consequence of politicians' attempts to protect their incumbency. It may, of course, result from the pressures of consensual decision making but, in this case, incremental growth rather than the more periodical and election-related pattern of the U.S. side should be a defining characteristic of USSR defense spending and procurement. However, the secrecy surrounding the deliberations and activity of such bodies as the Politburo mean that it is not possible to get a solid empirical handle on this hypothesis.

The second major and defense-related goal of U.S. politicians concerned the performance of the national economy—for which they could expect to be held accountable by the electorate. Does something similar occur in the Soviet Union? There is every reason to believe that the economic performance of the Soviet Union is related to defense at least as much as it tends to be in the United States. Nevertheless, the nature of the link is very different in the two countries. It should be remembered that a major goal of the Soviet Union, ever since the first quinquennial plan of 1928, has been to transform a relatively primitive peasant nation into a highly industrialized, technologically advanced and, if possible, self-sufficient power. Not only was this a goal in itself and a much desired demonstration of the virtues of the Bolshevik regime, but it was also viewed as a method of bolstering the nation's security (since the extent of economic progress would determine the amount and quality of resources that could be devoted to military ends). The link between economics and Moscow's military activity is thus important and will be discussed in this and subsequent chapters. It may not, however, be the most significant consideration for understanding Soviet arms-race behavior.

The principal goal of the Soviet leadership with respect to defense policy is almost certainly to achieve invulnerability to external military threats. Virtually all other needs are subordinated to the claims of national security and even a rudimentary acquaintance with Russian history should make this understandable. Indeed, few nations have experienced as many foreign onslaughts as have the Russians and the dread of bellicose foreign intentions with their associated human and material costs is always present and deeply ingrained. Even William Colby, former CIA director, has recognized that

> You will find a concern, even a paranoia, over their own security. You will find the determination that they shall never again be invaded and put through the kinds of turmoil that they have been under many different invasions. . . . [The Soviets] want to overprotect themselves to make certain that that does not happen, and they are less concerned about the image that that presents to their neighbours, thinking that their motives are really defensive and pure and therefore other people should not be suspicious of them.[19]

Given the historically conditioned sense of vulnerability, it is not altogether surprising that a perception of threat from the nation's major adversary should represent the principal determinant of Soviet military activity. Therefore, in order to understand what is most likely to induce a substantial shift in the Kremlin's defense posture, it should be useful to take another and closer look at the Soviet Union's responses to perceived U.S. challenges. It may be, for example, that for the USSR to deviate from the groove set by bureaucratic inertia, some important change in U.S. behavior is a necessary prior condition. While Soviet defense outlays do rise fairly smoothly, there are certain undulations that cannot be adequately explained purely by reference to domestic factors. Perhaps these are reactions to particularly significant reversals on the other side. The Soviets may not be naturally innovative in the design and choice of their strategic weapons, but they do introduce new systems on occasion and these departures from conservative inclinations should perhaps also be explained by major U.S. innovations and deployments.

MAJOR SURGES AND THE INTERNATIONAL CONTEXT

Let us begin by taking a fresh look at military budgets. Examination of the data reveals that, in addition to the general continuity, there are three periods of particularly rapid Soviet growth since World War II. These periods appeared in the early-to-mid 1950s, early 1960s, and the very late 1960s (see Figures 2.1 and 4.2). The first surge was, in all likelihood, a straightforward response to the upward lurch of U.S. defense outlays since 1950-51 at a time of military action in Korea and following the National Security Council Memorandum (NSC 68), which urged very substantial increases in U.S. military capability. Likewise, it can rather easily be argued that the steep spending curve of the late 1960s was a consequence of swelling U.S. outlays occasioned by the intervention in Vietnam.

The hump in the early 1960s cannot, however, be quite as easily explained in these terms. Although U.S. expenditures did increase somewhat between 1960 and 1962, the rise was altogether modest and actually turned into a decline (in real terms) which lasted until 1965. Therefore, if an exogenous stimulus was present, it seems more likely to have originated from Peking than from Washington. Sino-Soviet relations, which had been characterized by a strong dose of mutual suspicion for a number of years, deteriorated badly in the 1960s. By 1960 already, Soviet military and technical aid to China had been withdrawn amid increasingly acrimonious charges of revisionism (and worse), and soon it became clear that China had at least matched the United States as an enemy and perceived threat to Moscow. While the People's Republic of China possessed nowhere near the United States' military might, it did share a 4,150 mile border with the Soviet Union and had embarked on its own program of nuclear development, which led to a first detonation in 1964. Thus, while the rise in military spending can be interpreted as a response to a perceived external threat, the threatening agent was probably China rather than the United States. Indeed, the fact that perceived security threats to the Soviet Union originate from at least two distinct quarters may explain kinks in its arms-race conduct that are clearly not attributable to anything that Washington may have done.

The other aspect of the arms race with which this study is concerned, that involving particular strategic weapons, displays a less ambiguous picture of responses to actual or projected U.S. acquisitions. The clearest example is perhaps provided by the Soviet missile build-up, which began in the mid 1960s. Chapter 2 described how a subsequently acknowledged misapprehension about USSR long-range missile strength led to a crash program to develop a United States ICBM force. Yet hard data, which became available in the early 1960s, indicated that the "missile gap" actually favored the United States (in 1963, for example, the United States had 424 intercontinental missiles as opposed to a mere 90 Soviet vehicles). The disadvantage that this implied was made evident to the Soviets during the Cuban missile crisis and, consequently, they engaged in a build-up of their own, which enabled them to catch up with the United States in numbers of missiles (though not of warheads) by approximately 1970. As McNamara himself recognized, "Clearly the Soviet build-up is in part a reaction to our own build-up since the beginning of the 1960s."[20]

There are also other good examples. The Soviet MIRV program came unmistakably on the heels of successful U.S. developments in this area. The Soviets tested MIRVs in 1973, five years after the initial U.S. tests; U.S. deployment occurred in 1970, and the Soviet Union followed in 1975. Moscow's development of an atomic bomb was, as closely as can be reconstructed, also in the nature of a response. In 1942 the United States produced its first chain reaction and, in July 1945, detonated a fission bomb. This was followed by accelerated Soviet efforts, resulting in a USSR chain reaction little more than a year later and an atomic detonation on August 24, 1949. In 1960 the first U.S. nuclear-powered submarine carrying 16 Polaris submarine-launched ballistic missiles (SLBMs) was launched; the Soviet Union deployed SLBMs on nuclear-powered submarines in 1964.

The link between Soviet strategic endeavours and antecedent U.S. initiatives seems fairly well supported but some caveats are, nonetheless, in order. At times the Soviets have been the first to introduce a new type of system—as in the case of the SS-20 medium-range missile. Also Moscow has occasionally been guilty of anticipatory reactions to erroneously predicted future challenges. For example, George Rathjens has suggested that the Tallinn line (for which United States MIRVs were at first officially justified) was conceived by the Soviet Union as an element of a possible defense against the B-70 bomber,[21] which was never deployed.

The conclusion to which we are drawn is that, although major discontinuities and reversals in Soviet military budgets can be explained by perceived external threats, the United States cannot be considered their sole cause. There is some asymmetry here since the United States, unlike the Soviet Union, has only one potential adversary. When we move from overall budgets to major *weapons systems*, the situation is somewhat different, since it is unlikely that Peking has been, or indeed will be in the relevant future, capable of developing novel and sufficiently threatening weapons to necessitate a Soviet response in kind. On the other side of the race, one would expect an increase in Soviet defense activity to be a *sufficient* cause for a corresponding U.S. surge but not, however, a *necessary* condition since a variety of domestic political and economic drives are apt to produce the same effect. The difference with respect to the Soviet Union is that, for the Kremlin, other external rather than internal stimuli seem to be behind major increases in levels of military activity. Also, an *incremental* pattern of military growth, resulting from bureaucratic momentum, is likely to characterize the Soviet Union even in the absence of perceived increases in threats to the country's security. In addition to whatever theoretical interest it may carry, this asymmetry has evident consequences for arms-control and disarmament strategies. These will be discussed at length in subsequent chapters; at the moment, yet another aspect of USSR military outlays merits consideration.

THE POLITICAL ECONOMY OF SOVIET DEFENSE BUDGETS

In the previous two chapters, the economic causes and consequences of U.S. defense procurement were analyzed and found to be a significant part of the context of its military activity. While a major conclusion was that perceived economic needs do frequently kindle defense programs, the situation is quite different in the Soviet Union where such needs are more likely to have a *constraining* rather than a *stimulating* influence. The contrast is clearly due to the differences between centrally planned and market economies. Unlike the United States case, in a centrally planned economy of the Soviet type, one can assume that overall demand will always be in a position to match productive capacity. Although specific goods may be unsalable at times, there is no reason to fear recessions caused by unabsorbable surpluses at the aggregate level.[22] In fact, the problem for the Soviets is of an entirely opposite nature and tends to take the form of shortfalls in aggregate *supply*, that is, of an inability to produce sufficient output to satisfy expressed producer and consumer desires. Whether or not Western economies really are burdened by ultimately unabsorbable surpluses, there is little doubt that the Soviet economy is constrained by endemic shortages and, in such a situation, growth can only occur if the quantity of goods and services produced can be expanded.

The obvious implication for our concerns is that the resources available for military purposes in the Soviet Union will depend on the general volume of economic activity. Furthermore, within the context of the economy, military needs will compete in a direct manner (albeit from a strong position) with the claims of various other sectors. Given the nature of the economic constraints, trade-offs are probably more immediately evident in the Soviet Union than in the United States, and it can thus be expected that the least painful manner of increasing the volume of resources that can be devoted to defense purposes is to expand the economy (i.e., the level of production).

An examination of recent trends in both levels of economic activity (as measured by real GNP) and of military spending highlights their related upward movement (see Figure 4.3).[23]   The

FIGURE 4.3
Soviet Defense Spending and Economic Growth: 1950-80

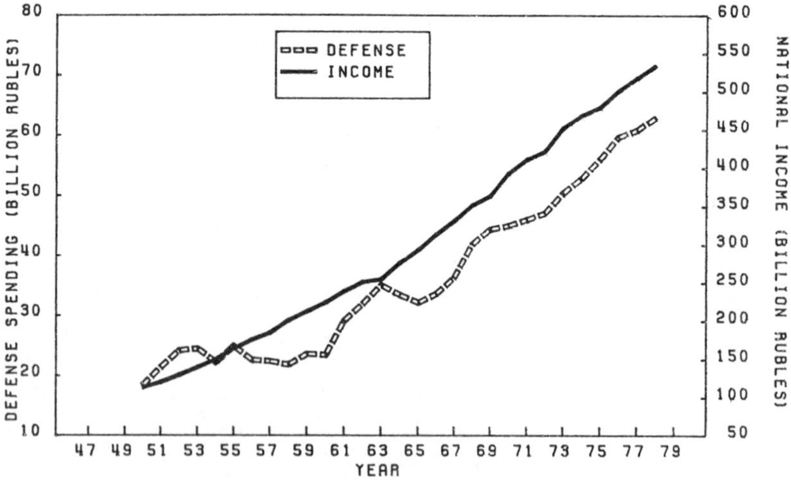

Note: Defense spending data are the same as for Figure 4.2. Soviet national income is measured in billions of rubles as reported in Robert Shishko, *Defense Budget Interactions Revisited*, The Rand Corporation, P-5882, p. 15. For 1976-78, I used the national income index (1970 = 100) provided by Herbert Block ("Soviet Economic Performance in a Global Context," U.S. Congress, Joint Economic Committee, *Soviet Economy in a Time of Change*, Washington, D.C., 1979, pp. 110-33) and adjusted the last known ruble figure (1975) on the basis of percentage increases in the index.

impression one receives is that U.S. military activities determine a floor below which Soviet efforts will not be allowed to fall, and the Soviets' own economy sets the permissible ceiling beyond which these efforts cannot go (as its rate of growth determines the opportunity costs that defense imposes on various facets of Soviet life). Thus, there is at least *one* major potential impediment on Moscow's desire to maintain a pace of military expansion commensurate with perceived security needs.

Nevertheless, the value of this information may be greatest in the long run, since the short-term relation between economics and defense is not as predictable as the overall trend. Cyclical fluctuations might exist within the secular relationship and yield information of considerable relevance to current policy. Specifically, it would be interesting and useful to determine how relative weights are assigned to military and nonmilitary needs by the political regime and how these weights may vary in the short run. If some systematic pattern to the comparative priorities accorded to these two categories of needs were found, it would describe a periodicity in the salience of the economic burden of defense. This, in turn, would have a predictive value similar to that which the electoral/economic cycle has for the United States. The existence of such periodicity is conceivable on several grounds. Economic life in the Soviet Union is guided by a set of plans of varying degrees of specificity among which the most important are the five-year and annual plans. Military force posture is also developed and procured in the context of plans of corresponding lengths that govern the activities of the Ministry of Defense and the various military-industrial ministries and that are coordinated with the plans of other economic sectors. It is therefore possible to modify the relative emphases on defense and civilian needs in annual plans while moving toward the overall quinquennial objectives. The question, then, is whether there are times when these emphases should be predictably expected to shift.

On the basis of a close examination of postwar USSR budgetary history, a British Sovietologist has concluded that these relative weights display a clear and predictable pattern across the typical five-year interval.[24] In particular, he found that nondefense needs fared best toward the beginning as well as the end of the plan, while the emphasis on defense would tend to reach a peak between the two. My own research indicates that, other things being equal, military increases will grow each year by 4 percent from the first to the third year and then decrease to the fifth—making growth largest in the middle and slightest at the ends.[25]

FIGURE 4.4
Soviet Military Spending and the Planning Cycle

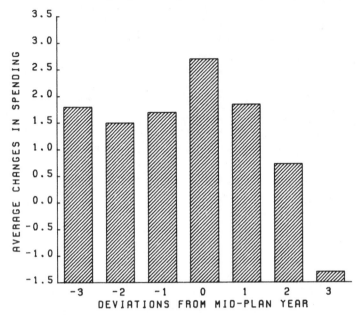

Source: Compiled by the author.
Note: Data used are estimates provided by the CIA and reported in Robert Shishko, *Defense Budget Interactions Revisited*, The Rand Corporation, P-5882. This information was supplemented by CIA, *Estimated Soviet Defense Spending: Trends and Prospects* (June 1978).

Figure 4.4 displays the average increment to Soviet military spending by order of year within the national economic plans beginning with the fifth Five-Year Plan (1951-55) and ending with the fourth year in the tenth plan (1979). The data include a period when the plan covered a seven-year period (1959-65) as well as one that spanned only three years (1956-58). The bar diagram plainly indicates a tendency for spending to experience a rise around the middle of the planning cycle and to taper off (not monotonically however) toward either end. (The most obvious exception is the year designated as − 3, which was the first year in the seven-year endeavour, and represents a single year rather than an average of repeated observations).

According to Raymond Hutchings, the initial high levels of civilian spending can be explained by a desire to get the plan off to a good start, while the surge at the end of the period is often necessary to ensure that the plan is, in fact, fulfilled. From another angle, Hutchings hypothesized that, in an economy characterized by tight aggregate supply and an overall priority given to defense, advocates of military programs may find it politically astute to relax their oppression of the other sectors at moments when this will mean most to planners and business organizations.[26]

Thus, while an electoral/economic cycle is discernible with respect to U.S. military procurement, so is there an apparent five-year-plan cycle to Soviet defense outlays. An important implication, of course, is that Moscow's defense behavior may be partly determined, at any given time, by a logic that is not understood by many U.S. observers, and that bellicose or peaceful intentions may be imputed to fluctuations that are *unrelated to immediate foreign policy considerations.*

Let us now turn to another aspect of the link between the Soviet economy and that nation's military activity. Much of the discussion of the impact of the arms race within the United States dealt with the opportunity costs it imposed on a number of social and economic needs. It should also be useful to examine the nature of these costs in an economy characterized by tightly constrained levels of output and where decisions concerning investment and production are taken out of the hands of individuals and placed in the hands of a centralized planning mechanism. The first question, then, is the following: how do military programs affect national economic performance defined in terms of growth in levels of production? While military security is an important goal to which economic growth is instrumental, it seems likely that Soviet investments in its defense capacity also produce some effect on the economy. In other words, the causal arrow may operate in both directions.

The expansion of output in the Soviet Union, as in any economy, depends on the increased use and effective combining of a number of inputs into production, principally, of capital (raw materials, plants, and equipment) and labor. The strategy of applying ever-greater quantities of both of these factors to produce a growing overall product is termed "extensive" growth. Until recently, it is this that has been the chosen Soviet approach to economic development. Indeed, the expansion of capital stock has been among the most impressive achievements of the regime and has resulted from the strong emphasis traditionally placed on investment, which even at the time of writing accounts for almost 30 percent of GNP (nearly twice the U.S. figure). Furthermore, the emphasis has been on the directly productive sectors of industry and agriculture to the detriment of areas like housing, transportation, and communication. These choices have generated economic growth rates of over 6 percent in the 1950s and over 5 percent per year in the 1960s. The momentum has since slowed down, however, and growth rates have dropped to less than 4 percent per annum in the 1970s with even lower rates anticipated in the future.[27]   As might be expected, this slowdown has moved in tandem with an increasingly sluggish growth in the economy's capital stock, whose rates have dropped by about 2 percent during this period (see Figure 4.5).

If the increasingly unimpressive growth rates are partly caused by insufficient new capital formation, one may wish to ask whether defense needs might bear part of the responsibility. That capital investment is adversely affected by lavish military outlays in an economy with rather limited economic resources should be obvious, and recent research underscores such opportunity costs. For example, one study covering the 1950s and 1960s found a pronounced displacement effect for nearly all categories of investment, since their growth rates tended to be most sluggish at times when defense budgets tended to rise most rapidly.[28]   Another

FIGURE 4.5
Average Annual Growth in Soviet Capital Stock

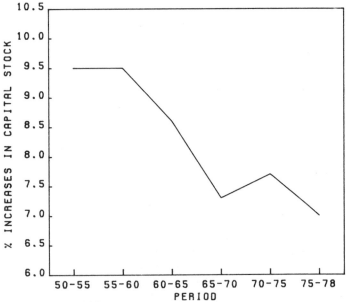

Source: Data are from Abram Bergson, "The Soviet Economic Slowdown," *Challenge,* Jan./Feb. 1978, p. 24 (for 1950-75); and from Central Intelligence Agency, *Handbook for Economic Statistics,* ER-79-10274, August 1979, p. 63 (for 1975-78).

study estimated that rises in defense spending occasionally lead to a fall in new investment of nearly the *full amount* of the increase.[29] Thus military spending detracts from capital formation; if this is not to have a seriously stultifying effect on economic growth, the second major input into production, that is, the labor force, would have to grow sufficiently to compensate for the squeeze on investment. While labor's contribution has been proportionately greater in the Soviet Union than in most Western economies, current trends do not bode particularly well for the future. The specter of serious labor shortages looms as a real possibility, and the relatively modest production plans for 1976-80 and 1981-85 indicate a clear awareness of the problem by Soviet planners.

According to an unclassified CIA report, annual additions to the working-age population, which averaged 2.5 million in the early 1970s, will decline to less than 0.5 million in the mid 1980s.[30] Although this would certainly create substantial problems, it should be noted that past increments to the industrial labor force have not been exclusively determined by the size of the working-age population but also by such considerations as the marginal increases in employment of women. Some efforts have also been made to shift a portion of the agricultural labor force into industry (a strategy that is limited by relatively low levels of agricultural productivity). Still, apart from such palliatives as extending the work week or shifting population from one geographical area to another, there are no evident solutions to the problem of labor shortage. Some responsibility for this situation must be borne by defense, which effectively sequesters a significant portion of the labor force.

In this regard, there is thus a fundamental difference between the two superpowers in terms of the impact of their military efforts. While defense is sometimes viewed as an expedient method of reducing unemployment in the United States, it may only be viewed as an aggravating influence on Soviet labor shortages, where it may further impair a growth that is already jeopardized by slackening rates of capital formation. Only a relatively small part of the problem is created by the armed forces. The civilian labor force numbers about 130 million persons while the figure for the armed forces is approximately 4 million. Therefore, if a demobilization were undertaken to reduce military personnel by a full 50 percent, for example, the corresponding addition to the work force would not exceed 1.6 percent of its previous size. The major drain on the labor force comes not from the armed services but from defense-related production that may account for a full 12 percent of the total work force according to an estimate that includes employment with a direct or indirect link to the military function.[31]   This is clearly a substantial burden on the economy and will make continued economic growth without arms limitation increasingly difficult.

On the whole, therefore, there is reason to believe that the traditional policy of "extensive" growth will encounter serious obstacles in coming years.   However, the situation is not entirely hopeless, since constraints on capital and labor availability can theoretically be obviated by increasing factor *productivity*, that is, the output associated with a unit of these factors of production. In fact, a realization of this fact has been apparent during the more recent five-year plans.   Officially sanctioned debates in the early 1960s, based to a large extent on writings of the economist Evsei Liberman, led to a recognition that overly specific central plans placed operational constraints on enterprises and stifled innovation as well as flexible performance.   Efficiency, and by implication productivity, was henceforth to be the major goal and its attainment was to be facilitated by giving greater independence and incentives to plant managers.   A first practical step in this direction was undertaken by the so-called Kosygin Reform of 1965 which, however, met with the resistance of numerous planners and even of some managers. It had effectively been abandoned by the end of the decade, and the focus shifted to the development or acquisition or productivity-enhancing technology.   One approach was to channel additional resources into high-technology industries, and another was to purchase advanced machinery and equipment in Western markets. While efforts have been made on both fronts, the results to date have not been very impressive and it seems unlikely that productivity growth will be sufficient to compensate for factor shortages in the relevant future.

While it is certainly possible to overstate the case, military programs must bear some of the onus for the Soviet productivity slump.   As in the United States, a considerable portion of the national research and development effort is geared to military needs.   Even more than in the United States, these needs make substantial claims on the most productive capital and manpower. In electronics, for example, defense requirements account for most of the output of integrated circuits, while they take approximately one-third of the product of the machine building sector.   It is also true that defense is in a position to place priority demands on the most qualified engineers and technicians who could, under different circumstances, make a particularly beneficial contribution to the civilian economy.   As far as the potential spinoff benefits that military research and development can provide to the civilian sector, the situation is probably similar for both superpowers—the highly specialized nature of contemporary military needs makes it increasingly unlikely that discoveries generated for such purposes will find appropriate nonmilitary applications.

CONCLUSIONS

What can we conclude about the dynamics behind the super-power military competition now that it has been examined from both sides? Perhaps the major conclusion is that the mechanisms that drive the arms-race behavior of the Soviet Union are only partially similar to those that apply to the United States. While initiatives on either side will usually represent a sufficient condition for a corresponding (equal or greater) reaction, these are not *necessary* conditions since, even in the absence of an objective challenge, a number of endogenous circumstances can produce very similar results. These conditions, moreover, are rather dissimilar between the two nations.

Major and discontinuous changes on the Soviet side do seem to originate from autonomous decisions taken by the top party leadership in response to real or perceived U.S. threats. Neverthe-less, even in the absence of visible U.S. initiatives, some incremental Soviet growth would probably occur anyway as a result of strong bureaucratic momentum (which subsumes the interests of the military elite) and an actual decline in U.S. programs and spending levels may not alter this fact. To the extent that a powerful constraining influence on USSR military growth does exist, it is most likely to be found in the increasingly onerous economic burden that the arms race places on the nation's economy.

Two factors make the situation in the United States seem even more complicated than in the Soviet Union. In the first place, a defining attribute of political pluralism is that political leadership is never free from powerful interest-group pressures. This fact makes it difficult for incumbents to take effective steps at curbing the military momentum even when this is thought to be advan-tageous after an overall assessment of internal and foreign policy needs. A related and substantial difference between the two nations involves the role of economic considerations. While there is little doubt that the Soviet economy suffers as a result of military claims, the U.S. economy is often thought to garner at least cyclical benefits from defense programs. The implication is that even relatively enlightened decision makers may have misgivings about creating dislocations, unemployment, and various recessionary symptoms (all of which might be experienced during their own incumbency) in exchange for hypothetical economic and other benefits sometime in an uncertain future.

The arms race is imbedded in circumstances proper to the domestic political and economic systems of the superpowers *in addition* to dynamics inherent in the interaction between the two nations. Any successful efforts at arms control or disarmament would have to take this into account, a fact that may make such efforts appear even more difficult than would be the case if their sole prerequisite were an elimination of objective conflicts of interest between the United States and the Soviet Union. In any case, the success of such endeavours would probably depend on the influence of those exceptional factors that actually do serve to constrain military growth and, since their salience may follow certain periodicities and trends, on the appropriate timing of important decisions. These points will be developed in greater detail in Chapter 7.

NOTES

1. See, in particular, Arthur J. Alexander, "Decision-Making in Soviet Weapons Procurement," *Adelphi Papers* nos. 147/148, 1978; Mathew P. Gallagher and Karl F. Spielman Jr., *Soviet Decision-Making for Defense* (New York: Praeger, 1972); Karl Spielman, *Analyzing Soviet Strategic Arms Decisions* (Boulder, Colo.: Westview, 1978); and Thomas W. Wolfe, "The Military Dimension in the Making of Soviet Foreign and Defense Policy," P-6024, The Rand Corporation, October 1977.
2. For example, Charles W. Ostrom Jr., "Evaluating Alternative Foreign-Policy Models: An Empirical Test Between an Arms Race Model and an Organizational Politics Model," *Journal of Conflict Resolution* 21 (1977): 235-265; Jacek Kugler, A. F. K. Organski, with Daniel Fox, "Deterrence and the Arms Race: Impotence of Power," *International Security*, 4 (1980):105-38; Hans Rattinger, "Armaments, Detente and Bureaucracy: The Case of the Arms Race in Europe," *Journal of Conflict Resolution* 19 (1975): 571-595.
3. Here I am following Jerry F. Hough, *The Soviet Union and Social Science Theory* (Cambridge, Mass.: Harvard University Press, 1977), chap. 2.
4. Ibid., p. 62.
5. Alexander, op.cit., p. 25.
6. Ibid., pp. 24-54.
7. Roman Kolkowicz, "Strategic Elites and the Politics of Superpower," *Journal of International Affairs* 26 (1972): 58.
8. Gallagher and Spielman, op.cit., p. 79.
9. These are the following ministries: Defense Industry, Aviation Industry, Shipbuilding Industry, Electronics Industry, Radio Industry, General Machine Building, Medium Machine Building (which covers nuclear devices

and warheads), and Machine Building.

10. This body is described in David Holloway, "Technology and Political Decision in Soviet Armaments Policy," *Journal of Peace Research* 11 (1974): 259-60; and in Jerry R. Hough and Merle Fainsod, *How the Soviet Union Is Governed* (Cambridge, Mass.: Harvard University Press, 1979), pp. 382-83.

11. On this point see John McDonnel, "The Soviet Defense Industry as a Pressure Group," in Michael MccGwire, Ken Booth, and John McDonnel, eds., *Soviet Naval Policy: Objectives and Constraints* (New York: Praeger, 1977), pp. 88-89.

12. Christopher Donnaly, "Military/Political Infrastructure," *The Soviet War Machine: An Encyclopedia of Russian Military Equipment* (New York: Chartwell Books, 1976); William Odom, "Who Controls Whom in Moscow," *Foreign Policy*, Summer 1975; Fred M. Kaplan, *Dubious Specter: A Second Look at the Soviet Threat* (Washington, D.C.: Transnational Institute, 1977).

13. *Kommunist Vooruzhenih Sil*, no. 21, November 1971, cited in Herbert Goldhamer, *The Soviet Soldier: Soviet Military Management at the Troop Level* (New York: Vrane, Russack, 1975).

14. These quotation are from Nikita S. Khrushchev, *Khrushchev Remembers*, Strobe Talbott, trans. and ed. (Boston: Little, Brown, 1970) p. 518.

15. This is the thesis of Vernon V. Aspaturian, "The Soviet Military Industrial Complex—Does it Exist?" *Journal of International Affairs* 26 (1972): 1-28; in a related vein, see Lawrence T. Caldwell, "The Future of Soviet-American Relations," in Lawrence T. Caldwell and William Diebold, Jr. (eds.), *Soviet-American Relations in the 1980s: Superpower Politics and East-West Trade* (New York: McGraw-Hill, 1981), esp. pp. 79-82.

16. It has, for example, been reported that a senior Soviet military representative to the SALT I meetings "took aside a US delegate and said there was no reason why the Americans should disclose their knowledge of Russian military matters to civilian members of his delegation. Such information, said Ogarkov, is strictly the affair of the military." John Newhouse, *Cold Dawn: The Story of SALT* (New York: Holt, Rinehart and Winston, 1973), p. 142.

17. Wolfe, op.cit., p. 31.

18. It has been observed, for example, that obstacles to technological innovation in the military sector had often been successfully surmounted by the political leadership, which overcame interdepartmental barriers to research and development efforts (e.g., in the case of ICBM development) and had removed administrative inhibitions to innovation. Holloway, op.cit., pp. 263-65.

19. Senate Foreign Relations Committee Hearings, *United States/Soviet Strategic Options*, Jan. 14, 19, March 16, 1977, p. 142.

20. Robert McNamara, *The Essence of Security* (New York: Harper & Row, 1968), p. 60.

21. "The Dynamics of the Arms Race," *Scientific American*, April 1969.

22. On this point, see Howard J. Sherman, *The Soviet Economy* (Boston: Little, Brown, 1969), chap. 9.

23. This relationship has been statistically analyzed in Paul Gregory, "Economic Growth, US Defense Expenditure and the Soviet Defence Budget," *Soviet Studies* 26 (1971): 72-80.

24. "Fluctuations and Interaction in Estimates of Soviet Budget Expenditure," *Osteuropa Wirtschaft* 18 (1973): 55-77.

25. Miroslav Nincic, "The Political Economy of Soviet Military Spending," Ann Arbor, 1980. Mimeographed.
26. Hutchings, op.cit., pp. 73-74.
27. See the various contributions to U.S. Congress, Joint Economic Committee, *Soviet Economy in a Time of Change*, Washington, D.C. 1979; also, Holland Hunter, ed., *The Future of the Soviet Economy* (Boulder, Colo.: Westview Press, 1978).
28. Stanley Cohn, "The Economic Burden of Soviet Defense Outlays," U.S. Ninety-first Congress, Joint Economic Committee, *Economic Performance and the Military Burden in the Soviet Union*, Washington, D.C., 1970.
29. Donald W. Green and Christopher I. Higgins, *SOVMOD I: A Macroeconomic Model of the Soviet Union* (New York: Academic Press, 1977), pp. 70-72.
30. "USSR: Some Implications of Demographic Trends for Economic Policies," ER 77-10012, Washington, D.C., January 1977, p. 2.
31. Daniel Galiik, "The Military Burden and Arms Control," in Hunter, op.cit., p. 136.

5

ARMS, STRATEGY,
AND SECURITY

The focus so far has been on the forces that propel the arms race and on the economic consequences of substantial and seemingly ceaseless military growth. Still, the professed justification for this kind of growth clearly does not involve counterrecessionary policy, bureaucratic momentum, or the appetites of the armed services but, rather, the claims of national security. It is these claims that, on both sides, are invoked to justify the recognized costs of the race and we must examine its effects by such criteria as well. Two major issues, in particular, should be addressed.

In the first place, it will be useful to assess the extent to which given security concerns have conditioned the specific content of the arms race at various times, an issue which, in the interests of focus, will be restricted to the competition in strategic weapons. To a limited extent, this question was addressed when we examined the role that military procurement and spending in one country played in determining defense endeavours in the other country. Nevertheless, this is not all there is to it. Decisions to develop or to deploy particular weapons are not justified exclusively in terms of the adversary's force posture but are often cast in terms of an articulated doctrine that establishes an explicit link between certain arms, strategic behavior, and national security. The doctrine seeks to determine which sort of hardware will best serve the nation's security and how it should be used. Our understanding of the strategic arms race will therefore be more complete if we examine to what extent security concerns, especially as treated in strategic doctrines, account for the acquisition of specific weapons. If it were to be concluded that their role in this regard is minor, we may also wish to reverse the question and ask whether the claims of security and the associated doctrines do not represent a rationalization of (rather than an explanation for) new strategic systems.

Quite apart from what might be claimed about the interplay between doctrines and weapons, it is necessary to confront the issue of the *actual* consequences of the strategic arms race for superpower security. Is either country more secure now than it was in 1970 or, for example, 1955? Before embarking any further, however, some conceptual clarification is called for.

Security, for any social entity, denotes the relative absence of effective threats to that which it values. Since we are dealing with nation states, we should thus attempt to identify what is most central to their value systems. Taxonomies are often awkward, but it seems that three types of values, which can be variously ranked, are particularly relevant. The first concerns the physical integrity of the nation's population and, here, security would refer to the absence of threats to its survival and health. The second, which is less sharply defined, involves the nation's material well-being and the concern would be with the safety of such things as resource endowments (or of access to external sources), capital stock, preferred economic mechanisms, etc. The third value encompassed by security bears on the chosen sociopolitical patterns and institutions of the nation, that is, on its normative order. The list, while not long, is relatively comprehensive and the assumption will be that each side seeks to protect its population, economy, and normative heritage from threats by the rival superpower. Given the concerns of this study, the relevant threats for our purposes will be those that inhere in armed hostilities.

Security can now be more specifically defined as a concept that reflects the *probability* that hostile military action will be directed against these values, and the *costs* to these values should this occur. For example, a weapon or an arsenal that diminished the probability of armed hostilities by making their costs prohibitively high might be neither more nor less valuable from the perspective of security than one that increased their likelihood by rendering the associated damage virtually insignificant. However, if probability were held constant while costs increased (or the former decreased with fixed costs) there would be a clear loss in terms of national security.

Both the examination of strategic *doctrines* (as applied theories of security enhancement) and of actual *achievements* in security will rely on this conception. In certain ways, of course, the two issues come together and, as a parenthetical illustration of this point, it could be argued that if these doctrines amount to no more than post hoc justifications for new weapons and codifications of the rules of strategic conduct that they impose, all that could be hoped for security would be to make the most of acquired military circumstances.

As a final bit of preliminary groundwork, the reader should recall that weapons can, theoretically, serve security by performing three possible functions.[1] They can, first of all, provide the means of *defending* against external threats, of fending off aggression, and of minimizing damage should it occur. A second function is one of *deterring*, designed to minimize the likelihood that a resort to defense will become necessary; this is usually done by threatening substantial retaliatory punishment to a potential aggressor. Third, military might can be called upon to perform a function of *compelling*, by forcing an adversary to do something it would otherwise not do or by depriving the adversary of something it would otherwise possess (for example, to disband an alliance, to forego a new weapon). While these functions overlap in certain ways (for example, the purpose of both deterrence and defense is to dissuade) they are quite different in others (for example, if defense becomes necessary then deterrence has failed; while compelling is meant to produce an active outcome, deterrence is meant to produce a negative result) and should, generally, be treated as distinct categories. Until recently, military power has usually been assigned a role of compelling or of defense; currently, however, the nuclear age has caused a partial displacement of these two functions in favor of the third. The cardinal tenet of much contemporary strategic thought was presaged, in 1946, by Bernard Brodie's perception that

> Thus far, the chief purpose of our military establishment has been to win wars. From now on, its chief purposes must be to avert them. It can have almost no other useful purpose.[2]

How was this supposed to work in practice as the strategic competition moved through its various phases? How did deterrence interact with weapons development and how has security been affected?

UNILATERAL ADVANTAGE AND MASSIVE RETALIATION

The Cold War, which had been intensifying during the late 1940s and early 1950s, was the major foreign policy problem of the new Republican administration as it assumed office in 1953.

Nevertheless, as the Korean War came to an end in July and with Stalin's death that same year, a strategy was sought that would avoid another costly engagement abroad. This was provided by the so-called New Look in defense policy which, under the rubric of Massive Retaliation, embodied the first explicit strategic doctrine of the nuclear era. The basic idea was simple and straightforward: any Soviet armed foray into regions deemed important to U.S. security would, according to John Foster Dulles, "encounter a great capacity to retaliate, instantly, by means and at places of our own choosing."[3] The impression purposely conveyed was that the United States would be willing and ready to respond, with the full force of its nuclear arsenal, to any USSR armed initiative even if this were only of a limited and conventional sort. Thus, for example, a thrust into Western Europe might not be met by dispatching a corresponding contingent of U.S. troops to the region but, conceivably, by a full-scale nuclear assault on the Soviet Union.

This was a doctrine of war avoidance, and hence of security, that was based on the conviction that deterrence could be ensured by threatening a retaliation that was disproportionately greater than the provocation. A rational government would prudently abstain from aggression under these circumstances and the need for future commitments of men and money to foreign wars would be removed. What are we to think of the doctrine in light of the framework we have set for ourselves?

Conclusions about the security-enhancing merits of this approach may depend on whether the matter is viewed from a static or dynamic perspective. In the first case, one would assume that the doctrine referred to a permanent situation, where the balance of nuclear power between the two rivals was frozen. Under such circumstances, the aim would have been to reduce the likelihood of U.S. involvement in conflict, which would in any case have had limited costs, to an insignificant level by threatening the certain and virtually total devastation of the Soviet Union should it initiate an armed provocation in certain parts of the world. In these limited terms, the strategic approach can be said to have made some sense. From the point of view that recognizes that major achievements on one side stimulate similar accomplishments on the other, it was plainly self-defeating. Faced with a dangerous inferiority, Moscow did its utmost to match the U.S. position and thus destroyed the doctrine's foundation.

The decisive blow to massive retaliation was delivered by the successful launching of Sputnik and by Washington's perception that the Soviets had acquired a long-range missile capability. An influential assessment of the situation created by strategic symmetry was Albert Wohlstetter's article in 1957 entitled "The Delicate Balance of Terror."[4] The principal problem, according to the article, was that the ability that each nation possessed to destroy the other led to a dangerously unstable situation by creating an incentive, in a crisis, to strike first in order to preempt a similar idea on the other side. Arms-race instability (the inability to control competitive military growth) had thus led to crisis instability (the risk that available weapons could transform crises into actual warfare). The security of both superpowers was now imperiled, perhaps more than it had previously ever been.

An important point, for present purposes, is that the doctrine of Massive Retaliation was the product of a given stage in the arms race. Whatever might have explained the U.S. decision to acquire nuclear hardware, technology, and associated resources, this conception of security was, to a significant extent, a rationalization for the strategic balance thus produced. When the doctrine was first conceived, only the United States possessed thermonuclear weapons while the Soviets had only the less impressive fission bombs. Though this edge was lost with the Soviet's detonation of its own fusion device in 1954, United States dominance was still ensured by its superior delivery capabilities. True, neither nation had intercontinental missiles at the time and each relied mainly on long-range bombers, but the *basing* of these bombers conferred a decisive advantage on the United States. It should be remembered that surprise is essential in a confrontation of this type and that even a B-52 (a very advanced plane at the time) took about 11 hours to reach the Soviet Union from the United States. For this reason, it was significant that the United States had bases in Europe and in the Pacific from which Soviet targets could be quickly reached, thus guaranteeing their destruction. More than anything else, therefore, the state of the race in bombs and delivery capability explained the appeal of Massive Retaliation to the United States.[5] In the post-Sputnik era of relative parity, the strategy became irrelevant and, because of the crisis instability it created, security may well have been lower than before the first detonation of a nuclear device. In other words, a situation where probability was relatively high and costs were low was superceded, in the late 1950s, by a situation where both became simultaneously high. By definition, therefore, the move to a major missile capability seemed to decrease security and a new nuclear doctrine was called for.

DETERRENCE AND MUTUAL ASSURED DESTRUCTION

A first adjustment to the changed circumstances was to jettison the strategy, which no longer carried much conviction, of all-out retaliation for limited provocation. The idea was that options should be relatively flexible but that, on the whole, responses would be of a similar nature (a conventional attack on Europe, for example, would call forth defense with conventional forces as long as possible).

Deterrence was now mutual and based on the expectation that nuclear retaliation would follow a nuclear attack and that this would preclude the occurrence of either. The major condition was the retention, by both sides, of a second-strike "countervalue" capability. This term refers to the ability to destroy those *non-military* targets that the enemy values most, notably civilian population, urban centers, and economic installations. That this should be achieved by a *second*-strike implied the possession of a nuclear arsenal capable of weathering an initial full-scale assault well enough to counter with an unacceptable level of damage on the attacker. Knowing that intolerable devastation could not be avoided, no first strike would ever be hazarded.

If this were to work, however, it was necessary to ensure the "survivability" of one's delivery force, a need that encouraged the accelerated procurement of systems that were relatively invulnerable to nuclear attack, such as the Polaris submarine (whose development had been undertaken in the 1950s). It also led to the hardening, on both sides, of ICBM silos and, at one stage, to sympathy for ABM systems.

Efforts were made in the United States to articulate the doctrine as clearly as possible. Not only was the function of a second strike explained, but an effort was also made to determine what an unacceptable level of assured destruction would involve, as well as to estimate the amount of destructive force that would be needed to inflict the necessary amount of retaliatory damage after a first strike had been absorbed. In his final appearance before the House Armed Services Committee, Robert McNamara argued that sufficient devastation for deterrent purposes would include roughly one-quarter of the USSR population and half of its industrial capacity[6] or, in other words, about twice the losses absorbed by the Soviet Union during World War II. The level of destructive power considered necessary to achieve this was computed to be in the vicinity of 400 "equivalent megatons" (EMTS).[7] Since U.S. strategic forces were based on the concept of a triad, including land-based missiles, submarine-launched missiles, and bombers, it was calculated that each should have the ability to deliver this amount even if the other two legs of the triad were destroyed. In 1978, these figures were slightly revised by Secretary of Defense Harold Brown who defined the necessary amount of assured damage to include at least 200 Soviet cities,[8] raising threatened losses to approximately one-third of the population and nearly two-thirds of the adversary's industrial capacity.

How had security fared as a result of these developments? Clearly the idea was that the probability of conflict would decrease proportionately to the level of anticipated damage (on a second strike), a hypothesis to which the United States now seemed to give bilateral application. On a prima facie basis this is not implausible, yet a sense of unease with the doctrine may be expressed on several grounds. To begin with, moral arguments can be raised against the idea of deterrence via countervalue threats and, indeed, the notion of wiping out innocent population in the name of security should raise some fairly basic ethical questions even for the hard-nosed military planner. The question of *direct* concern here, however, is whether superpower security was effectively enhanced by the new force postures and by the strategic doctrines by which they were justified. An affirmative answer would be appropriate only if two possible criticisms could be dealt with adequately. One involves the matter of whether these principles of deterrence were fully accepted by the Soviet Union; if not, the foundation of the approach would clearly be shattered. Another concerns the implicit postulate of this doctrine: that the adversary will act in an almost totally rational manner.[9]

Let us begin with the matter of Soviet conceptions. The strategic debate is usually not public in the Soviet Union, and we know considerably less about the Kremlin's views on deterrence by mutual destruction than we do about those of the United States. Nevertheless, and despite occasionally differing opinions on this point, the basic logic *does* appear to be accepted with some variants by Moscow.[10] This acceptance, in turn, derives from two perceptions that are central to USSR strategic thinking.[11] The first is that nuclear war would be a calamity of tremendous proportions for both sides—that neither could hope to escape unprecedented levels of destruction if it were to occur. Not only are the inevitable human and material losses acknowledged, but serious stress is also placed upon the likely costs of nuclear warfare to the Soviet political order (the maintenance of which is probably a first priority). As one observer explains it:

Soviet military-political doctrine warns that the course of military conflict can exercise a "reverse effect" on the political systems of states at war . . . that military setbacks often exacerbate tensions in domestic politics and undermine the legitimacy of the government in power.[12]

The second belief to which Soviet strategists adhere is that the scope of nuclear war cannot remain limited, that is, that its effects cannot be moderated by the progressive and controlled use of nuclear weapons. *Any* use therefore, is to be avoided by all means. The major difference between the official thinking of the two sides, at least until recently, has been the Soviet readiness to challenge the assumption of the necessarily symmetrical nature of the devastation that would ensue. While each side would suffer unprecedented losses, these should be even heavier on the U.S. side, assuring the Soviets of at least a Pyrrhic victory. Thus, rather than setting an absolute level of assured destruction as the condition of deterrence (for example, x percent of the population and y percent of the economy), the USSR notion emphasizes *relatively* more destruction for the assailant as a guarantee that the United States would not attack.

This is certainly a different doctrinal twist but it does nothing, as far as I can tell, to invalidate the concept of mutual deterrence through a powerful and certain retaliatory capacity. It is sometimes asserted that the Kremlin views actual nuclear warfare as a viable means of promoting its political goals, but the evidence seems to point the other way. In an interview in the *New York Times*, the head of the Political-Military Division of the Soviet Institute of the United States and Canada observed that: "Our doctrine regards nuclear weapons as something which must never be used. They are not instruments for waging war in any rational sense. They are not weapons with which one can achieve foreign-policy goals."[13] Thus, the mismatch between strategic doctrines in the mutual assured destruction (MAD) era may have been less substantial than is often believed.

The assumption of *rationality*, however, is more problematic. The justification for the new weapons (e.g., nuclear-missile submarines) was predicated on their ability to decrease the probability of warfare to an insignificantly low level, and this assumes a perfectly rational adversary. Any doubt cast on this assumption would weaken both the doctrine and the justification for the weapons. The problem, of course, is that rationality could be definitely disconfirmed only if either side actually did launch a nuclear attack contrary to the doctrine's prediction—in which case we would no longer be in a position to care anyhow. Under less cataclysmic circumstances, an assessment of the assumption's credibility would have to depend on one's beliefs concerning individual and organizational behavior. This author's perception is that, apart from the risk of messianic fanaticism by governments under no one's control, it is extremely unlikely that either side, knowing the extent of the punishment it could not hope to avoid, would wantonly invite its own devastation for the satisfaction of incinerating the adversary's society.

Given the amount of destructive power that both superpowers had, for a variety of reasons, acquired by then, deterrence by mutually assured destruction may have been a reasonable strategy, but only under the circumstances of that particular era. On ethical grounds it is clearly repulsive yet, from the narrow viewpoint of security under the constraints of existing weaponry, this was surely a vast improvement on the situation of crisis instability that preceded it.

One attractive feature of MAD, from the perspective of arms control, was that it provided a ceiling for necessary destructive power and, hence, a rationale for limiting at least U.S. arms behavior (and making it independent of Soviet conduct).

If the United States were in a position to inflict the predetermined amount of damage on the Soviets with a second strike, further Soviet acquisitions need not be matched. The essential thing was that each leg of the triad should be able to deliver at least 400 MTEs even if the other two were totally destroyed. By the late 1960s it was estimated that this capacity had been achieved and the security-related rationale for further growth (particularly that which did not contribute to a second-strike capacity) should have been hard to justify. The extent to which this growth did occur, therefore, may serve as a partial test of the actual influence of prevailing security concerns, as codified in strategic doctrine, on the development and procurement of weapons. It seems, on the basis of observed arms-race behavior, that the influence of these concerns is modest. Despite the doctrine, technological developments and, eventually, acquisitions continued their ineluctable march and a relation between arms and security, which appeared to have been obtained, became increasingly tenuous.

MIRV, the system that produced an initial impetus to strategic revisionism, is a case in point. It will be recalled that development of MIRV was undertaken in the 1960s and became operational by 1970. By 1977 the United States had deployed the system on 550 Minuteman ICBMs and 496 Poseidon SLBMs. The initial justification, as described in Chapter 2, was to offset the anticipated Soviet ABM program and, thus, to guarantee sufficient destruction of the Soviet Union if necessary *despite* the missile-defense measures. Otherwise, it was argued, MAD and security would be jeopardized. While the explanation may seem plausible when put in these terms, subsequent events indicate otherwise. Soon, the USSR system was discovered to be far more modest than had been initially estimated and was, furthermore, apparently designed for protection against bombers rather than missiles; in any case, ABMs were limited by mutual agreement in 1972. Thus, if objective security needs dictated by MAD were the reason for contemplating MIRVs, later developments should have led to their total or partial abandonment. Despite the vanishing rationale, the U.S. program continued at full speed and, since a major development on one side is a sufficient, albeit not always necessary, condition for a response by the other side, a corresponding Soviet program was soon initiated. MIRV development continued apace and the United States soon had a total of 9,000 warheads, many times more than would have been needed if the assured destruction of 200 Soviet cities (many of which are of modest size) was sought. Also, while the Russian warheads were still rather inaccurate in the 1970s, superior technology had made those associated with United States MIRVs capable of increasingly impressive precision. The need for this could not be justified in terms of a countervalue strategy either, since cities and industrial complexes represent sprawling and relatively "soft" targets that do not have to be hit with pinpoint accuracy to ensure their destruction. Events since MIRV do nothing to dispel the impression of a dubious link between weapons acquisition and extant security doctrine.

A major new U.S. development, initiated in 1972, was the cruise missile—a small, drone shaped and self-propelled vehicle that could be deployed on airplanes (ALCMs), submarines (SLCMs) or launched from the ground (GLCMs). The ALCM, which is both far more accurate and much cheaper (though considerably slower) than ICBMs, has recently been deployed on B-52 bombers with a 700 KT warhead. These payloads can be delivered with the extreme precision of 0.01 nautical mile thanks to an advanced guidance system. While this weapon is potentially one of the most effective components of the U.S. arsenal, its relevance to MAD has never been clear; rather, its natural application has always been for the destruction of specific *military* targets such as weapons installations or command centers. It is, therefore, a counterforce, rather than countervalue, weapon and its function seems as closely related to compelling and defending as to deterring.

Similar conclusions can be drawn about the most recent developments in the area of submarine and SLBM technology. Despite their comparative invulnerability to attack, a major disadvantage of submarine-launched missiles relative to their land-based counterparts has traditionally involved a lower level of accuracy. Although this would not make a less appropriate countervalue system, many spokesmen for naval interests were unhappy with this element of comparative inferiority. Part of the problem has been that, to hit a target with a certain measure of accuracy (e.g., 0.5 nautical miles), the submarine would have to know its location with an even greater degree of exactitude—something that has, until recently, been unattainable. Nevertheless, the development of the inertial-guidance system[14] has reduced the problem considerably and there is reason to expect that the satellite global-positioning system[15] will transform SLBMs (Trident II missiles in particular) into highly accurate counterforce weapons. Like the cruise missile, this could not be adequately justified in terms of MAD, and a revised rationale, via a new strategic doctrine, was necessary.

Nor have the Soviets been passive during this time. In the course of the 1970s, they developed a more powerful and somewhat more accurate fourth generation of ICBMs (the SS-17, SS-18, and SS-19) and a fifth generation has recently been flight tested. The Soviet MIRV was initially tested in 1973 and deployed on land-based missiles (the SS-18) two years later. In addition, the Soviet Union produced a tactical bomber (the Backfire) with some strategic capability and has deployed a new "Delta-class" ballistic missile submarine. Presently, the Soviets have deployed 2,504 strategic delivery vehicles of which more than 650 ICBMs and 950 SLBM launchers are MIRVed. While the relative inaccuracy of this weaponry has precluded a counterforce capability so far, this does indicate a willingness to pursue strategic growth with at least the same enthusiasm as the United States.

COUNTERFORCE WEAPONS AND STRATEGIC REVISIONISM

Pressures to modify U.S. strategic views were apparent by the early 1970s. As security claims could no longer be plausibly invoked under the old terms of strategic reference, new doctrinal efforts were needed to justify the latest, weapons. Accordingly,

Secretary of Defense James Schlesinger argued for a policy of "flexible targeting" in order to maintain options in addition to all-out nuclear assaults should deterrence break down. In his 1975 annual defense report, he specifically called for an approach that would allow for

> A series of measured responses to aggression which bear some relation to the provocation, have prospects of terminating hostilities before general nuclear war breaks out and leave some possibility for restoring deterrence.[16]

The argument was not that MAD should be altogether discarded, but that the range of nuclear responses should be expanded. What was needed, it seemed, was the ability to conduct limited nuclear warfare, to target military installations and missile silos, and to reduce collateral damage when possible and desired. Such missions, in turn, would necessitate precisely those attributes possessed by the U.S. systems that have just been described (and most of which were at or beyond the development stage at that time).

Even so, there was some hesitancy to depart from the previous conception of security by means of mutually assured destruction. When the Carter administration stepped into office, the president reaffirmed his commitment to the traditional approach while Harold Brown, the new defense secretary, began by downplaying counterforce.[17] Soon, however, the clamor of new programs became overwhelming. The MX missile entered the development stage and called for congressional funding; its expensive price tag (variously estimated at between 30 and 80 billion dollars), and the controversy surrounding the system (on questions ranging from performance to its ecological impact)[18] meant that powerful justifications were needed. Another new missile, dubbed the Maneuverable Reentry Vehicle (MARV), with a variable postboost trajectory and increased accuracy, was also being developed. In 1980 its advanced version (AMARV) was flight tested[19] and displayed an ability to evade Soviet interceptor vehicles and to correct its trajectory to ensure delivery within a fraction of a nautical mile—this too required a rationale. In addition, tactical nuclear weapons suitable for use in actual war theaters (particularly in Europe) became a significant component of the total force posture. None of these weapons had any logical place within MAD, and a commitment to counterforce options and limited nuclear warfare became indispensable. In July 1980 President Carter signed Presidential Directive 59, requiring

U.S. nuclear forces to be able to undertake precise and limited strikes against military facilities in the Soviet Union. Assured destruction of cities was not abandoned, the repertoire of possible destruction was simply expanded according to the dictates of increasingly sophisticated weapons technology.

Is a similar development occurring in the Soviet Union? Since there has never been a perfect symmetry between the strategic thinking of the two superpowers, a comparison of the doctrinal impact of new weapons is not always feasible. Specifically, there would be less of a contradiction between deterrent aims and a war-fighting capacity in the context of a strategic doctrine that has traditionally asserted that deterrence can best be achieved by acquiring the ability to inflict *relatively* greater damage on the assailant. Nevertheless, acquired or desired military resources do influence Soviet strategic pronouncements as well, and two examples, concerning both limited nuclear engagements and MAD, will illustrate this. To begin with, the USSR perspective on nuclear warfare does not recognize the feasibility of limited and precision exchanges of the sort envisaged by Washington. Rather, the contention that nuclear weapons can be used in a controlled and modulated manner is emphatically rejected. Moreover, it is the state of their strategic technology that may provide the explanation for this argument since, despite some progress, the accuracy of Soviet warheads does not match that of the United States. For example, the U.S. Minuteman III with Mark-12a warhead has (at the time of writing) a CEP of 600 feet, while the current figure for the SS-18 is 1,100 feet; the Trident I, by some accounts, has managed to obtain a CEP of 800 feet, whereas the present figure for the Russian SSN-18 is 1,800 feet.[20] Thus, Soviet achievements in weapons technology do not allow the same doctrinal link to be established between arms and security as in the United States. Nonetheless, advances in accuracy are taking place and recently announced tests of a long-range cruise missile by the USSR[21] (and continued work on their own MARV system) may change Moscow's approach as well.

A second illustrative observation is that an important function of strategic doctrine in the Soviet Union, as in the United States, is simply to rationalize military growth. In fact, it can be argued that the idea of deterrence via the ability to inflict relatively greater damage on the adversary is less an expression of deep beliefs than an attempt to ensure continued defense expansion. The point is that accepting a concept of deterrence by a finite amount of assured destruction might place a natural ceiling on new acquisitions and developments. The concept of greater *relative* damage, on the other hand, is conspicuously open-ended and suggests no obviously definable limit to military needs. The logic does not seem to have escaped Soviet military spokesmen. Raymond Garthoff, possibly the foremost U.S. analyst of Moscow's strategic policy, recently reported a debate that took place in the specialized Soviet press on the notion of nuclear warfare. Attacking the position of certain military theorists who maintained that nuclear war could not be won in any meaningful way, General Bochkarev, Deputy Commandant of the General Staff Academy, complained with some asperity that

> In other words, the armed forces of the socialist state . . . will not be able to set for themselves the goal of defeating imperialism and the global nuclear war which it unleashes . . . and our military science should not even work out a strategy for the conduct of war . . . in this case, *the very call to raise the combat readiness of our armed forces and improve their capability to defeat any aggressor is senseless.* (emphasis added)[22]

The gist of the matter comes through rather obviously. As Garthoff observes, "It is clear what is troubling General Bochkarev. The entire rationale for supporting Soviet military efforts is seen as undermined."[23]

A link between acquired weaponry, desired weaponry, and professed strategic beliefs is, to all appearances, as present in the Soviet Union as it is in the United States. In the context of counterforce posture, what effects have these links produced on the security of the superpowers?

COUNTERFORCE AND NATIONAL SECURITY

Unlike MAD, which seeks to decrease the probability of a nuclear exchange by making it prohibitively costly, the new approach lays far greater emphasis on cost reduction. However, it is often maintained that this strategy causes a more dangerously volatile situation than any which has been experienced in previous stages of nuclear history. Therefore, there are claims and counterclaims and it will be useful to begin with the arguments that can be adduced in favor of the new posture, that is, to try to understand why, in the words of a recent RAND publication, we should "learn to love (even lust for) first-strike counterforce capabilities."[24]

The arguments that attribute security-enhancing functions to counterforce flow, as far as I can tell, from three convictions.[25] The first concerns its apparently superior deterrent qualities, the second involves its imputed ability to control destruction should deterrence fail by limiting the collateral damage of warfare, and the third bears on the ability to destroy the Soviet Union's nuclear arsenal in a preemptive strike should war appear imminent. I will attempt to explain the reasoning behind these beliefs as well as to present some grounds on which the new strategy may be subject to criticism. Whatever its merits, however, it is clear that an exclusive reliance on nuclear weapons for purposes of deterrence has been abandoned and that their functions now include defending and, possibly, compelling.

The reasons for assigning superior deterrent abilities to highly accurate weapons seem intuitively compelling. If, it is argued, the only conceivable use of nuclear weapons is to destroy the other side's population and economy in retaliation for similar devastation directed at oneself, its relevance is limited to the most implausible strategic contingency. In other words, it is merely the least likely form of Soviet aggression that would be deterred, and many assaults of a lesser scale could be discouraged only by relying on conventional forces. While this may be feasible where such forces are evenly matched, the assumed preponderance of Soviet conventional power in both Europe and parts of Asia tends to decrease the credibility of an effective U.S. response. If, however, the United States were to maintain *limited* nuclear options for possible engagements in such regions, deterrence against more modest (but more likely) threats would be improved as well. Thus, the range of conflicts that can be avoided will, by this theory, be extended by expanding the range of application of nuclear weapons.

Even if deterrence broke down, it would be well to avoid a total holocaust of the type encouraged by MAD by keeping mutual destruction from becoming indiscriminate. According to one scenario, nuclear arms would be used only to exchange military targets (e.g., airfields and missile silos) and their precision would substantially limit collateral damage to civilians. In other words, the most objectionable forms of destruction would be avoided. In another variant, discrete nonmilitary targets would be attacked ("taken out") on the basis of strict reciprocity. For example, one city of a certain size might be sacrificed on each side after which hostilities would terminate with no further escalation of the violence. In both cases, the costs of a breakdown of deterrence would be considerably mitigated—an achievement made possible by the accuracy of offensive weapons and the controlled destruction this allows.

The third manner in which a counterforce posture could, under certain circumstances, increase security is by providing the United States with the capacity to destroy, as nearly as possible, the enemy's strategic force with a preemptive first strike. Thus, if tensions were sufficiently acute to presage nuclear conflict, a decisive first blow would limit the damage that the other side could impose with the full power of its arsenal. Clearly, however, this ability would require weapons (such as the MX missile) capable of striking extremely close to "hard" targets like missiles in thick concrete silos or, perhaps, underground command centers.

On the whole, all of this sounds reasonable from the perspective of national security. Since much of it would help reduce the costs to innocent civilians beyond that which MAD would entail, it may appeal on ethical grounds as well. Nevertheless, this whole brand of strategic revisionism has encountered a barrage of criticism which, if accepted, could imply that security has never been as threatened as it is now despite the substantial opportunity costs imposed by the new developments and acquisitions.[26] It seems to me that the strongest criticisms address two logically distinct dangers. The first involves the possibility that, despite the claims that are made, the *destructiveness* of nuclear warfare cannot really be controlled with the new weaponry. Obviously, this concerns the most central rationale for the new strategic approach. The second possible danger refers to a real increase in the *probability* that war would occur under the new circumstances. If either of these possibilities seem plausible, it would be difficult to argue that national security has increased; if both are accepted, however, the threat would seem greater than it has ever previously been.

Let us begin with the contention that, arguments to the contrary notwithstanding, restrained destruction could not be ensured in a nuclear engagement, no matter what the initial intent might have been. The major issue, in this context, is whether the amount of collateral damage could indeed be accurately anticipated and effectively controlled merely because of the accuracy of the new weapons. In this author's view, there are rather solid grounds for questioning the contention. Even if only a limited exchange were involved, high-priority targets in a counterforce duel would include such things as submarine facilities and command centers many of which are situated near sizable population concentrations. Moreover, not all of the effects of nuclear weapons can be confidently estimated. The destruction associated with the actual blast produced by an atomic bomb can be anticipated with some accuracy if the characteristics of the target and the target area (e.g., "hardness" and concentration of objects) are known. Secondary damage caused by the fires that would be ignited by the explosion cannot, however, be calculated in advance, since this is dependent on variable conditions of wind, humidity, etc. Least predictable of all are the effects, many of which are delayed, of radioactive fallout: there is (fortunately) little experience from which to assess the biological consequences of this fallout, and the total dose received would, in any case, be contingent on such imponderables as the dissipation of gamma radiation (which depends on meteorological conditions), the amount of contaminated food that is ingested, and so forth. Even the U.S. Office of Technology Assessment, in its most recent attempt at grappling with some of these problems, has observed that "the effects of nuclear war that cannot be calculated are at least as important as those for which calculations are attempted. Moreover, even these limited calculations are subject to very large uncertainties."[27]

The point is that if the effects of nuclear weapons can only be approximated in the roughest manner, it is not at all obvious how one could "fine tune" their impact to modulate the damage inflicted and thus maintain a controlled reciprocity. Rather, it seems quite possible that each side could impose more devastation than intended, thus vitiating the expectation of balanced destruction and encouraging an escalatory process that neither may thereafter be able to control.

Apart from the problem of insufficient knowledge for adequate control, there is also the unavoidable matter of human nature. One should consider that the idea of flexible and graduated response assumes that people at both ends of the conflict will behave in a totally dispassionate manner and exercise magnificent self-control throughout. Emotions are altogether absent from such scenarios and supreme rationality prevails. It is assumed that the U.S. government and people would look with clinical detachment upon the incineration of, say, Detroit and compute that a reasonable response would be the elimination of, for example, Murmansk. A similar assumption is made of the Soviets. Yet, it can be strongly argued that large portions of one's people would not be viewed as irrelevant pawns on the chessboard of nuclear strategy and that the impulse to punish, rather than simply to match, would soon push both nations far higher up the escalatory ladder than had initially been anticipated.

A further and related issue may be involved as well. It seems that even the limited use of nuclear weapons eliminates a crucial psychological threshold between conventional and nuclear warfare.

This, in turn, may remove a major inhibition to embarking on a process that may, thereafter, possess no naturally prominent barrier to further escalation. In other words, it may be considerably easier to escalate within the same general category of weaponry than to make the qualitative jump from one category to another—*unless* the distinction between the two had been purposely blurred by the prevailing strategic doctrine and weapons. Thus the decision to engage in nuclear conflict, as the continuation of what had begun as a conventional engagement, may become easier to take despite the intentions that are initially professed.

There are, quite simply, a number of reasons why control over the course of a nuclear exchange might escape the superpowers. Yet the notion of tightly controlled escalation is essential to the rationale for the new force posture and if this assumption should prove shaky, one may wish to conclude, along with a former deputy director of the CIA, that,

> A limited nuclear conflict presents a major risk of uncontrollable escalation so that almost no gain is worth risking an increase in the probability that it will occur.[28]

An obvious implication of this is that if conventional attacks must be deterred, the safest way of doing so is by fortifying one's *conventional power* rather than by invoking the nuclear option (but this may be another topic).

Not only can it be contended that the likelihood of assaults on a *limited* number of civilian or military targets by nuclear means is now enhanced, it is also possible that *large-scale* attacks on an entire missile force may be much more likely. One of the most significant characteristics of the new delivery vehicles is their apparent ability to destroy land-based missiles in hardened silos. Indeed, the third argument for counterforce explicitly justifies this capacity in terms of security needs. Nonetheless, this sort of capacity may also be viewed as a cause of acute crisis instability, where each side is tempted to hazard a first strike in situations of exceptional tension. The point is that if both superpowers have the ability to wipe out the other's ICBM force (and a substantial part of the bomber and submarine forces) then, if a serious crisis were to occur (e.g., over the Persian Gulf), each side will know that a first strike by the other may disable its arsenal and may thus have an incentive to preempt by being the one to attack first.[29] Eventually, the motivation on both sides may become so strong as to make the initiation of an attack very likely. This is, once again, the sort of situation against which Wohlstetter had warned in 1957. Admittedly, the existence of a relatively invulnerable submarine force (particularly on the U.S. side) reduces the danger of such a development in the immediate future but advances in antisubmarine warfare technology may eliminate this safety factor before long.

Obviously, the extremely large scope of the attack assumed in this type of scenario would make substantial collateral damage virtually inevitable—something that military spokesmen are not always eager to recognize. For example, when arguing for a counterforce capability in 1974, James Schlesinger claimed that a Soviet attack on all 1,504 ICBMs would result in approximately 800,000 deaths which, in itself, might not be enough to guarantee a full countervalue response by the United States. The Soviets, therefore, might not be deterred from launching such a strike.[30] This figure is, however, disputed by the estimates of the Office of Technology Assessment which, on the basis of its own research, computes that the number of victims would range anywhere from 2 to 20 million within the first 30 days.[31] If the situation is at all symmetrical in terms of Soviet casualties, it would seem unlikely that either side could avoid catastrophic civilian losses if such an attack were to occur.

On the whole, we may be in a position where an improbable attempt at limiting the damage that nuclear engagements would occasion is increasing the probability that such conflicts could occur and at similar levels of destruction to those that would have been involved in the previous strategic approach. If this seems like a reasonable inference, one is forced to conclude that, after another fiscally lavish round of the strategic arms race, after another wave of foregone economic opportunities, superpower security may actually have declined. Thus both nations are worse off as the result of a process that, despite the fact that many of its roots are domestic, they seem unable to control. At the same time, the doctrines by which the new weaponry is explained and matching rules of strategic conduct proposed tend to be codifications and rationalizations of the stage in the race to which we have been driven rather than optimal guides to national security.

Should we conclude that nuclear weapons inevitably drag us down a path of ever-decreasing security? The answer may not be wholly affirmative, but the circumstances where security is an actual beneficiary appear to be exceptional. To explain, let us consider two properties of the nuclear-arms competition: the first involves the comparative rate of growth of the antagonists' strategic capabilities; the second concerns the relative emphasis on offensive and nonoffensive weapons by both sides. Offensive weapons will be defined as those whose function is a preemptive strike or the attainment of decisive advantages in a war theater (e.g., a MARV system, ground-launched cruise missiles, etc); nonoffensive weapons will be those intended to destroy incoming vehicles or to provide retaliatory deterrence (e.g., ABMs, Poseidon SLBMs). If we just designate capacity growth as equal or unequal, a simple two-by-two table can be presented. Four possibilities are included in Figure 5.1 and it can be argued that security will benefit in *only one case*. Let us examine them sequentially.

1. The first case, that of a relatively equal increase in offensive capabilities, has characterized several stages of nuclear history and notably (but not exclusively) the late 1950s and, if there is some Soviet progress, the current period of rapid counterforce weapons development. The major consequence for security is the crisis instability that ensues.
2. The second case was characteristic of the U.S. missile build-up in the early 1960s and may be dominant in the 1980s if the MX, AMARV, and other programs are not matched by corresponding Soviet systems. Whereas in the previous case, each side has the motivation to strike first when crises become acute, in this case the underdog has the incentive to preempt when relations

FIGURE 5.1
Security and Strategic Arms Races

Relative Capability Growth

		Equal	Unequal
Strategic Emphasis	Offensive	1.	2.
	Nonoffensive	4.	3.

deteriorate sufficiently for fear of being left hopelessiy behind and exposed to the threat of the leader's aggression or blackmail. However, if a judicious management of bilateral relations inhibits tensions from reaching a point where the lagging party is tempted to strike first in a now-or-never context, a situation akin to that prevailing in the very early 1960s may exist. These circumstances should, however, change when the underdog *does* manage to catch up, leading back to a situation like Case 1, which is at least as unstable.

3. The effects of an unequal competition that stresses nonoffensive capabilities may be similar to the one characterized by the discrepant development of offensive systems. Again, the nation that perceives that it is being outrun has an incentive to preempt before the adversary is in a position to launch a nuclear attack with total impunity. However, this is not a simple case and an exception would occur if, for example, the nonoffensive capability of the loser is an inadequate match for the *offensive* power that the leader has retained.

4. If we assume that the newly acquired nonoffensive systems can virtually nullify the effects of a previously acquired offensive capacity, this may be the only case where *neither side has an incentive to strike.* This is true even in a context of acute crisis or steadily sharpening conflicts of interest.

The point is that the instances where a pure Case 4 situation can be attained are rare and the fact that there is often a "gray zone" between offensive and nonoffensive weapons does not simplify matters. Even if such problems could be eliminated, and both sides were to concentrate exclusively on nonoffensive systems, the optimistic scenario would require their closely matched rate of development and their clear superiority over existing offensive weapons.

In addition to purely strategic considerations, it should be remembered that much of the danger inheres in the *simultaneous* occurrence of a dangerous arms-race scenario (Cases 1-3) *and* a severe deterioration in political relations. While true security would be obtained only if crisis instability were not appreciably increased by political tensions (as in Case 4), under more probable circumstances astute diplomacy and mature efforts at dealing with (or transcending) conflicts of interest are indispensable palliatives.

My entire discussion of the probability of warfare has assumed that the initiation of hostilities would follow a considered decision on both sides. An issue that will be only briefly mentioned is the possibility that nuclear war may be accidentally triggered. On June 3 and June 6 1980, successive alerts indicating a Soviet missile attack were caused by a malfunctioning computer accessory (a 46 cent electronic chip).[32] Seven months earlier, on November 9, 1979 a war-game tape simulating a limited attack by Soviet SLBMs was accidentally fed into the live system of the North American Air Defense Command in Colorado.[33] The alert lasted a harrowing six minutes before the error was recognized; in the meantime, jet interceptors were scrambled and missile bases put on alert. There is no reason to think that false alerts could not have occurred on the Soviet side as well. The point is that the more weapons are deployed, and the more complicated they and the associated systems become, the greater will be the risk of error and, consequently, of accidental catastrophe. "We have created a world in which perfection is required if a disaster beyond history is to be permanently avoided."[34] It is daunting to reflect that we will be increasingly dependent on a quality that has never been achieved.

What does the future hold? While it is difficult to anticipate the cumulative effect of the arms race on security for the next decade or two, there are some inklings of the directions the actual race may take, and indications are that much of it may involve space-related systems.[35] This, moreover, is likely to be the most open-ended and costly arena of military competition yet.

The increasing reliance on satellites for strategic ends, current developments in space technology, and advanced work on military applications of laser and charged-particle beams, all presage future trends. The Soviet Union, which appears to have a lead in this area, has tested so-called "killer" satellites, which are designed to incapacitate those used by the United States for reconnaissance, missile guidance, and communications.[36] The United States, in turn, is responding with a major program of its own. Both nations have invested considerable effort and resources in acquiring a laser-beam capacity for strategic purposes; these beams, which travel at the speed of light and embody a rate of fire several thousand times that of any known weapon, have been successfully tested by the United States[37] and will probably be deployed within the current decade. Other systems related to engagements in space are also being developed and, as remaining technical problems are resolved, [38] bureaucratic, corporate, scientific, and other constituencies will coalesce behind the programs. Alarming predictions about the other side's plans or achievements will be aired in both nations and, in all likelihood, qualitatively new weapons will join existing arsenals in an unprecedented concentration of destructive might. While their exact nature may not be predictable at present, new doctrines will be demanded and provided to justify future acquisitions and to explain why, along with appropriate rules of conduct they will enhance national security. Some of these weapons may serve a nonoffensive function (for example, a laser operating in the relative vacuum above the atmosphere could serve as an ABM device by destroying incoming missiles), while others will have an offensive role (for example, satellites, or beams used from a space platform, could neutralize early-warning systems prior to attack). Their aggregate effect, nevertheless, is unlikely to produce a Case 4 situation.

CONCLUSIONS

Strategic doctrines are designed, in large part, to justify the weaponry that the arms race has imposed on both the United States and the Soviet Union. Their relation to actual security is thus rather tenuous and, with the transition to a counterforce doctrine, security may actually have declined. In fact, an arms race is likely to enhance security only in the improbable case that it leads to equally rapid growth in essentially defensive systems. This, however, would be quite atypical and superpower control over the conditions of their security may become increasingly elusive.

NOTES

1. These distinctions are insightfully discussed in Thomas Schelling, *Arm and Influence* (New Haven, Conn.: Yale University Press, 1966), esp. chap. 2; also in Robert J. Art, "To What Ends Military Power?" *International Security* 4 (Spring 1980): 3-35.
2. Bernard Brodie, *The Absolute Weapon* (New York: Harcourt, Brace, Jovanovich, 1946), p. 52.
3. Quoted in Michael Mandlebaum, *The Nuclear Question: The United States and Nuclear Weapons, 1946-1976* (New York: Cambridge University Press, 1979), p. 51.
4. Albert Wohlstetter, "The Delicate Balance of Terror," *Foreign Affairs* 37 (Jan. 1959): 209-34.
5. While this was the most important reason, it was not the only one. Another consideration of the Republican administration was of an economic nature, since deterrence by dint of the atomic bomb was seen as cheaper than if it

were assured by conventional troops. For a government that was much concerned with balanced budgets this was important.

6. David Ziegler, *War, Peace and International Politics* (Boston: Little, Brown, 1977), p. 79.

7. Equivalent megatons represent the explosive power that would be produced by the detonation of the same number of one-megaton bombs. This is a meaningful concept since the EMTs of a bomb are inferior to its raw megatonnage.

8. *Annual Report, Department of Defense Fiscal Year 1979* (Washington, D.C.: U.S. Department of Defense, 1980), p. 55.

9. The concept of rationality in strategic thought is analyzed by Anatol Rapoport, *Strategy and Conscience* (New York: Schocken Books, 1969), pts. I, II; and by Philip Green, *Deadly Logic: The Theory of Nuclear Deterrence* (New York: Schocken Books, 1966), Chaps. 5, 6.

10. One matter should be clarified at the outset. A number of authors have contended that the USSR adheres to Clausewitz's maxim by which war is a legitimate extension of politics and that, therefore, the Soviets may be planning to fight and win a nuclear war in order to further their political ambitions abroad (see, for example, Richard Pipes, "Why the Soviet Union Thinks it Could Fight and Win a Nuclear War," *Commentary*, July, 1977). This does not seem to be an appropriate interpretation of Soviet doctrine. While Moscow's theory does stress the existence of a powerful link between militarism and politics, this appears to refer to the motivations of dominant classes within capitalist nations who pursue their class-based interests by violent means—both internally and externally. War, from the perspective of Soviet theorists, *is* "a continuation of politics" but *not* a "legitimate instrument of politics." As one U.S. author remarks:

> In this context it is evident that when the Soviets defend the dictum that war is a continuation of policy as valid even in the nuclear age, they are not suggesting, as some Westerners contend they are, that nuclear weapons can and should be used as practical instruments of policy. Instead, the Soviet spokesmen are arguing that the Marxist-Leninist theory of war is still valid and that, if a nuclear war does start, it too will occur because certain classes within a nation are pursuing a policy by violent means.

(Robert Arnett, "Soviet Views on Nuclear War," in William Kincade and Jeffrey Poro, eds., *Negotiating Security: An Arms Control Reader* (New York: Carnegie Endowment for International Peace, 1979). See also Fred M. Kaplan, *Dubious Specter: A Second Look at the Soviet Threat* Washington, D.C.: Transnational Institute 1977); and B. Byely et al., *Marxism-Leninism on War and the Army* (Moscow: Progress Publishers, 1972).

11. See, for example, Raymond L. Garthoff, "Mutual Deterrence and Strategic Arms Limitation in Soviet Policy," *International Security* 3 (Summer 1978): 112-48; and Christopher D. Jones, "Soviet Military Doctrine: The Political Dimension," *Arms Control Today*, October, 1978.

12. Jones, op.cit., p. 4.

13. Lieutenant-General Mikhail A. Milshtein interviewed by Anthony Austin in "Moscow Expert Says US Errs on Soviet War Aims," *New York Times*,

August 5, 1980.

14. This involves a complex system of gyroscopes, accelerometers, and computers whose function it is to relate the movement and speed of the vessel in all directions with respect to true north in such a way that, if an initial position is known, the system will furnish continuous information on the ship's position.

15. This will allow even greater accuracy by relying on a constellation of 24 navigation satellites.

16. Quoted in Leon Sigal, "Rethinking the Unthinkable" *Foreign Policy* (Spring 1979): 35-51.

17. The Carter administration's movement from MAD toward counterforce during its first two years is traced in Jeffrey D. Poro, "Counterforce and the Defense Budget," *Arms Control Today*, February 1978.

18. Some relevant articles are: "GAO Says MX is Facing a Host of Uncertainties," *The Washington Post*, March 7, 1980; "MX Proposal Stirs Stiff Opposition," *Aviation Week and Space Technology*, December 31, 1979; Colin S. Gray, "The MX ICBM: Why We Need It," *Air Force Magazine*, August 1979, pp. 66-71; "MX: The Missile We Don't Need," *The Defense Monitor*, Oct. 1979; William H. Kincade, "Will MX Backfire?," *Foreign Policy* (Winter 1979-80): 43-48; and Donald Snow, "MX: Maginot Line of the 1980's," *The Bulletin of the Atomic Scientists* 36 (1980): 20-25.

19. See Bruce Smith, "Advanced Reentry Vehicle Flight-Tested," *Aviation Week and Space Technology*, February 11, 1980: 43-45.

20. Accuracy figures are from Paul F. Walker, "New Weapons and the Changing Nature of Warfare," *Arms Control Today*, April 1979.

21. Richard Burt, "Soviets Said to Test Cruise Missile with a Long Range," *New York Times*, February 2, 1979.

22. Garthoff, op. cit., p. 120.

23. Ibid., p. 120.

24. Carl H. Builder, "The Case for First-Strike Counterforce Capabilities," P-6179, The Rand Corporation, July 1978.

25. Some relevant references are Builder, op.cit.; Paul Nitze, "Assuring Strategic Stability in an Era of Detente," *Foreign Affairs* 54 (1976): 207-32; L. E. Davis, "Limited Nuclear Options: Deterrence and the New American Doctrine," *Adelphi Papers*, no. 21 London: International Institute of Strategic Studies, 1975/76); Richard Rosecrance, "Strategic Deterrence Reconsidered," *Adelphi Papers*, no. 116 (London: International Institute of Strategic Studies, 1975).

26. See, for example, Donald M. Snow, "Current Nuclear Deterrence Thinking," *International Studies Quarterly*, 23 (Sept. 1979): 445-86; Sidney D. Drell and Frank Von Hippel, "Limited Nuclear War," *Scientific American*, November 1976; Hans J. Morgenthau, "The Fallacy of Thinking Conventionally about Nuclear Weapons," in David Carlton and Carlo Schaerf, eds., *Arms Control and Technological Innovation* (New York: John Wiley, 1976) pp. 255-64; and Leon Sigal, op. cit.

27. *The Effects of Nuclear War* (Washington, D.C.: Office of Technology Assessment, 1979), p. 3.

28. Herbert Scoville, Jr., "Flexible Madness," *Foreign Policy* 14 (Spring 1974): 168.

29. In a pioneering and sophisticated article advocating a version of counterforce strategy, Bruce Russett of Yale advocated deterrence by the threatened

destruction of Soviet conventional power, its domestic security forces, and military production facilities, rather than its population. However, in order to avoid crisis instability, he suggested that Soviet strategic weapons, particularly those with a second-strike function, should be explicitly excluded from the list of threatened targets. While this could obviate the incentive to launch a preemptive strike, it involves a crucial yet fragile assumption: that the Soviets can be made to believe that weapons designed to destroy their military forces and political control apparatus would not also be used against their ICBMs. Since great accuracy is needed for the first sort of function, the associated weaponry would be well suited for ICBM destruction as well. Thus their doubts should appear entirely reasonable, and it does not seem possible to avoid the destabilizing effects of this strategy. "Assured Destruction of What? A Countercombatant Alternative to Nuclear Madness," *Public Policy* 22 (1974): 121-38.

30. See Drell and Von Hippel, op. cit., pp. 144-45.
31. Office of Technology Assessment, *The Effects of Nuclear War*, p. 4.
32. Richard Burt, "False Nuclear Alarms Spur Urgent Efforts to Find Flaws," *New York Times*, June 13, 1980.
33. A. O. Sulzberger, Jr., "Error Alerts US Forces to a False Missile Attack," *New York Times*, November 11, 1979.
34. Lloyd J. Dumas, "Human Fallibility and Weapons," *The Bulletin of the Atomic Scientists* 30 (1980): 15-20.
35. For an introduction to some of the issues, consult, for example, Richard Burt, "New Killer Satellites Make Sky War Possible," *New York Times*, June 11, 1978; Barry L. Thompson, "Directed Energy Weapons and the Strategic Balance," *Orbis*, January 1980; John Parmentola and Kosta Tsipis, "Particle Beam Weapons," *Scientific American*, April 1979, pp. 54-65; Donald Snow, "Over the Strategic Horizon," *Arms Control Today*, November 1979; "The New Military Race in Space," *Business Week*, June 1979, pp. 136-49; and Richard Garwin, "Are We on the Verge of a New Arms Race in Space?," *The Bulletin of the Atomic Scientists* 37 (1981): 48-55.
36. Bernard Weinraub, "Brown Says Soviets Can Fell Satellites," *New York Times*, October 5, 1977; and Richard D. Lyons, "New Weapons Could Blind Spy Satellites," *New York Times*, May 18, 1980.
37. Richard Burt, "Experts Believe Laser Weapons Could Transform Warfare in the Eighties," *New York Times*, February 10, 1980.
38. As far as particle-beam weapons are concerned, the major obstacle to their deployment is the fact that the linear accelerators by which the beams are produced weigh several tons, which means that they cannot be based in space. If, however, they are based in the atmosphere, these beams (like lasers) disperse with a rapid loss intensity.

6

THE POLITICAL ECONOMY
OF THE ARMS TRADE

The principal concern of this book is with the programs that the United States and the Soviet Union embark on, and the expenditures which they undertake, with the professed intention of deterring or of responding to attacks on their own homeland or on that of their immediate allies. While this accounts for the bulk of their total military endeavour, it does not cover it entirely, since substantial efforts are also directed at arming other, often remote, nations in a quest for various diplomatic and economic gains. These international transfers are dominated by the superpowers and are rapidly becoming a significant aspect of global military activity. While such dealings are not new, and they indeed have a long history, they are currently distinguished by several features that endow them with a new salience. The principal features are probably the following: (1) the recent surge in the international transfer of weapons and related equipment; (2) the growing proportion of military goods that are disseminated through trade rather than aid; (3) the upgraded sophistication of the items involved; and (4) the increasing share of the global purchases of armaments by the developing nations.

These arms transfers, which involve some of the most volatile regions in the world, are often held principally responsible for the human and material destructiveness of many local conflicts. They involve some of the poorest nations and have thus also been charged with diverting scarce resources away from pressing developmental needs, prompting one author to remark that,

> There is a resultant trend towards greater equality between developed and underdeveloped countries in military equipment rather than in economic growth and standards of living.[1]

Since the major suppliers of armaments are the two super-powers, it should be useful to address some of the issues involved, at least for the space of one chapter. Current trends will be examined and the motivations of providers and recipients, as well as the consequences for both, will be discussed. An entire volume would no doubt be needed to do the topic justice by dealing with it in a comprehensive fashion. Nevertheless it would create a glaring gap to neglect the issue altogether even in this book.

To place things in proper perspective, it should be pointed out that even the superpowers are not without their competitors in this area. While the United States and the Soviet Union account for the bulk of all arms exports, a number of other nations have carved out substantial portions of the market for themselves.[2] In the decade preceding World War II, Britain was the second largest exporter of weapons in the world, a position that it lost as it divested itself of its colonial empire and of the far-flung military commitments that went with these possessions. While Britain no longer enjoys such a preeminent position in the international arms trade, the growth of the nation's defense industry still relies heavily on an export market in which India and several Middle Eastern countries are the major buyers. France, which has recently surpassed the United Kingdom, experienced a rather late start as a leading supplier of military equipment. However, it has grown rapidly since the 1960s, often by replacing its major competitors in countries where political restraints and inhibitions precluded continued sales (for example, in South Africa or India and Pakistan during their armed conflict). Although the Middle East accounts for most French sales, its ship-ments span many other regions of the world. Other major exporters include Italy, West Germany, Czechoslovakia, and Israel. Figure 6.1 describes the relative proportion of the market accounted for by the principal suppliers.

While the superpowers do not have an exclusive claim on arms transfers, they do represent the principal arsenals for the rest of the world, and their willingness to function in such a capacity has been particularly pronounced since the mid-1970s. Together they have accounted for over 70 percent of the total (the United States leading with more than 40 percent) and seem unlikely to relinquish their dominant positions anywhere in the foreseeable future. The trajectory that they have followed is depicted in Figure 6.2.

Aside from the growing volume of military transfers, there has been a steady reduction in that proportion of the total that is furnished on aid-like terms. As late as the 1960s, most of what the superpowers provided was allocated to chosen nations in the context

FIGURE 6.1
Major Exporters' Share of Military Market: 1977–80

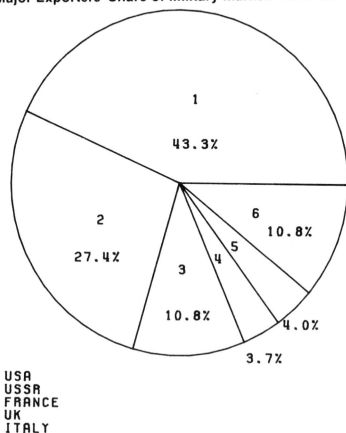

1 USA
2 USSR
3 FRANCE
4 UK
5 ITALY
6 OTHER

Source: Data are from Stockholm International Peace Research Institute, *World Armaments and Disarmament, 1981* (London: Taylor and Francis, 1981), p. xxi.

of various aid programs. Soviet military transfers, in particular, were distinguished by their apparently generous terms. Although the equipment was usually dated and did not include the more sophisticated items that the Soviet Union's own armed forces had at their disposal, a number of nations turned to Moscow for their military needs for reasons ranging from political compatibility to a dearth of hard currencies. But things have changed in recent years and the gifts, easy credit terms, or repayment in commodities have given way, more and more, to payment at value, in hard cash, and usually upon delivery. At the same time, increasingly sophisticated

FIGURE 6.2
The Superpowers' Arms Exports: 1969–78
(in millions of dollars)

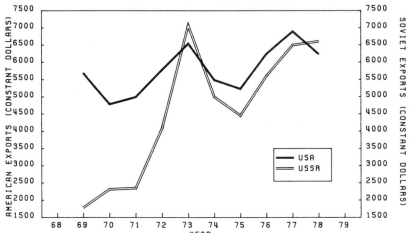

Source: Data are from *World Military Expenditures and Arms Transfers* (Washington, D.C.: U.S. Arms Control and Disarmament Agency, 1980).

(and hence expensive) items have replaced much of the obsolete weaponry that had previously dominated Soviet export arsenals. The arms trade has become relatively big business for the Soviet Union.

The United States, for its part, has traditionally sold more than it has furnished on grant-like terms. Even so, sales have grown at a considerable pace. U.S. military equipment is made available in two principal forms:[3] foreign military sales (FMS) and military assistance grants (MAP). In 1967, at just over $1 billion, the former was approximately four times as great as the latter. Thus, although most recipients had to pay the full price, a fair portion of the total was shipped abroad as part of overall foreign-aid programs. But this meant that much military assistance was financed by the U.S. taxpayer and therefore limited by fiscal constraints and congressional scrutiny. More recently, at values hovering around $8 billion, FMS is nearly ten times greater than MAP, meaning that a much larger part is being paid for by the foreign recipient. When we speak of military transfers now we are, thus, referring essentially to the international arms trade.

Not only has the amount that is traded risen fast, there has also been a simultaneous qualitative upgrading of the material provided. Gone are the days, which in chronological terms are admittedly not very distant, when military exports (particularly to the Third World) consisted chiefly of dated firearms and other rudimentary surplus, which had since been replaced by new generations of equipment in the exporters own services. In fact, the technological sophistication of the exports is one of the most striking aspects of the recent situation. The ultramodern weaponry furnished by the United States to the Middle East illustrates this point. Iran, for example, which was the United States' most lavish customer under the Shah, bought fighter planes and destroyers that were as advanced as those procured for the United States' own armed forces. Saudi Arabia's and Israel's purchases put them in virtually the same league. The Soviet Union has recently offered for purchase abroad such items as MIG-23 fighters armed with the most modern air-to-air missiles, F-62 tanks, and Frog and Scud surface-to-surface missiles, as well as the most modern antitank weaponry.

The businesslike proliferation of arms has thus moved along two dimensions: a growing volume of weapons that are being diffused within the international system (horizontal proliferation) and the spread of more and more advanced and destructive weapons (vertical proliferation).

Yet another significant aspect of international arms transfers concerns, not the identity of the suppliers or the type of equipment offered, but the nature of the recipients of this military material. The tendency during recent years has been for the locus of demand to shift from rich nations to poor nations and from there to even poorer nations. Contrary to what basic economic logic might suggest, demand has grown fastest in countries where the opportunity costs are the greatest—a fact that many observers view as the most distressing aspect of current military commerce. Figure 6.3 illustrates the rapid rise of military exports to the Third World from 1961 to 1980.

As late as the 1960s, European nations were the major, and seemingly the most natural, recipients of U.S. arms. Not only were arms shipments to democratic allies not politically controversial, they were also commended by the latters' ability to pay. Nevertheless, after the Middle East war of 1973, and the associated increase in the price of oil, the market shifted and soon the locally embroiled but newly rich nations of the region came to account for 60 percent of military orders from the United States. U.S. eagerness to sell to customers in this area can no doubt be explained in terms of diplomatic as well as economic motives; still, there may have been considerable satisfaction in recuperating some of the money that had just been expended on the skyrocketing OPEC oil

FIGURE 6.3
Third World's Arms Imports: 1961–80
(in millions of dollars)

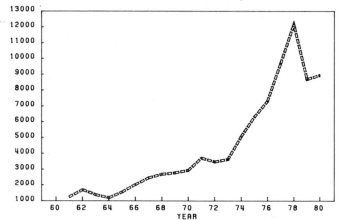

Source: Data are from Stockholm International Peace Research Institute, *World Armaments and Disarmament, 1981* (London: Taylor and Francis, 1981), pp. 184–85.

bill. That exports should have been thus reoriented is not entirely surprising, and while one would be concerned about the effects on the potential level of violence in this part of the world, one may not be overly concerned at the opportunity costs involved for, say, Saudi Arabia. Even more disturbing has been the fact that, since 1975, arms exports to nonoil-producing countries, that is, to some of the very poorest economies, have risen faster than those to either industrialized nations or OPEC. For example, U.S. sales to Kenya, Ethiopia, and Zaire increased almost eightfold in one year; thereafter, they came to include nations such as Chad, Sudan, and, most recently, Morocco as well. Nor has the Soviet Union been passive in this respect. In addition to its traditionally copious transfers to Cuba, the USSR market came to include Uganda and Tanzania in central Africa, Algeria and Libya in north Africa, Syria, Iraq, and, currently, North Yemen in the Middle East, as well as Peru in Latin America.

Thus the international arms trade is characterized by several significant trends and can be described from a number of perspectives. Two questions are, nevertheless, fundamental if the process is to be adequately understood. The first concerns the incentives that a nation, particularly a developed one, might have to export military equipment, as well as the consequences of this willingness. The second looks at the coin from the other side by inquiring into the motives and effects of these purchases for developing nation importers. Both perspectives are important, albeit for different reasons. Let us begin with the suppliers.

THE UNITED STATES, THE SOVIET UNION, AND MILITARY EXPORTS

Why do the superpowers export large quantities of sophisticated equipment and why, in addition, have these exports been growing so significantly recently? Assuming that there is a real demand for such items, why is it to the advantage of an industrialized and powerful nation to respond to the demand?

It is unlikely that any single factor should, in and of itself, have the explanatory power to answer adequately these questions, and the analysis of exports is certainly no simpler than that of procurement for purely national needs. When examining the latter, three categories of needs that could be served by military programs were identified. These were national security, the direct political interests of incumbents, and economic prosperity. While the second category is less relevant in this case, national security, as well as a variety of objectives of a diplomatic nature, can clearly be promoted by arms transfers, as can a number of economic goals. The effect of military sales on these two categories of policy objectives will therefore be examined. Moreover, these are not entirely independent categories, since levels of attainment on one may be contingent on the success of the other. Thus arms exports may occasionally serve one sort of goal indirectly, by dint of its effect on the other; these contingencies will also be examined.

Let us begin with the role of diplomatic and security-related considerations, both of which can be subsumed under the more general rubric of *political* objectives.

Arms Exports and Political Goals

Of all the ends that are overtly acknowledged by the official promoters of foreign military sales, attempts to acquire friends and leverage abroad are most frequently mentioned. This is often cast in terms of denying one's rival an international advantage and, in this respect, military exports represent a projection of East-West competition in regions that are essentially remote from the initial issues behind the superpower rivalry. As a recent Brookings study reported:

Whatever the nature of the regimes it supported, security assistance was
viewed as the first step toward a positive US influence and as a hindrance
to other, undesirable sources of supply.[4]

It seems that similar motives have guided Soviet programs,
and there are several manners in which the provision of weaponry
can, in principle, contribute to such aims. Specifically, these may
be affected in three ways: by bolstering a recipient regime's
security from internal threats; by ensuring its loyalty; or, finally,
by affecting a regional balance of power. These policies will be
examined one by one.

The first manner in which arms transfers can serve the
supplier's political purposes is by buttressing the position of
regimes that are sympathetic to the interests of the provider but
that face internal threats to their security. The purpose of
furnishing arms and other related equipment is then to strengthen
the regime's control by giving it the means to fortify its coercive
apparatus. Several examples illustrate this method of shoring up a
government whose ouster might usher in a regime that is un-
sympathetic to the superpowers' interests. Shipments of U.S. arms
to Brazil during the past 15 years or to Iran under the Shah can
certainly be accounted for in these terms, as can Soviet transfers
to Algeria or to the Uganda of Idi Amin. The fact that these were
of dubious ultimate value does not affect the suppliers' intent.

The second manner in which the arms trade can affect the
attainment of a superpower's political objectives is by enticing a
government with which significant interests are shared not to
backslide in its support of the mentor's goals. If it is insufficiently
supportive of these goals, supplies may be curtailed or reduced; if
it extends its commitment, the supplies may be increased or
qualitatively upgraded. Since military equipment is the sort of
commodity that is avidly sought by many developing nations, this
would seem to provide exceptionally effective leverage for the
superpower. While there are several reasons for the intensity of
this demand (and the issue will be dealt with presently), the
proliferation of military or of military-controlled regimes has
probably contributed to the perceived political efficacy of arms
transfers. Indeed, if we assume (as seems reasonable) that the
power and status of a military establishment depends on the
material means that it possesses, can display, and ultimately
employ, and if we further assume (as is obvious) that this equipment
is expensive and, as a rule, unavailable domestically, then it is only
a short step toward recognizing that the continued good will and

accessibility of the actual supplier is very important to the military's corporate interests. Governmental policies that alienate such a supplier may be expected to provoke retaliatory action, and the military itself cannot be expected to undertake such policies. A dominant political role of the armed forces may not be an essential condition for the effective exercise of external leverage via military supplies, but it is most probably a contributing factor.

The third fashion in which U.S. and Soviet transfers may be intended to bolster their position (particularly vis-à-vis one another) is by affecting local power balances. Where regional politics are competitive or conflictual, each superpower may attempt to extend its sphere of influence by dint of a well-armed and well-equipped client state. While the idea behind the arms transfer is to acquire general commitments of support, the specific intention in this instance is to deter or confront expansionist ambitions by the clients of the superpower's rival (or to engage in expansionism one-self via the regional proxy). Local arms races or actual warfare may thus be conditioned by what is in essence a superpower competition. For example, when conflict erupted in the Horn of Africa over the Ogaden region, Moscow decided to supply the military needs of the larger (and presumably more important from a strategic point of view) Ethiopia; this prompted the United States to play the same role with respect to Somalia and to express a willingness to contribute to the defense needs of the Sudan. Soviet aid to Libya, which seemed to have designs on northern Chad, caused Washington to consider also supplying the latter nation. In addition, when Kenya felt threatened by the Soviet-equipped regime in Uganda, it received a dozen United States F-5 jets.

One interesting aspect of all this regional jockeying is the relatively low weight that is given to questions of ideological compatibility compared to those of a more directly realpolitik ilk. Despite its professed preferences, the United States has furnished arms to nations that can scarcely be described as model democracies; in fact, for Third World nations, a right-wing orientation has frequently sufficed to qualify them as arms recipients. Neverthe-less, there have been exceptions, such as the readiness to supply arms to the nominally Marxist Somalia. Nor has a commitment to Marxism been the principal criterion in the Soviet choice of clients. Despite a rhetorical support of revolutionary movements and governments, Moscow has not been averse to supplying regimes that had banned or repressed communist organizations—as the examples of Egypt, Libya, or Guinea illustrate. Pragmatic benefits rather than ideological palatability have provided the ultimate guidelines for the choice of recipients for the weapons of either superpower.

Thus there are at least three sorts of reasons for arms transfers to developing nations. The question that one is then inclined to ask is whether these deliveries do, in fact, perform the anticipated functions. Although it is never certain that the link between policy goals and policy instruments are correctly perceived by decision makers, current trends in arms transfers make the issue very relevant in this instance.

To place the issue in proper perspective, it is important to distinguish between the short-term and long-term effectiveness of this tool of diplomacy and of security policy, since the difference may be significant. In fact, it is in the short run, and after an initial infusion of military equipment, that the effectiveness of arms transfers may be greatest. By placing substantial repressive resources in the hands of a favored regime, the balance of coercive power will often tilt toward that regime and away from its domestic opponents, thus decreasing the immediate likelihood that it will be dislodged. A similar effect will usually be produced on the client's position vis-à-vis a local rival, since the probability that the client will be overpowered or intimidated may be reduced in the short run. It is also likely that the recipient's immediate response will be some combination of gratitude and acknowledged further dependence (due, for example, to its need for spare parts, training in the use of the equipment, etc.). Nevertheless, these are all only *proximate* effects and it can be argued that in the long run, even sustained arms transfers are less likely to produce the desired results.

In the long run, for example, it tends to be increasingly difficult to ensure the stability of an unpopular regime simply by providing it with the tools of repressive control. Its opponents will rarely be passive and their probable response is to acquire more or better weapons for their own use from the rivals of the regime's supplier. They can also be expected to improve their organization and the effectiveness of their operations. The advantages that the regime initially enjoyed may therefore be neutralized after some time. For example, the United States-equipped, and apparently all-powerful, National Guard in Nicaragua incited the Sandinista rebels to upgrade their own equipment and organization and, ultimately, to overthrow the Somoza dictatorship.

Furthermore, the opposition can often benefit from the alien stamp that extended military dependence confers on the regime and from the popular distaste that this engenders. The United States role in Iran, for example, was underscored by its massive military sales to the Shah and this fact was partly responsible for the popular mobilization against his regime. A similar pattern seems apparent with respect to the Soviet role in Afghanistan.

Thus, there is no guarantee that the longevity of a disliked regime will be very significantly extended by providing it with military equipment; instead, the policy may ultimately be counterproductive. Also it can be expected that the regime that displaced the client government would be hostile to a nation that supplied its political enemies with the means of coercion. In addition, the new rulers will have inherited much of this equipment, which they may then make available for the military edification of the superpower's rival, transfer to unpalatable third parties, or employ to undermine the supplier's local interests.

Similarly, increasing the military might of even a politically stable regime in the game of regional jockeying may not, in the long run, contribute to the regional preeminence of one's client. As the initial supplier's rival bolsters the power of its own friends, the ultimate result may simply be to promote an arms race by proxy, with the position of neither side improving significantly but with more destructive consequences should armed conflict eventually occur.

In addition, it is very difficult to ensure the long-term allegiance of client nations in politically volatile parts of the world. Somalia, for example, was the first black-African nation to sign a treaty of friendship with the Soviet Union and even went so far as to provide Moscow with a naval facility at Berbera. Yet, following Soviet support for its archenemy Ethiopia, the Somalis expelled their former associates and turned to the United States for political and military help. Ethiopia, which while officially nonaligned had relied on U.S. military equipment, became later dependent on the Soviets. As another example, the Sudan was once aligned with the Soviet Union but has since tilted toward the West and adopted a particularly vociferous anti-Soviet stance. Similar claims could be made for Indonesia and, to a lesser extent, Egypt.

Thus continued support and allegiance may not always be purchased in exchange for weapons. For example, my own research on the effects of military dependence by a Third World nation on the United States indicates that this does not reduce governmental hostility toward the United States.[5] Even if arms could buy friends, another problem would be that the supplier cannot always control the use to which the arms are put and may find itself in a diplomatically awkward situation should its weapons be used for purposes it does not condone—as with Israel's use of U.S. planes in its bombardment of Iraq.

On the whole, it is doubtful that the long-term political and military interests of either superpower are well served through arms transfers. Immediate gains may be achieved, but such success will frequently be counterproductive. Should we then consider their continued adherence to this policy instrument as evidence of a lack of rationality and perspective? The appropriate answer may not be affirmative. Clearly the decision not to shore up an imperiled but politically compatible or useful regime, or the decision not to arm a friendly nation that is facing a military threat from a rival's client, may seem altogether irresponsible to the suppliers' decision makers. The dangers of inaction are immediate and, while the policy may backfire in the long run, the distant future is always discounted more heavily than the near future—particularly since the long-term consequences will be faced by different incumbents, while the immediate rewards will be reaped by the current decision makers. Thus, whatever the ultimate wisdom of such policies may be, arms-transfer decisions can be related to perceived political needs, and one would find it difficult to argue that this is, in the politically relevant context, an instance of irrational behavior.

Still, this answers but part of our question. While diplomatic and security concerns may account for arms transfers in general, it does not necessarily explain arms *sales*, since either aid or sales could, in principle, serve the desired purpose. Yet, the increase has, for the most part, been manifested by surging *sales* rather than by a growth in the volume in military *aid*. Furthermore, it is arguable whether political and security needs have, in fact, increased in tandem with the arms trade; rather, it was precisely at a time of relative détente that sales mushroomed on both sides. It appears that the situation might be one in which these needs determine a floor below which military shipments should not be expected to fall, but they are less useful in explaining fluctuations at higher levels. Perhaps we should expand our inquiry by including, in our analysis, the second set of needs that are connected to the arms trade, that is, the possible economic gains that this might produce for the supplier.

Arms Exports and Economic Gains

A greater emphasis is placed on economic motives by authors of a radical bent than by those within the mainstream of U.S.

social science; yet, there is a consensus on the potential relevance of this sort of consideration and virtually no analyst would dismiss it offhand. Also there is good reason to believe that economic and security-related needs are not entirely independent, and that the former may, in addition to their autonomous import, be instrumental to the attainment of security goals as well. Specifically, arms sales may have a beneficial impact on military production for national security, a fact that provides a link between the two categories of goals.

It is often considered desirable that defense productive capacity should exceed the immediate demands of a nation's armed forces, that is, one should maintain an ability to produce beyond those levels that are suggested by peacetime defense needs. Factors of production, such as labor, plants, and machines, are thus permanently mobilized at a level that makes a smooth and rapid expansion of military production possible should this be necessary. Peacetime military exports (which can be curtailed in times of acute security needs) are frequently considered a good way of ensuring that there will be such a capacity. Admittedly, this is not particularly pertinent to the supply of strategic weapons that are stockpiled; additional production of such weapons would be neither relevant nor possible after the onset of nuclear war. But for arms and equipment that are designed for more conventional forms of warfare, the previous considerations are very relevant, given the unpredictable duration of hostilities conducted on this basis. Such considerations are, at least in the United States, also officially acknowledged. A study prepared for the Senate Committee on Foreign Relations explains that,

> Production for exports helps to maintain a warm mobilization base by reducing the extent to which industrial capacity lies idle or underutilized, and to keep total output potential above peacetime domestic requirements, thereby providing reserve capacity for emergency use. Production for exports makes it possible to avoid the dispersal of skilled and experienced labor teams, and by keeping some production lines active forestalls the necessity to incur large start-up costs and to expand production of certain items rapidly during an emergency.[6]

Thus an economic effect, excess defense production capacity, is instrumental to a security goal—military readiness in case of an emergency. The second manner in which sales abroad can produce economic consequences that are of relevance to national security is by reducing the costs of military procurement for domestic purposes. The development of new weapons typically involves high research and development costs (many of which are ultimately never redeemed) and the actual production of old or of new items usually implies very substantial overhead outlays. Given the size of fixed costs, the price of these products for the nation's armed forces will partly depend on the economies of scale that can be realized. These, in turn, may be contingent on the extent to which export markets are available. Obviously, this will not have the same meaning for all nations. For countries with small internal defense markets (e.g., Great Britain or France), the procurement of certain items would not be possible without export outlets; for other nations, particularly those with substantial internal defense markets, it might matter less. Even for superpowers, however, foreign markets will lead to a reduction in domestic unit costs and it is unlikely that they are oblivious to this fact. For example, in specific reference to the savings created by lower procurement costs, the aforementioned Senate report reckoned that,

> according to conservative estimates for military sales corresponding in volume and composition to orders placed in fiscal year 1976, the sum of savings to DOD from all sources reached 827.7 million in fiscal year 1975 dollars and exceeds 1 billion dollars if less conservative estimates are used.[7]

These figures may not be overwhelming but neither are they trivial. By itself, the need to control the cost of weapons and equipment for one's own forces may not be a sufficient explanation for overall levels of arms exports, but, in conjunction with other reasons, it helps illustrate the causal process behind these transfers. As the unit costs of increasingly sophisticated weapons have risen very considerably in recent years, this should also help account for both the absolute increase in such sales and their growth relative to military aid.

It is, predictably, more difficult to assess the role that such factors play in the Soviet Union where, unlike the United States, there are only the vaguest official justifications for arms sales and very little (if any) scholarly work on their economic context. The Stockholm International Peace Research Institute (SIPRI), which has produced some of the most authoritative works on the arms trade, stated in a 1975 publication that "Soviet arms-supply policy has primarily served political interests, and economic interests have been secondary."[8] This policy may have been changing however. Most of the data on which SIPRI's conclusions are based did not extend beyond 1972 and may not be as appropriate to subsequent years. As has been observed, Soviet equipment had traditionally been furnished at very favorable terms. It cannot, therefore, have had much of an impact on the costs of domestic procurement. Also the dated nature of most items sold abroad meant that they were not the output of current production lines and, hence, probably unrelated to a desired slack in Soviet military industry.

Nevertheless, Soviet policy has been shifting, and increasingly sophisticated weapons are now being made available to foreign buyers at more and more realistic prices and very often on a hard-currency basis. This leads one to infer that arms sales may, to a growing extent, be serving similar functions for both of the two leading exporters.

This is not the whole story however. Even if both the United States and the Soviet Union regard military exports as a way to maintain excess defense capacity and to reduce unit costs, the role of economic factors seems even more significant when balance-of-payments effects are also taken into account. Although this is important to both nations, it may be particularly relevant to the Soviet Union.

It is widely understood that Moscow's foreign-currency needs are substantial and growing. The increasingly unimpressive rates of national economic growth, which were described in Chapter 4, were largely attributed to the sluggish expansion of overall productivity. While this could conceivably have been redressed by the economic reforms proposed in the 1960s, the remedy was precluded by the opposition of bureaucrats and party conservatives who feared for their hold over the levers of control. The other option was to boost productivity via imported technology. This has, in fact, been the apparent aim of the Soviet leadership during the past decade, but the policy has encountered a number of obstacles. Foremost among these problems is the fact that the Soviet ruble is not convertible into the hard currencies of the West; thus, the only obvious way of generating the foreign exchange needed to purchase the technology of the industrialized economies is via the Soviet's export earnings. But the quality and level of sophistication of Soviet manufactured foods has discouraged foreign demand for their products, while the export-earning potential of its raw materials is insufficient. One way of obviating the problem would be to acquire the means of payment through Western credits, and this had appeared to be a real possibility until the Jackson-Vanek amendment to the 1973 Trade Reform bill foreclosed this solution as far as U.S. credits were concerned. Some foreign exchange is acquired by borrowing on European currency markets; the sums are not momentous and, in any case, loans must be repaid.

Armaments, on the other hand, are eagerly sought since even the poorest nations have demonstrated their willingness to squander scarce reserves of convertible currencies for the purchase of military hardware. Not only have Soviet exports to the Third World traced a steeply ascending curve lately (see Figure 6.4), but the very nature of the policy has also changed. The most obvious change is reflected in Moscow's increasingly businesslike stance; while prices are still lower than those for comparable U.S. material, prices have been increasing and there has been a recent insistence on payment in hard currency and upon delivery. Already in the late 1960s, for example, Egypt was no longer permitted to pay for its arms with cotton. Even during the airlift to resupply the Arab states during the 1973 war in the Middle East, the Soviets insisted on immediate cash payment. Without emergency help from Saudi Arabia, Egypt could not have paid the bill, and this certainly led to that nation's growing coldness toward the Soviet Union.

According to the CIA,[9] the Soviet trade surplus with the Third World was $800 million in 1976 and $1.2 billion in 1977; it would, however, have been a *deficit* without military sales, which added up to $1.5 billion and $2 billion in each of the two years respectively. As the Center for Defense Information recently pointed out, "Economic pressures will tend to make the political credentials

FIGURE 6.4
Soviet Arms Exports to the Third World: 1961–80

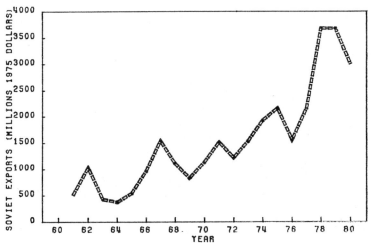

Source: Data are from Stockholm International Peace Research Institute, *World Armaments and Disarmament, 1981* (London: Taylor and Francis, 1981), pp. 186–87.

of would-be customers less important than their credit rating."[10]

Balance-of-payments considerations are not limited to the Soviet Union but are also relevant to the United States. Deficits have existed since the 1950s, but these were initially accepted as necessary for the pursuit of foreign-policy objectives and were not considered reflective of any serious economic problems. Dollars flowed out in reconstruction aid to war-devastated allies and to pay for a direct military presence abroad, which was necessitated by the Cold War. Even as U.S. corporations began applying dollars toward the acquisition of foreign branches and subsidiaries, the overall favorable balance of trade sufficed, until the late 1960s, to maintain confidence in the dollar and to ensure its acceptance as the leading international currency. At that time, however, the surplus became a swelling deficit and the world decided that it had far more dollars than it needed or wanted. The rush to convert this currency into gold led to the suspension of convertibility in 1972 and to the decision to float the dollar which, in many respects, signalled the end of the postwar Bretton-Woods system. Chronic balance of payments deficits have since caused the dollar's eroding value with respect to other leading currencies.

Several factors can account for this turn of events. The domestic unpopularity of the Vietnam war made the Johnson administration wary of financing it through taxation and forced a reliance on massive deficit spending. Inescapably, this led to powerful inflationary pressures and, thus, to the increasing costliness of U.S. goods to foreign buyers. Furthermore, compared to the performance of its main economic competitors, U.S. productivity gains have not been particularly impressive. While this can be partly attributed to exports of technology via direct foreign investment in other industrialized nations, U.S. military production must, as pointed out in Chapter 3, bear some of the onus. The ultimate consequence has been that goods produced within the United States have become less competitive abroad. Since this was the case, it is scarcely surprising that efforts should have been made to mitigate the economy's balance-of-payments problems and that the benefits of arms sales for this purposes should have been recognized.

The United States' reliance on arms sales abroad for balance-of-payments reasons should not, of course, be overestimated and such considerations are, in any case, likely to matter more in the Soviet case given that nation's hard-currency problems. Nevertheless, even for the United States this seems to add yet another dimension to an economic context with a direct bearing on the arms trade.

Thus, in addition to purely political reasons, it may be economically attractive on several grounds to sell military equipment abroad. The incentives are powerful for both superpowers and the level of their exports should not be unexpected. Still this information is more interesting for what it tells about the propensity to furnish arms than for the light it sheds on the ultimate consequences of this willingness. It tells us merely that economies that are already quite prosperous may operate even more smoothly in the *short run* if they engage in military transfers. The most serious economic consequences of this commerce are, however, experienced by the Third World nations, which are the fastest growing importers, and the eagerness of superpowers to sell is far less paradoxical than the readiness of governments of relatively impoverished nations to accept the costs that their own involvement in this trade entails.

ARMS TRADE AND THE THIRD WORLD

An apparent willingness to serve as markets for superpower military exports is one aspect of the recent militarization of developing societies. The rule of juntas, the demise of mass-based politics, and the deflection of scarce resources for military purposes are part of a multifaceted trend that emerged clearly in the 1960s and has since become a defining characteristic of Third World politics. Although a substantial literature on this topic has emerged in Western social science,[11] no true consensus has evolved on the nature and desirability of such militarization—a fact that is exemplified in the divergent evaluations of military government.

According to one school of thought, the indigenous officer corps represents a force capable of freeing these nations from the rule of retrograde oligarchies and of eradicating corrupt and ineffectual political practices. For example, one of the early exponents of this view argued that the military in developing nations, due to the salutary influence the West has had on them, represents one of the most competent, devoted, and organized domestic forces.[12] Owing their position to merit, officers were considered unlikely to sympathize with social conventions wherein rewards are granted by ascription; rather, they would strive to promote social mobility. They were also expected to socialize conscripts to their own value systems, which diverged in many respects from that of civilian authorities. Possessing an appropriate value system and a rational approach to development, it should be scarcely surprising that the military enjoys such political prominence in the Third World or that it is frequently compelled by events to perform the functions that civil authorities traditionally view as their own.

Contrary to this view, it has been argued that historical evidence does not support the contention that the military promotes progress in the Third World but that the contrary appears to be true.[13] While these critics may agree that the military does play an autonomous political role, they argue that this is not the result of advanced organizational structures or of modernizing values. Rather, it is due to the single-minded pursuit by the military of its own corporate values which are, as often as not, at variance with the overall societal interest.

Thus, even at the most general level, there is considerable scholarly divergence on the consequences of militarism in the developing nations. When we turn to its specifically economic results, we find not only academic divisions but even greater disparities between that which intuition dictates and that which social science seems to have revealed. Intuitively it may appear evident that the military purchases of developing nations would make substantial claims on slight incomes. Domestic savings, and reserves of foreign currency in particular, are typically insufficient to finance needed investment in social overhead or productive facilities; this being so, one would expect prospects for development of many Third World nations to suffer if the scant resources are allocated primarily to officers salaries or to the purchase of armaments.

The contrary claim has, nevertheless, been made and empirical data has been marshalled to support it. In a study entitled "Defense and Economic Growth in Developing Countries,"[14] Emile Benoit claimed to have found a positive correlation between the share of Gross Domestic Income devoted to defense and growth rates of civilian GNP. The finding is clearly surprising and the author buttresses his conclusion with a number of theoretical explanations. The principal arguments involve: (1) the claim that a powerful military establishment promotes the sort of political stability on which economic performance is ultimately contingent; (2) the classical argument that military outlays may boost aggregate demand and reduce idle industrial capacity; (3) the role of defense programs in promoting infrastructural development (roads, communication networks, etc.); and, (4) the issue of the overall modernizing attitudes and Western values that are imputed to military elites.

Before scrutinizing these arguments, it should be observed

that, even if the postulated association did exist, its nature could be misstated. For example, the causal arrow could operate in quite the opposite direction, that is, it may be that rapidly developing nations can *afford* to spend proportionately more on defense rather than that high rates of military spending induce accelerated economic growth. Also a correlation between military outlays and economic growth might not denote *any* causal relation between the two but simply reflect a spurious association (it could, for example, be argued that a close relationship with a superpower might account for an infusion of aid for both purposes, as in the case of South Korea). Finally, and in order to keep things in proper perspective, it should be pointed out that there is little reason to believe that such a relation should also apply to that portion of military spending that is devoted to the acquisition of military material produced by a foreign economy.

Let us, however, consider the data. In order to gain a more rigorous handle on Benoit's assertion, data on the ratio of military outlays to GNP were collected for 79 developing nations for the period from 1972 through 1976. This was also done for changes in GNP during the same period, and an average military spending ratio score (m) as well as an average GNP growth score (E) were computed for the five-year period. The latter was then regressed against the former. A plot of the relationship as well as the regression equation are displayed in Figure 6.5.

FIGURE 6.5
Military Imports and Economic Growth in the Third World

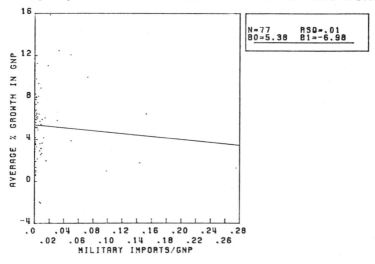

Source: Compiled by the author.

A visual examination of the scatterplot suggests that there is no discernible association. This is statistically confirmed by regressing growth against arms imports. Such purchases explain a bare 1 percent of the variance in economic growth, and the regression coefficient, while negative, has not even the weakest claim to statistical significance ($t = 0.73$).

Not only is the data not very supportive of the hypothesis, but its theoretical underpinnings are also debatable. I have already pointed out that the fourth explanation, which concerns the military's attitudes and values, involves assumptions on which there are very divergent opinions. At most, however, they seem *occasionally* valid. One would, for example, find it difficult to argue that Colonel Qaddafi is deeply imbued with Western values and goals or that Idi Amin's rule, for example, was characterized by the rationality associated with effective developmental efforts In less obvious examples, Alfred Stepan[15] has argued that the Brazilian military did not display more organizational stability than did the civilian authorities who preceded them, while Uma Eleazu[16] observed that, in West Africa, the army has not proven to be a modernizing agent and that it lacks, in any case, the experience of civilian administrations.

The suggestion that military programs promote infrastructural development is not unassailable either, although occasionally this point may also be valid. Specifically, it has been argued that the infrastructure that is developed for military purposes is only tenuously related to nonmilitary needs.[17]

It is also necessary to deal cautiously with the argument that military procurement in developing nations serves to reduce what would otherwise be excess, and hence idle, productive capacity. While there are a few developing economies with an industrial capacity that is more than equal to the effective demand that the economy can generate, these are plainly the exceptional cases. Scant capital formation in the past, and an economy historically biased toward exports of cash crops or of raw materials, has usually meant that indigenous production is barely able to meet domestic needs and much less to generate a surplus of any kind. It is indeed very misleading to attribute to the Third World the functions of defense spending that its advocates claim for it in industrialized economies.[18] As far as our immediate concerns go, an additional point should be made. The matter of overall military outlays aside, the purchase of weapons from abroad could have no bearing on idle productive capacity even if this could be assumed to exist. Where imports are involved it is obvious that the employment, multiplier, and other effects occur within the exporters economy, while the only result from the point of view of the buyers is an outflow of scarce hard currencies. Without this foreign exchange, the ability to purchase the capital equipment and technology needed for industrialization is further limited.

Pursuing the matter of foreign exchange, one may point out that not all capital formation is endogenously generated in the Third World but that much of it is the result of activities of multinational corporations. This has a bearing on our immediate concerns, because it has been suggested that militarism in general, and arms imports in particular, tend to encourage foreign investment. Although the link may not be immediately apparent, it has been argued that foreign capital might consider a politically potent and well-armed military establishment as the sort of condition that provides for a hospitable climate for multinationals. The idea is that this deters the rise of left-wing nationalism which, these companies might fear, would constrain their freedom of activity or even lead to the outright expropriation of their assets. It has also been claimed that the interests of the military may be directly linked to those of the foreign investor.[19] This is because the army's demand for arms from abroad creates a need for foreign exchange which, in turn, leads the military to encourage an influx of multinational corporations as a means of generating the required hard currency. The question of whether direct foreign investment is ultimately beneficial to host economies aside, one can inquire whether militarism does indeed lead to an inflow of foreign investment. My own impression is that while this may have been true of early years (the 1960s in particular), there are progressively fewer multinationals that still consider a well-armed and repressive right-wing regime as a sufficient guarantor of their interests. The Brazilian generals, for example, may seem to embody all of the qualities that imbue investors with an easy feeling of security. Yet, since the early 1970s, the military regime has enacted a surprisingly restrictive body of legislation concerning these companies in apparent response to a realization that military's internal legitimacy required a relatively tough stance toward these investors. Multinational corporations are simply among the most visible targets for frustrated nationalism, and there is a fairly widespread realization, even among right-wing military regimes, that it is often politically more expedient to restrain the foreign economic agent than to use armed repression to punish hostility toward these firms. Obviously not all multinationals feel threatened nor are the governments of all host countries equally ready to restrict their freedom of operation. Certainly a number of circumstances determine how free a rein foreign firms will enjoy,[20] but the extent to which the polity is militarized (even if the regime is clearly conservative) may now rank unexpectedly low on the list of considerations likely to be deemed most important by the foreign investor.

It is furthermore not obvious that the entry of multinationals is synonymous with the inflow of foreign currency. In fact, it has been observed that much direct foreign investment in the Third World relies principally on money acquired from local financial institutions and does not involve a significant transfer of currency from the investor's economy to that of the host nation.[21] Profit repatriations, on the other hand, may mean that a net financial drain on the developing economy can occur despite the physical presence of real capital (principally plants and machinery) accounted for by the multinational investor.

Thus, even without addressing the controversial questions of the net economic effect of direct foreign investment on Third World nations, there is not much reason to assume that there is a strong rationale for the imputed link between this investment, military regimes, and weapons imports. At present, military regimes are no guarantee of favorable treatment for multinationals and should not, in this author's opinion, be considered a major predictor of their desire to enter a particular developing nation. Quite simply, other considerations might weigh much more heavily in their decision. Even if they do enter, however, they may not be the best source of the means needed to finance the purchase of arms and related equipment from abroad.

There appears, therefore, to be a substantial price and few economic justifications for lavish military imports. Ultimately, the losses are reflected in the opportunity costs to the developing nations, that is, in the foregone opportunities in terms of social well-being for exceptionally deprived societies. Indeed, according to a study submitted to the United Nations by Bruce Russett and David Sylvan,

> for the "average" developing country with a population of 8.5 million and a GNP per-capita of around $350, the first $200 million worth of arms imported would a/ add 20 additional infant deaths per 1000 live births; b/ decrease life-expectancy by 3 to 4 years; and c/ result in 13 to 14 fewer literate adults out of every 100.[22]

Despite the harmful effects, such purchases are endemic, copious, and show no strong signs of abating for many countries. This is probably because they are not *intended* to perform primarily economic functions for the buyers. While suppliers are apparently driven by the expectation that arms sales will provide economic as well as political and security services, the overriding concern of the recipient governments tends to be with the latter sort of functions. The question then is whether this is really the optimal way of achieving such goals. I have already addressed this matter in the discussion of the sellers' motives but some elaboration may be useful here.

By acquiring substantial military power, the recipient nation often wishes to increase its ability to deter a regional enemy with whom it has serious territorial, ethnic, or ideological disputes. Even in this regard, it would seem that military imports are not very beneficial. Virtually all of the armed conflicts that have occurred during the past several decades have involved Third World nations that were armed by industrialized countries. Arms have typically been competitively provided by the superpowers to each side. The outcome has been a series of local arms races reminiscent of the race that links the suppliers themselves. The precise effect of arms races on the *probability* of conflict occurrence has not yet been conclusively demonstrated (though see Chapter 1) but, while it cannot be confidently stated that this ineluctably leads to war, it is virtually certain that such competition does not, short of nuclear deterrence, *decrease* the likelihood of this outcome. It may, of course, be the case that defense from attack rather than peace through deterrence is really desired and, indeed, this is often the stated aim. But, declamations to the contrary notwithstanding, aggression frequently tends to be the real goal. Independently of the issues of the incidence of war, there is the matter of its human and material costs and there is certainly ample evidence that the *destructiveness* of these conflicts when they do occur is greatly increased by the possession of vast arsenals of sophisticated weapons. To the extent that security is a function both of the probability of conflict and of its costs assuming that it would occur, one would find it difficult to argue that security in the Third World has benefited from military purchases abroad.

Often, of course, military imports are intended to mitigate *internal* threats to a regime's security and, here too, the benefits are dubious. Earlier in this chapter, I have argued that the ultimate consequence of a militarized regime is quite likely to be an increasingly well-equipped and well-organized opposition, with no net amelioration of domestic stability. But even a real coercive advantage over political opponents may not resolve the problem of security in the long run. Indeed, it would be misleading to assume that the ultimate viability and longevity of a political regime is exclusively a matter of rifles, soldiers, and jails. It is, more fundamentally, a matter of the ability of government to adapt to the needs and preferences of those whom it encompasses. While a regime can maintain some distance from the precipice by dint of overwhelming coercive power, and even provide itself some additional time to shape a new basis of support, it cannot stave off its natural political descent unless it enjoys a sufficient modicum of legitimacy. Legitimacy, as political scientists are well aware, is granted principally on the basis of performance, that is, of the regime's demonstrated ability to deliver the tangible and symbolic goods which its public demands. The point is that the impression of security that massive repressive power provides frequently leads a government to discount the need to cultivate its legitimacy via political performance. It becomes not only oblivious to the necessity of meeting public needs, but it is also rarely in a position to effectively acquaint itself with these needs should it wish to do this. In a climate of fear, censorship, and sycophancy, such information simply does not flow easily from society to the political elite. Repression stifles performance and deprives the government of the foundations on which it could build its legitimacy, and this will typically decrease the long-term likelihood of its survival—with or without military force.

NOTES

1. Alva Myrdal, *The Game of Disarmament* (New York: Pantheon Books, 1976), p. 141.
2. For descriptions of some trends, see Michael Mihalka, "Supplier Client Patterns in Arms Transfers: The Developing Countries, 1967-1976," in Stephanie Neuman and Robert E. Harkavy, eds., *Arms Transfers in the Modern World* (New York: Praeger, 1979), pp. 49-76; also, Jo L. Husbands, "A World in Arms: Geography of the Weapons Trade." *The American Geographical Society*, March-April 1980, pp. 1-10. See also Stockholm International Peace Research Institute, *World Armaments and Disarmament: SIPRI Handbook 1981*, (London: Taylor and Francis, 1981), chap. 4.
3. There is also a third form, which is represented by commercial sales. These are not mediated by the government and involve, as a rule, light firearms. These sales, which typically represent 10 percent of the U.S. total, are, nevertheless, subject to the obtention of an export license from the government.
4. Philip J. Farley, Stephen S. Kaplan, and William H. Lewis, *Arms Across the Sea* (Washington, D.C.: The Brookings Institution, 1978), p. 34.
5. Miroslav Nincic, *Determinants of Third World Hostility Toward the United States*. Ph.D. dissertation, Yale University, 1977. See also David Sylvan, "Arms Transfers and the Logic of Political Efficacy," *Military Issues Research Memorandum ACN 78041*, Carlisle Barracks, Pa., Strategic

Studies Institute, U.S. Army War College, 1978.

6. *Arms Transfer Policy* (Washington, D.C.: Senate Committee on Foreign Relations, 1977), p. 50.

7. Ibid., p. 48.

8. Stockholm International Peace Research Institute, *The Arms Trade with the Third World* (New York: Holmes and Meier, 1975), p. 78.

9. Central Intelligence Agency, *Changing Patterns in Soviet-LDC Trade 1976-1977*, ER78-10326, May 1978, p. 2.

10. "Soviet Weapons Exports: Russian Roulette in the Third World," *The Defense Monitor* Jan. 1979:3.

11. For example, see Samuel Decalo, *Coups and Army Rule in Africa* (New Haven, Conn.: Yale University Press, 1976); John J. Johnson, ed., *The Role of the Military in Underdeveloped Countries* (Princeton, N.J.: Princeton University Press, 1962); Henry Beinen, ed., *The Military and Modernization* (Chicago: University of Chicago Press, 1964); and Eric Nordlinger, *Soldiers in Politics: Military Coups and Government* (Englewood Cliffs, N.J.: Prentice-Hall, 1977).

12. Lucian Pye, "Armies in the Process of Political Modernization," in Johnson, op.cit.

13. Eric Nordlinger, "Soldiers in Mufti," *The American Political Science Review* 59 (1970): 1131-48.

14. Emile Benoit, *Defense and Economic Growth in Developing Countries* (Lexington, Mass.: Lexington Books, 1973).

15. Alfred Stepan, *The Military in Politics: Changing Patterns in Brazil* (Princeton, N.J.: Princeton University Press, 1971).

16. Uma Eleazu, "The Role of the Military in African Politics: A Reconsideration of Existing Theories and Practices," *Journal of Developing Areas* 7 (1973): 265-86.

17. J. C. Hurewitz, *Middle Eastern Politics: The Military Dimension* (London: Pall Mall, 1969).

18. See, for example, David K. Whynes, *The Economics of Third World Military Expenditures* (Austin: University of Texas Press, 1979).

19. For example, by Robin Lukham, "Militarism and International Dependence," in Richard Jolly, ed., *Disarmament and World Development* (Oxford: Pergamon Press, 1978), pp. 35-36.

20. A good treatment of these circumstances can be found in Theodore Moran, "Multinational Corporations and Dependency: A Dialogue for *Dependentistas* and *Non-Dependentistas*." Paper delivered at the 1976 Meeting of the American Political Science Association, September, Chicago.

21. The issue is discussed in Constantine Vaitsos, "Foreign Investment and Productive Knowledge," in Guy Erb and Valeriana Kallab, eds., *Beyond Dependency* (Washington, D.C.: Overseas Development Council, 1975), pp. 75-95.

22. "The Effect of Arms Transfers on Developing Countries." A report to the United Nations Group of Governmental Experts on the Relationship between Disarmament and Development, July 1980.

7

ARMS LIMITATION:
SOME DOMESTIC POSSIBILITIES

There has never been a dearth, from either superpower, of statements lamenting the escalating arms race. Neither has there been
a lack of resolutions, conferences, and negotiations with the
professed intention of curbing military growth. As mentioned at
the very beginning, these efforts have usually fallen short of
promises and expectations: from the ill-fated Baruch Plan (which
the Soviet Union rejected), to the Non-Proliferation Treaty of 1970
(which placed limits on all signatories but its major-power sponsors)
to the apparently still-born SALT II treaty (which was to compensate
for reductions in certain systems by encouraging the expansion of
others), the gap between apparent desires and actual performance
has been interpreted either as evidence of hypocrisy on both sides
or as proof of the sisyphean nature of the arms-controller's task.
Questions of sincerity aside for the moment,[1] it is true that the
conditions that propel superpower military programs are objectively
much more powerful than those available to restrain them and,
while this lopsidedness is generally recognized, the remainder of
this study will attempt to assess whether the circumstances that
have made this true of the past and the present are likely to hold
for the future as well. The principal question will be: To what
extent can these circumstances be affected by conscious policy?

The persistence of the arms race over three full decades and its
apparent resilience to arguments of political and economic rationality may not provide much basis for optimism, yet even 30 years is
too short a period for total resignation. Ultimately, both policies
and their empirical context do change, and there is some hope that,
even here, changes may be for the better.

A few preliminary clarifications are in order at this point. Let us begin by again referring to the distinction between growth of overall military expenditures and the introduction of new weapons systems. Will policies designed to control one also be effective in curbing the other? A qualified affirmative is probably appropriate. When the determinants of arms-race behavior were discussed, similar factors were seen to affect both dimensions. Usually, of course, this is because the two are logically related, but this need not always be the case. It is sometimes possible, for example, to spend more by raising officers' salaries than by acquiring new arms; a new weapons system (even a particularly deadly one) could theoretically be cheaper than its predecessors. Nonetheless, even when these two aspects are disassociated, the same categories of determinants tend to be behind their growth. Bureaucratic interests, strategic calculations, or economic imperatives can drive mushrooming budgets as well as new acquisitions of hardware. Thus, while the same specific cause will not be behind each individual decision on either type of growth, most of these decisions will flow from the same general *category* of causes. The implication is that, while the technical issues will differ somewhat, anything which can serve to neutralize the causes of one sort of growth should also facilitate the job of controlling the other.

Another necessary clarification concerns the ultimate goals of policies that are intended to counter military growth. Just how ambitious can they be? There is some room for maneuver here and added specificity is called for. A distinction is usually made between disarmament and arms control and it may be that their respective prerequisites differ. Disarmament involves the reduction (by some unspecified amount) of existing stocks of weapons. While the former may seem like the more ambitious goal, this is not necessarily the case. Modest disarmament *may* be less desirable than far-reaching arms control. The latter is also a broader concept since it concerns the modalities of use and deployment of existing weapons (for example, measures designed to avoid accidental launchings) as well as numerical limits. Nevertheless, not all facets of arms control are of concern to this particular study, which deals mainly with the qualitative and quantitative expansion of the superpowers' military machines and the most destabilizing weapons in particular. Thus the relevant aspects of arms control are those that concern such increases, and they could involve either a flattening of growth curves (arms limitation) or their actual reversal (disarmament).

Although the principal focus will be on arms limitation, one can inquire whether similar conditions and policies are apt to affect *both* goals. In other words, if one were to discover a remedy, which if applied in a certain dose, would cause the arms race to level off, might one also conclude that the race could actually be reversed by increasing the dose? It is clear that this will not always be true, and an example will illustrate the point. For instance, if the rate of U.S. military growth is conditioned by the size of the gap between the economy's productive potential and its absorptive capacities, this rate should decrease as the gap narrows. However, if absorptive capacity were suddenly to *exceed* output, it does not follow that *disarmament* would ensue since reducing existing weapons inventories would have no obvious bearing on the new economic situation. Thus, while it is usually possible to move an object more slowly by pulling less rapidly on an attached string, it may not be possible to move it backward by pushing on the string. The analogy does not always apply, but the general point should be kept in mind.

What future can one anticipate for arms limitation? If the apparently ineluctable expansion of military programs is explained by the fact that, for both superpowers, *incentives* propelling growth are much stronger than the *constraints* on such growth, the solution seems obvious: incentives should decrease or the constraints should increase, or both should occur. Although modifications in either case might result from conditions that had not been explicitly sought as a matter of arms-limitation policy, one should not rely on the benevolence of secular trends or incidental events. Conscious efforts must be made to influence the pertinent variables and the first task is to select those that are most promising.

At least two criteria are useful in guiding the choice. Although it was argued that several variables have some effect on arms-race behavior, not all are equally potent from a causal standpoint. The first criterion of variable selection should, therefore, be one of causal *impact*. At the same time, variables that propel the race most forcefully or that could, if encouraged, frustrate it most effectively may be least responsive to policy control. Thus malleability is another important consideration, and the aim should be to find those variables that embody an optimal combination of potential impact and manipulability.

This study began with a discussion of the interactive dynamics that may be behind military growth, that is, with the suggestion that each side's activities are simply responses, albeit at times overdrawn, to the other's previous, current, or anticipated activities. The question now is whether the process can be halted or, better yet, made to operate in reverse. In other words, is it possible to generate a closed cycle of mutual *retrenchment* or can one, at least, achieve immobility by an agreement to simultaneously freeze force postures and spending levels? On the whole, retrenchment is unlikely because, as I have pointed out, the model focuses on what is, for both sides, a sufficient but not always necessary cause for further military endeavours. Simply, the arms race is fueled by powerful internal motives as well. Thus either superpower would be disappointed if it decided to eschew anything that could be interpreted as a unilateral military initiative and expected the other country to stabilize the situation by doing likewise. In other words, if nothing were done to control *internal* drives on both sides, then even unilateral restraint (assuming it could be engineered somehow) might be met by endogenously driven growth on the other side. This, in turn, would result in righteous anger and maybe even an accelerated race. The failure of the Soviet Union to respond to the decrease in U.S. defense spending in the early 1970s and the surge in U.S. military activity that ensued illustrate the risk. However, if the domestic determinants of each side's defense behavior could be controlled, it would then be feasible to concentrate on the reactive dynamics. The reasoning, moreover, is as applicable to the arms trade as to the arms race.

This chapter will examine the conditions that are likely to affect these domestic drives and will discuss the feasibility of affecting the process with explicit policy interventions. The central argument will be that objective economic problems are likely to increase the appeal of arms-race curbs for the Kremlin and that this, in turn, should provide a helpful context for weakening the link between economic and military interests within the United States. The latter is thus the area where initial policy should be directed. Should both of those things occur, a solid foundation would exist for addressing the problem of Richardsonian dynamics.

ECONOMICS AND ARMS LIMITATION

While most of the variables that were examined in previous chapters had the effect of accelerating the arms race, economic conditions could actually exercise a restraining role with regard to Soviet behavior. In the long run, this may also be true for the United States but, in the short run, this applies most evidently to the Soviet Union where there is an unambiguous and directly visible tradeoff between military growth and civilian prosperity.

Thus, to the extent that there is an immediate impetus to checking superpower military momentum, it is likely to proceed from economic constraints on the Soviet Union. This will, therefore, be our point of departure.

The Soviet Union and the Burden of the Arms Race

Despite the current and anticipated economic difficulties that the Soviet Union must face, its past record has had much to commend it. While the picture is somewhat blurred by the problems of measurement,[2] the estimated 6 percent growth rate of the 1950s and the 5 percent of the 1960s are extremely respectable—not quite on par with the records of Japan or Israel but, nevertheless, better than those of many Western industrialized nations. Past performance notwithstanding, certain uncomfortable truths are likely to become increasingly evident.

To begin with, earlier rates of growth were considerably superior to those experienced more recently, and even these may come to look good when compared to rates that are expected for the future. Furthermore, the opportunity costs that military programs impose on other economic sectors, and on Soviet society as a whole, may become even starker in coming years than they had recently appeared.

As was pointed out in Chapter 4, the USSR economy, unlike most market economies, has never experienced a mismatch between aggregate demand and supply. This is precluded by a centralized and comprehensive planning system designed to balance the supply of resources with the demands involved in the pursuit of selected economic targets.[3] The principal instruments of the system are a set of material plans involving physical quantities of goods and services, and a monetary counterpart in the form of financial plans designed to balance producer needs with credit availability and consumer income with the volume of available goods. Equilibriums and flows between sectors are charted on the basis of modern methods of input-output analysis. Plans are as ambitious as the most optimistic interpretations of economic reality will countenance and are related, in a rather mercantile fashion, to overriding national political goals.

The very explicitness and tautness of the system clearly reveal the tradeoffs involved in the pursuit of certain goals and, most apparently, the sacrifices in terms of consumer goods and producer durables occasioned by the Soviet commitment to military growth.

Unwelcome though such sacrifices may be to those who are on the losing side, this need not always present a serious political problem for the leadership. This is particularly true when the potential for friction is mitigated by rapid economic progress since, even when one's own share of the pie does not increase proportionately to overall economic expansion, some consolation will be derived from the fact that it is growing respectably in *absolute* terms. The military might be getting ever richer but the citizen is, at least, becoming less poor. However, when economic growth becomes sluggish, even this consolation may be unavailable and the potential for dissatisfaction increases. If Soviet growth, therefore, does indeed level off appreciably, the decision to continue subordinating public welfare to the claims of armed security should become politically more risky. Despite the implications, such a slowdown is very likely.

The most serious problem, that of productivity, seems intractable in the near future for a number of reasons.[4] Apparatchiks, for example, are loath to relinquish their control over economic decisions and tend to oppose decentralizing (and probably efficiency enhancing) reforms. Managers, who feel the pressure to meet the immediate targets set by planners, are often disinclined to disrupt operations in order to introduce innovations in their methods of production. Systemic problems aside, much Western (or at least United States) technology may not be available in coming years. To a certain extent, this will be because of continuing hard currency shortages, but a more profoundly political impediment to technology transfer will be the climate of the heightened East-West tension created in recent years and which is unlikely to dissipate soon.

In addition to torpid productivity growth, there is the problem of the impending labor shortage, which will have a major impact on production; demographic trends render an early solution to this problem unlikely. In addition, the sluggish rates of capital formation, which are increasingly characteristic of the economy, will limit yet another factor of production. Finally, the Soviet Union's decreasing self-sufficiency in oil will deprive the economy not only of easy access to sources of energy but of an important raw material as well (for making synthetics).

Soviet growth rates might still not appear excessively low by the standards of many other nations, yet they will be paltry relative to the nation's past performance and, especially, its future needs. This, of course, carries certain implications: if consumption is to be increased (both to bolster regime legitimacy and to enhance labor motivation) and if the decline in capital investment is to be checked (so as not to jeopardize future capital availability yet further), lavish military production may have to be curbed. What the actual consequences of this state of affairs will be for arms limitation is uncertain, but a number of scenarios can be suggested and the extent to which one or another prevails will depend on the political context accompanying the slowdown.

Some Soviet Scenarios

The most appealing prospect would be to have the Kremlin decide, as the weight of the economic troubles sink in, that the bulk of the nation's resources should be redirected toward the civilian economy. This would involve an explicit shift of past priorities to the benefit of light industry, agriculture, and the Soviet consumer. In this scenario, as each sector's prospects look dimmer, a reversal of the traditionally lopsided pattern of priorities would occur to the benefit of those that had been most deprived in the past. While the gains to both the Soviet citizen and the cause of arms limitation would be evident, it takes a very sanguine bent of mind and a cavalier attitude toward the historical record to assign much credence to this eventuality. Specifically, it would assume an improbable behavior on the United States side and a disregard for the acute security concerns that are so much a part of the Soviet character.

In a more realistic scenario, the new economic situation will have to be taken into consideration, but the relative importance given to military and civilian needs will remain unchanged. The growth of both sectors will suffer but according to the political weights traditionally assigned to each by the regime.

The meaning of such scenarios can be clarified by visually depicting their assumptions and implications. Let us assume, for present purposes, that the two principal policy goals of the Kremlin, i.e., the "goods" it most wants to acquire, are the enhancement of military power, and the development of the civilian economy. The quantity of both goods that can be produced is determined by the nation's total economic capacity, which must be apportioned between the production of military and civilian goods. By depicting military goods produced (M) on the vertical axis in Figure 7.1, and civilian goods (C) on the vertical axis, we can draw a line (PPa) representing the *additional* combinations of *both* that can be produced for a given *increase* in overall economic capacity. This is also termed the "production-possibility curve" in economic literature.

PPa's curvature illustrates the assumption of diminishing returns,

FIGURE 7.1
Economic Constraints on Soviet Military Growth:
A First Scenario

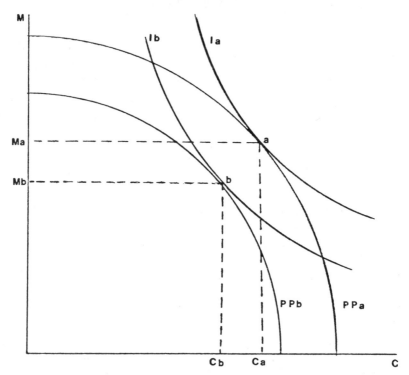

which characterize the tradeoff between M and C; the idea is that the more of one that is being produced, the larger the relative increment of the other that could be gained by shifting factors toward its production and away from the first.[5] This embodies an economic concept: it shows the additional combination of "guns and butter" that the Soviet economy could produce for a given level of capacity growth. It does not tell us, however, which combinations will actually be desired by the political leadership. This is determined by how much M and C are valued and is a matter of *political* preference. An "indifference curve" (denoted Ia) can be used to depict a hypothetical set of M and C combinations that the Kremlin would consider equally acceptable. The curve's slope measures the terms on which a little of one sort of good would willingly be sacrificed to obtain a little more of the other.

Thus the indifference curve describes which combination of

military and civilian goods the Soviet leaders might *desire*, while the production-possibility curve shows those which they could *obtain*. The point of tangency between the two (point a) depicts the hypothetical combination that will actually be produced—in this example, a quantity Ma of military goods and a quantity Ca of goods for the civilian economy.

Let us now assume that, because of constraints on USSR economic capacity, the additional amounts that can be produced in the future decline, that is, the production-possibility curve shifts inward although the rates of return for M and C (and hence the tradeoffs in production) remain unaltered. The new situation is shown by PPb in Figure 7.1. If we also assume that the slope of the indifference curve does not change, that is, military and civilian goods are valued in the same ratio as before, the new curve will be Ib and the new point of tangency will be point b. This is the second of our scenarios: the growth of both sorts of goods will have suffered but in some constant proportion.

This prospect has some foundation in recent history, since movements in Soviet defense outlays have borne a relatively constant relation to economic growth. At the same time, extrapolation might be risky. The crucial, yet questionable, assumption is that of an indifference curve of unaltered slope, that is, the idea that the relative importance that the Kremlin attributes to the two sectors will not be affected by the changing context accompanying the slowdown. The very first scenario, which assumed a *decrease* in the relative emphasis on military needs as economic problems set in, was dismissed as overly naive. The current scenario, depicted in Figure 7.2, which assumes the opposite, might be somewhat more plausible. Here, as the production possibility curve moves inward (from PPa to PPb) the amount of additional military goods that are produced decreases very slightly, while the civilian sector bears the brunt of the economic difficulties. Such a situation could be encouraged by several circumstances. To begin with, this could be brought about by a changed distribution of power within the Soviet elite. It has been suggested that a major line of fissure separates a heavy-industry/defense group (which favors a stronger emphasis on defense) from a group representing the interests of light industry and agriculture (which tends to champion the Soviet consumer). If the former were to further strengthen its position at the expense of the latter, a modified indifference curve for the regime would ensue. For example, if the West and its predatory intentions could be blamed for the economic difficulties, the probability of such a power shift would be increased. A generally

FIGURE 7.2
Economic Constraints on Soviet Military Growth:
A Second Scenario

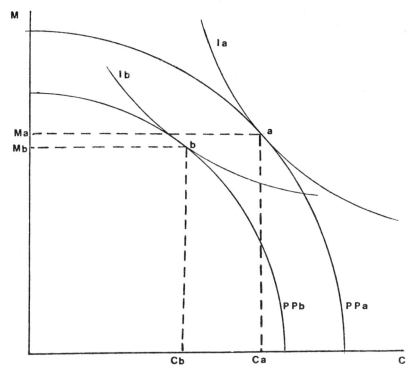

hostile Western stance, an increase in Sino-Soviet tensions, or too intimate a collaboration between Washington and Peking could tilt the indifference curve to the military sector's advantage.

These are all discouraging prospects but there is, nevertheless, one condition under which a more significant reduction in defense procurement could occur *despite* a change in official priorities. If, as the indifference curve inclined in a military direction, the production-possibility curve tilted the *opposite* way, a countervailing influence would be produced. In other words, if, as the regime wanted to increase production of military relative to civilian goods, it also found that it could produce the latter more efficiently (which is not the current case), the ultimate outcome might be the same as when neither slope changed despite the retrenchment in overall economic growth. This is illustrated in Figure 7.3. The key assumption is that the production of goods connected to civilian needs becomes *relatively* more efficient as economic capacity grows less rapidly. Though not very plausible as an overall scenario,

FIGURE 7.3
Economic Constraints on Soviet Military Growth:
A Third Scenario

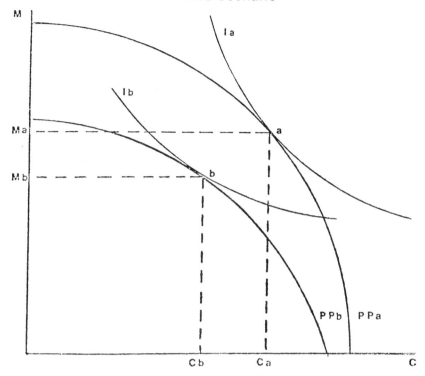

it could occur if the slowdown were accompanied by a movement from "extensive" to "intensive" development strategies, which increased the benefits of shifting the more productive resources from the military to the civilian sector (thus changing the slope of PPb in the desired direction).

While each of these prospects bears heavily on arms limitation, actual policies leading to a *favorable* scenario would probably flow from other sources. For example, a hypothetical Soviet unwillingness to further slant the indifference curve toward defense would probably come from a need to revitalize the regime's legitimacy in the eye's of the Soviet public. Although the consumers' mentality is not as pervasive in the Soviet Union as in the United States, it cannot be assumed to be altogether absent. The Soviet citizen will clearly settle for less than his U.S. counterpart, but it is overstating things to claim that "Russian consumers are appeased if there is a supply of bread, cabbage, potatoes and Vodka, an occasional shipment of oranges and a chance once in a while to go to a Western movie."[6] Promises can be deferred only so long without losing credibility, and the increased exposure to Western achievements cannot have failed to induce a sense of relative deprivation. Ultimately, a willing grant of legitimacy may elude the regime of any moderately industrialized nation that consistently frustrates the expectations of its consumers. Even if the general principle has escaped the Kremlin, it should have taken some heed from the violent eruptions of consumers' dissatisfaction, which threatened the Polish regime twice in a decade.

In sum, it is hard to believe that the Soviet leaders would not prefer to alleviate their military burden. Still they would probably not do so under all circumstances. USSR authors may claim that a relaxation of tensions was desired even at the height of the Cold War, since it "was acutely necessary for the restoration of the Soviet economy, for raising the standard of living of the people,"[7] but the fact remains that the people's standard of living will never have precedence over security needs. If necessary, a tradeoff between consumer ire and defense readiness could be resolved by increasing repression to squelch the former rather than by deemphasizing the latter, and *external* factors will probably be instrumental in guiding the regime's choices. The point is that, while the slowdown is not the product of purposeful policy, its consequences for levels of Soviet military activity will be, and it is this that the United States is in a position to influence. Washington must be expected to react to Soviet behavior as it deems prudent, but it should certainly avoid military initiatives that the Soviets cannot relate to their own previous or current behavior and that they would, consequently, interpret as further evidence of a gratuitously threatening external environment. And since the most damaging initiatives of the sort originate from domestic drives, the focal point of U.S. arms-limitation efforts should be the control of internal instigations to expanded defense activity.

Several categories of endogenous inducements to new U.S. procurement and augmented budgets were proposed, and one is led to inquire which one of these provides the best combination of causal impact and policy manipulability? Is it the economic context? Or, is it the bureaucratic drive? Or, perhaps, something else? My own view, as the reader may have anticipated, is that the first of these categories may provide the least discouraging point of departure.

Arms Limitation and the U.S. Economy

The discussion of the effect of economic needs on U.S. defense activity may have left the reader somewhat perplexed. On the one hand, it seemed that governmental spending is perceived by political leaders as a necessary complement to the private economy; on the other hand, the opportunity costs and baneful side effects of lavish military outlays make this a questionable tool of economic policy. Then why is this particular type of spending so frequently relied upon for economic ends?

Two explanations were suggested for this apparent paradox. To begin with, the beneficial cyclical effects are easily identifiable and virtually immediate, while the politician's horizon may not extend beyond the next election. Furthermore, there is the general distaste of U.S. citizens for substantial governmental participation in economic life. Washington is held accountable for the economy's performance but is unwillingly accorded the instruments with which to affect it. If governmental spending is, nonetheless, deemed necessary, it is likely to generate least resistance when the claims of military security can be invoked.

There are, moreover, some less apparent explanations for the economic function with which defense outlays are vested.[8] It is noteworthy, for example, that military spending usually does not displace the private entrepreneur. Since it supplements, but does not supplant private demand, it does not generate opposition from the business community. Furthermore, modern military equipment has a very restricted longevity, which means that there is almost always scope for new production. This is not true of many other forms of public spending: a school, once constructed, is likely to fulfill its function for quite some time and, barring occasional maintenance, the street or highway built with public funds will preclude similar construction on the same route for a long period.

Defense spending is highly expandable for yet another reason.[9] When a civilian product becomes obsolete, a new model can often be manufactured with only a slight modification of the machines and equipment that yielded the previous one. Thus new production frequently involves the final good alone. In contrast, the complexity and highly distinctive nature of many items of modern military hardware call for correspondingly specific tools and machinery, which means that the final good and the capital good are tightly linked. Consequently, it is often not enough to retool existing machinery; one must also produce basically *new* versions of this.

Therefore, there are a number of powerful reasons that may account for the apparent predilection for military procurement over other forms of governmental spending or, indeed, over efforts at directly stimulating the private sector. In addition, when political considerations enter the picture, it becomes clear why such programs appeal to many elected and appointed officials despite their long-term costs. Fundamentally then, significant arms limitation could entail the dissipation of a component of economic activity that, whatever its shortcomings, looms large in the process of national income generation. Even if there were no actual *disarmament*, a substantial reduction in new procurement would threaten the government's ability to act on the economy and would cause at least temporary dislocations for a number of social groups and individuals.

Let us assume, however, that in the interest of avoiding international conflict, it was decided that the state should relinquish this tool of macroeconomic policy and commit itself to extensive arms limitation. What would the likely economic impact be? Ultimately it would surely be beneficial, but a number of relatively painful immediate effects would probably be felt—and it is these that would be on the minds of the union leaders whose membership is engaged in weapons productions, of mayors whose cities are threatened by the closing of bases and military-industrial facilities, of defense firms whose contracts are not renewed, and so forth. Under these circumstances, political authorities will fear being held accountable for the inevitable short-term dislocations, and the decision to curb the arms race (as well as military exports) would be easier to take if it seemed that the proximate effects would not be too severe. What evidence do we have of their likely nature?

A modest body of research has been conducted on the consequences of conversion from military to civilian production. Though not as voluminous as could be hoped, it does shed some light on the nature of the problems that can be anticipated and, thus indirectly, on some useful directions for arms-limitation policies. A recent study, involving econometric modelling, was conducted by Roger Bezdek for the period 1975-80. The author assumed a hypothetical reduction in the Defense Department's budget of 30 percent, which would be compensated by an equivalent increase in spending for education, health, public assistance, and environmental programs. On the basis of a multiequation model of the U.S. economy, he calculated that net output and employment would *rise* by 2.1 percent above the level that would otherwise have been expected. On the other hand, a hypothetical *increase* in defense spending of 30 percent over the same period would cause a loss of 1.3 percent in output and jobs compared to a "base forecast." This suggested that, even in the short run, no losses would be experienced if the cut in military outlays were associated with a simultaneous increase in public spending for civilian needs. [10]

Reassuring though this may be in principle, the assumption of such a compensatory increase is heroic. Despite its obvious desirability, spending for environmental protection, housing, or public health is just not the sort of stuff that kindles the political ardour of the man in the street to the extent that defense against an ignoble enemy does. Yet we are assuming that something has happened to motivate the government to address these problems (perhaps a feeling that the Soviets can be induced to cooperate in the venture because of their own difficulties) and this, perhaps, will affect the U.S. public as well. Notwithstanding the difficulties, let us assume for the moment that military reductions can be balanced by new forms of public outlays, or perhaps, by a successful tax cut and that, therefore, the *macro*economic problem can be resolved. Even so, there would remain problems of a *micro*economic nature involving the reorientation of firms, households, and communities, which had previously relied on the military sector for their sustenance and prosperity, to civilian endeavours. The transition would not be totally smooth but it might not be overly painful either, particularly if intelligently conceived policies could reduce the friction. This is an important matter since the ability to convert from military to civilian activity can be viewed as the crucial fulcrum around which efforts at curbing the arms race will revolve. It can, in fact, be argued that conversion is one of the few areas where explicit policy is capable of making a substantial difference. A rough idea of the promises and pitfalls of such policy can be acquired from the experience of communities and firms that have, at some point, undergone the loss of military installations and defense contracts. After surveying this experience, I shall make several additional proposals for advancing the cause of conversion.

The Community's Experience

Either because of a process of partial demobilization (e.g., following the end of a war) or because of a redirection of military priorities, numerous U.S. communities have faced the closure of defense-oriented plants or the termination or relocation of military bases. Although the impact on any particular community depends on regional characteristics and specific circumstances, some generalizations on the basis of historical experience can be made. The consensus of observers is that readaptation and recovery are possible and that, while some problems are inevitable, the process is not unduly lengthy or painful.

For example, when Dow Air Force Base near Bangor in Maine was closed in 1968, the former military facilities were converted to yield the Bangor International Airport, which now services both domestic and international flights. In addition, part of the former base was devoted to industrial expansion and was eventually used as a location for five new manufacturing plants (as well as a Hilton Hotel located next to the airport). Another portion of the former facility was used as a campus for a community college.[11] A further example is provided by the Springfield Armory, in Springfield, Massachusetts, which had existed since 1794 and which was the city's third largest employer when the decision was made in 1964 to terminate its activities. Again, however, the community did not suffer long-term adverse consequences. Some of the armory buildings were conveyed by the government to the Commonwealth of Massachusetts for the development of Springfield Technical Community College. Other buildings were purchased by the city and successfully leased to newly attracted industries, including the Digital Equipment Corporation and the Milton-Bradley Company. Altogether, nine industries came to occupy the former armory site.[12] Yet another instance of successful conversion in the immediate post-Vietnam period was provided by Middletown, Connecticut. When Pratt and Whitney layed off 1,600 workers because of a cutback in military orders, the community's future looked bleak. Yet good local leadership and assistance from the federal government led to the inflow of several new industries and increasing employment. Total recovery was accomplished in about five years.[13] On the basis of a study of 22 communities where defense installations had to convert to civilian use, the president's Economic Adjustment Committee reported that, for a total of 45,429 jobs that were lost due to closings, fully 72,426 new jobs were eventually created as a result of conversion.[14]

Although these are all encouraging findings, a number of caveats should be made. In the first place, most of these studies were conducted by governmental bodies with a responsibility for successful conversion and there is generally little indication of how the sample of observed cases was selected or of its representativeness. Also, many (but not all) of the successful cases of conversion were recorded in the mid-to-late 1960s, which was a period of a rapidly growing national economy when it was not difficult to attract new industries and other commercial activity. Under less auspicious economic circumstances, the conversion process might have been less swift and smooth.

Nevertheless, with an opportune combination of fiscal and

monetary policies and vigorous local leadership, it is likely that many of these successful community efforts could be replicated at other times and in other places. This would rarely be totally pain-less. Transition troubles must be expected and a period of increased unemployment and dislocation may be inevitable: affected com-munities must acquire the vacated facilities, new activity must be attracted or created, often new skills have to be learned, and so forth. In any case, not all communities will be equally affected; those with base closings, for example, will usually have less trouble than those that experience the shutdown of a military-industrial plant. Also, the amount of planning that accompanies the conver-sion process is a major predictor of successful recovery. Yet, under most plausible circumstances and with a modicum of government aid, recovery should be expected within a few years.[15] To will-ingly accept even this level of transition pains implies some political will and is never an altogether easy decision to take. Under the proper circumstances, however, the difficulties would not appear too formidable.

The Experience of Industry

The regional perspective is only one of the two focuses through which the issue of conversion can be viewed; the second is that of the defense industries that suffer a loss of military orders. Not only do communities have to attract new forms of economic activity, but firms and plants with a substantial prior reliance on Department of Defense contracts and subcontracts must find new work and markets. Although the evidence has not been as systematically amassed and as rigorously studied in this case, there is some experience from which lessons can be drawn. Perhaps the foremost lesson is that earnest industrial transition from military to civilian work is difficult and infrequently attempted.[16] There is thus less ground for encouragement than there was at the community level.

Part of the problem has involved a lack of sufficient manage-ment motivation; those responsible for such efforts have simply not tried hard enough. Most often, this has come from the percep-tion that civilian business opportunities were neither sufficiently plentiful nor remunerative to justify the risks and exertions involved in conversion efforts. The problem of the perceived inadequacy of rewards is further reinforced by the generous earnings (for an operation that is free of most market risks) allowed by the Pentagon to its contractors and which are rarely replicable in the civilian economy. Ultimately rewards must provide the motivation for conversion and most industry estimates do not rate them very highly. However, the difference between military and civilian markets may make the transition rather difficult, even with the best of intentions.

To begin with, quality requirements are quite dissimilar in the two markets. Performance and tolerance levels are very demanding for advanced military products, work is meticulous and involves extremely sophisticated scientific knowledge and technological skills, and virtually no deviation from standards is permitted. While great stress is placed on quality, cost tends to be treated fairly casually. Since demand is typically for a modest number of complex goods, production is conducted on a low-volume basis with little opportunity for economies of scale. Moreover, the umbilical link to the U.S. Treasury that defense contractors enjoy makes this a secondary concern.

All of this is in stark contrast to the civilian economy. Technical sophistication is less crucial in most sectors, and performance standards are less demanding. On the other hand, cost is a prime determinant of profitability and quality is often sacrificed on the altar of competitive pricing. Thus, for example, a company engaged in residential construction may prosper nicely by using inferior materials if the effect is to reduce costs. Likewise, shoddy workmanship in products ranging from office equipment to children's toys may be forgiven by the market if the price is right. This cannot be assumed of the Pentagon's demand for strategic missiles, communications satellites, or modern combat helicopters. The nature of the respective reward structures is there quite different. Moreover, the commercial sector has forced those in business to acquire the marketing skills exacted by a competitive marketplace. In contrast, an ability to research the market or to engage in aggressive advertising is not very relevant to the military producer who deals with a single wealthy customer on an established basis. For the latter, skills at negotiating with bureaucracies and adroit lobbying is a surrogate for effective marketing.

Over all, the firm accustomed to the high-cost, high-performance, and frequently low-volume world of the military market finds it difficult to redirect its operations to the cost-conscious and competitive civilian market. It often has neither the ability nor the predilection to try. This is an obvious impediment and, despite several success stories,[17] there have been many instances of failure in the transition from one sector to the other; consequently, firms have tended to eschew conversion via the internal development of commercial products.

Although authentic conversion of this kind does not have an impressive record of success, there have been more modest efforts at reducing corporate dependence on military orders. One strategy has involved diversification to other forms of high-technology work within the public sector (for example, NASA) or the application of acquired skills to restricted parts of the private sector (for example, electronics or the civilian aerospace industry) where demand has warranted it. Such attempts have, nonetheless, been rather restricted. Another approach has involved mergers with companies outside the military sector, and particularly, with those firms that possess the marketing skills lacked by defense contractors. The financial community, for its part, has sought to encourage diversification as a means of mitigating the possible consequences of an exclusive reliance on a single customer (although investment bankers have favored diversification by acquisition rather than on the sole basis of the internal development of commercial products).[18] Efforts of this sort have often been successful, but it must be recognized that they are considerably less ambitious than straightforward conversion. Nevertheless, such efforts are valuable and, if diligently pursued, they would reduce the unwelcome side effects of military cutbacks and decrease the business community's apparent aversion to arms limitation.

The conclusion give grounds for neither enthusiastic optimism nor abject pessimism. While industrial conversion needs additional encouragement if it is to help mitigate apprehensions about the economic consequences of military cutbacks, the problems are probably not insurmountable. However, it would call for at least as much institutional effort and governmental involvement as is required for the resolution of comparable economic challenges (the energy problem, for example). This applies not only to conversion at the industrial level but also at the community level; in addition, some *direct* attention to the problems of displaced workers may be necessary. A few rather limited governmental endeavours in this area have been recorded but additional efforts would certainly be needed.

The Role of Government

The official interest in conversion has been remarkably tepid, and relatively little has been attempted at either the executive or the congressional levels. Nevertheless, some encouragement can be derived from the fact that, where the government has decided to get involved, it has also demonstrated its ability to make a difference. In this regard, the most significant of the rare efforts has been the creation, within the Department of Defense, of the Office of Economic Adjustment (OEA) which, while a palliative rather than a solution, is still a step in the right direction.[19]

The initiative for establishing this body was taken by Robert McNamara in 1961 to allay some of the problems caused by the closing of 95 unnecessary bases to free additional funds for missile procurement. During its first decade, the OEA was almost exclusively concerned with the effects of base and depot closings but, since 1970, it has extended its activities to cover communities affected by shutdowns of military-industrial plants as well. It acts principally as an advisory body to affected communities. Although it lays the greatest emphasis on local initiative for recovery, it does promote readjustment by offering, in collaboration with a number of federal departments and agencies, technical advice and, occasionally, financial help. Thus it may engage the Labor Department to help with employment services, or it might call upon the Commerce Department for advice on how best to attract new industries to the region, or to furnish grants from the Economic Development Administration. In the beginning, it relied exclusively on the funds of other agencies but was endowed with its own source of funds in 1973. So far, assistance has involved several hundred million dollars and over 150 communities.

The major shortcomings of these endeavours have concerned both scale and timing. Most obviously the OEA is not set up to anticipate difficulties and prevent their emergence. It enters the scene only after a crisis strikes, as in a community that is jolted by a substantial loss of employment. Also its resources are really quite modest. While several hundred million dollars may have been spent, this is a paltry sum compared to, say the 30 to 80 billion dollars that the projected MX missile system alone could cost. Of course, even if these problems were somehow surmounted, it would still be true that the OEA approaches the problem from one angle only. While it is designed to deal with affected communities, it has no capabilities to promote conversion at the level of the actual defense industries, that is, where the problem seems most intractable. Nor does it directly address the needs of those who have lost their military-related employment. The OEA surely represents a useful first step and its successful operation may dampen resistance to military cutbacks; nevertheless, by itself it is inadequate to encompass the magnitude of the total economic problem.

What is needed is a public program that would: (1) be automatically activated when problems caused by decreased military activity arise, and (2) provide more adequate resources than the OEA, given its essentially advisory nature, is in a position to provide. The principle behind such a program, even apart from its obvious pragmatic benefits, is entirely defensible: the gains from arms limitation include a general increase in security and economic welfare; the major costs are those associated with the temporary dislocations and employment losses occasioned by defense curbs. This being so, it seems appropriate that the minority that bears the temporary pains should be compensated by the majority that reaps the ultimate benefits.

As its principal focus, such a program would be designed to ease, but in no way to prolong, the period of transition to alternative employment for those whose jobs have been sacrificed to the goal of arms limitation. A substantial part of the benefits would consist of direct monetary compensation to cover income loss caused by the dislocation and covering the period of time needed for the employee to find a job that is similar to or better than the one lost. In addition, the benefits would include assistance in the acquisition of new skills (perhaps up to two years' schooling) as well as relocation expenses occasioned by the search for new employment. Of course, it should be kept in mind that we are not treading on virgin territory. In fact, the program would in many ways be similar to the compensation provided, under the Trade Adjustment Assistance Program, to U.S. workers who are adversely affected by free-trade policies advocated and pursued by the U.S. government. The principle of compensation for dislocations caused by the pursuit of the collective good is similar. In addition to the principle, there is a powerful pragmatic aspect since a major anticipated boon would be to dispel the misgivings that certain portions of the public may have about the employment consequences of a retrenchment from militarism.

Even this, however, would not directly tackle the problem of the firm for which defense orders are a substantial part of total business, but, here too, some effective policies may be available. The major efforts of the government in this regard should be directed at designing and legislating fiscal incentives to compensate for some of the risks involved in the transition to civilian production. There is a long tradition of using fiscal inducements in the pursuit of policy goals and, in this area as well, it may be necessary to furnish special tax considerations to companies bearing temporary financial reverses through their conversion programs. Alternative sorts of contracts should also be considered for firms that suffer a substantial reduction in defense orders and should involve skills that were specifically relevant to the company's previous military orientation. The development of public transportation networks could, in many cases, provide a useful alternative source of activity; the further expansion of civilian space programs would also provide an area of compensating procurement and employment for those with the requisite skills. One interesting type of high-technology function, which a number of former defense contractors would be well suited to perform, involves the development and production of the ultrasophisticated equipment of arms-control verification—the sensors, reconnaissance instruments, and decoding equipment (e.g., for telemetric information); this equipment is essential for negotiating curbs on military growth, and the need would increase with the process of arms limitation. It would be appealing to have former defense producers actively involved in quelling the development and deployment of new military products.

The strategy of diversification through acquisition could also be facilitated. While the purely economic rationale for antitrust regulation as a way of preserving a competitive market structure is sound, it may be desirable to institute a special regime for conglomerates involving defense firms that are seeking to reduce their heavy reliance on military orders by acquiring commercial companies. Some violence would obviously be done to antitrust tenets, but the greater economic danger would surely be produced if efforts at loosening this dependence were not facilitated. Again, it is a matter of intelligently prioritizing several desirable objectives.

There are, therefore, a number of promising strategies that could be pursued. A good outlook for conversion would not provide the prime motivation for curbing the arms race—this should flow from the security dangers and nonmilitary economic costs that it entails—but it could ease the process once it got underway. In order to place this in proper focus, it will be helpful to pause, get our bearings, and compare this emphasis on conversion with alternative approaches that also involve domestic variables.

At the outset of the chapter, I suggested that the proper strategy is to act forcefully on the internal determinants of national military behavior either before or simultaneously with action on the dynamics of interactive feedback (to the extent that it does occur). It was also proposed that it would be best to focus on that variable, or set of variables, embodying a combination of strong causal effect and easy manipulability. That none of the previously examined determinants of the arms race possess these qualities in an optimal fashion is amply evident; nevertheless, some variables hold more promise than others, and this is particularly evident when external and objective circumstances commend them as logical points of departure.

For our purposes, the most significant such circumstance involves the increasing economic constraints that the Soviet Union will have to face in coming years and whose effect could only be nullified by a further slant of regime values toward military security. Obviously, this syndrome of economic difficulties in not a variable for policy purposes per se, and any U.S. attempt to further jeopardize the Soviet economy would probably encourage the compensating shift in values.[20] The manipulable, and probably effective, variable from a policy standpoint is the degree of dependence of the U.S. economy on defense activity. If this dependence could be sufficiently weakened through meaningful conversion, there would be fewer instances of activities and initiatives that the Soviets could not causally relate to their own behavior. Their environment would seem less hostile and this, in turn, might induce a tapering off of Soviet military growth (due to the absense of adverse indifference-curve shifts in the face of economic difficulties). Under such conditions, dealing with the relevant Richardsonian dynamics might become a manageable task.

But the world is not so simple. Even if all of this could somehow be engineered in the face of practical and political difficulties, it would not eliminate all of the endogenous instigations to militarism. As was pointed out in previous chapters, organizational routines and momentum, vested interests of the defense establishment, and technological stimulation would still remain a problem. What should be done about these aspects of the matter? My judgement, which I shall proceed to argue, is that these influences are less directly malleable than the economic connection seems to be. At best, they can be restrained but not quashed. However, even this would probably be facilitated by a Soviet slowdown, U.S. conversion, and a generally propitious international climate.

THE RESIDUE OF DOMESTIC DRIVES

I discussed at some length the momentum fostered by bureaucratic and organizational dynamics within both superpowers. These dynamics are, both from the point of view of interest aggregation and policy implementation, typical of all complex modern societies. They manifest themselves in two ways. To begin with there is a tendency for bureaucracies and other established organizations to adopt routine operating and goal-setting procedures that impart a mechanical character to their activities and make it difficult to move their conduct from established grooves. The incremental component to military growth, in particular, may be an outcome of this form of institutional behavior in both nations. In the second place, these dynamics are also manifested in the pursuit of vested organizational interests, which usually include the expansion of resources and responsibilities. Thus some part of the force posture of both superpowers emerges, not so much from articulated security and economic needs, but from the day-to-day activities of numerous bureaucratic units pursuing their routines, habitual expectations, and definitions of their corporate weal.

The point is that the number, power, and relative autonomy of such bureaucracies and public organizations is a product of: (1) the volume of problems that public policy must confront; (2) the specialized knowledge and skills that are called for by their complexity, and (3) the need for uniformity and predictability in their resolution. It is scarcely surprising that the activities of the organizations vested with these tasks are relatively impervious to shifting preferences at the pinnacle of political authority. As William Taubman has pointed out,

> Soviet governmental behavior reflects not only the Politburo's deliberated political purpose but also the mode of operation of complex large-scale organizations that even a powerful central leadership cannot always and everywhere control. [21]

The situation might not be dissimilar in the United States despite the very different basis of political organization. As Franklin D. Roosevelt, an astute political manipulator, remarked,

> The Treasury is so large and far-flung and ingrained in its practices that I find it almost impossible to get the action and results I want. . . . But the Treasury is not to be compared with the State Department. You should go through the experience of trying to get any changes in the thinking, policy and action of the career diplomats and you'd know what a real problem was. But the Treasury and the State Department put together are nothing compared with the Na-a-vy. . . . To change anything in the Na-a-vy is like punching a feather bed. You punch it with your right and you punch it with your left until you are finally exhausted, and then you find the damn bed just as it was before you started punching it. [22]

The bureaucratic substructure has, therefore, an impact on

national policy that is independent, in part, of official preferences. Yet the ability of governments at least to check the influence of their *military* establishments when arms limitation requires is critical. Neither government will wish to constantly second guess and challenge the estimates that the armed services make of their own needs, but each should have the ability to prevail when major military desires conflict with political goals that are deemed to be in the national interests.

As I have suggested, the Soviet leadership appears to be in a more favorable position than its U.S. counterpart in this regard. Simply, the distribution of political power in the Soviet Union is such that the military is rarely in a position to impose its preferences on those (probably infrequent) occasions when they run counter to the objectives of the party elite. The question is whether the reverse situation is true, that is, can the Politburo force its own policy on a recalcitrant or hostile military establishment? Instances where the two have openly disagreed are rare, but what we have been able to observe indicates that, within plausible ranges of arms limitation and favorable international circumstances, the party leadership does prevail. Khrushchev's military policy, announced before the Supreme Soviet in January 1960, is a case in point.

While Stalin's emphasis on conventional forces and sheer manpower ("the permanently operating factors") dominated USSR strategy in the early postwar decades, Khrushchev determined, partly for economic reasons, to deemphasize the role of the traditional forces in favor of a more explicitly nuclear posture. Rather than finance the needs of the new strategy by added slices of military spending, he decided to cut the resources of the ground and naval forces by as much as one-third and to reallocate this to the nuclear rocket force. Predictably, Khrushchev's axe created much bitterness and resentment within large portions of the military establishment and occasioned a number of significant dismissals. Eventually, rising international tensions (particularly the new crisis over Berlin) caused him to modify his position and to expand *all* sectors of the defense machine, but the principle of ultimate civilian primacy even on strategic matters was affirmed. This does not mean that it is a costless matter to thwart the armed services (the military establishment that had helped Khrushchev in his earlier challenge to Malenkov offered no support when he was ousted by Brezhnev and Kosygin in 1964). Still, when the party leaders are willing to absorb risks of this sort they probably can prevail even in the face of the marshals' ire.

The normative principle of civilian supremacy in matters of overall military policy is also clearly present in the United States, but the situation is politically more complicated, since the distribution of political power characteristic of polyarchical arrangements makes it possible for the administration to be effectively challenged by a coalition of forces including the military. It is not that the United States armed services want to protect their interests more fiercely than do their Soviet counterparts; they simply have more means of promoting them. The defense establishment's ability to seek allies within the legislative branch makes a substantial difference. Adam Yarmolinsky, a former Defense Department insider, sheds light on some methods that can be used:

> The Pentagon takes a "carrot and stick" approach to Congress. The biggest contract awards have tended over the years to go to key members of the military committees, who in turn usually vote for the Pentagon's program. One former White House assistant said a special technique was employed by the services whenever the White House or the Secretary of Defense vetoed one of the services' favorite projects or wanted to buy something it did not want. "In this case," he said, "the service lines up a friendly Congressman to plant questions when the chief of staff of that service or another high-ranking officer appears on the Hill. The Congressman will ask the officer his 'professional' opinion on the weapons system, as opposed to official Defense Department line." Then, he said, after the officer rendered his opinion, "the friendly faction on the committee has a field day criticizing the Secretary of Defense for not doing something the service chief thinks is in the national interest."[23]

Nor is the military forced to lobby alone. The overlap between its interests and those of a number of other influential groups provides it with natural partners. Most of these allies are not integrated into formal structures of political authority (unlike the Soviet case) and can effectively agitate against arms-limitation measures that damage their vested interests. Therefore, it is frequently just not feasible for political leaders to oppose programs with substantial military, industrial, and congressional support.

The policy implications of all this will differ depending on whether one is dealing with (1) the regular bureaucratic patterns that keep military trends on a steady path, or (2) with the occasional surges caused by the coincidence of military preferences with those of powerful interest groups. As for the former, an attempt to quell the normal expression of organizational politics and routines may not be a promising first step on the path to arms limitation. The Soviet Union does have an established party supremacy and a correspondingly centralized network of political authority, but it also has a conspicuously large and unwieldy bureaucracy with interests that are often impervious to shifting official policy goals. The force is great but so is the counterforce. Less is encompassed by the bureaucratic clasp in the United States but, in this case, the power that the political leadership can wield in its regard is correspondingly slighter. Any substantial change here would involve a considerable strengthening of hierarchical authority and the absorption of a far larger part of public activity into the government's direct embrace; this would also involve subordinating much scientific and technological work to explicit political priorities. None of this is either feasible or desirable.

As for the second category, neither nation can dismiss the need to bring *major* defense programs and activities in line with national policy objectives rather than with the vested interests of the military establishment and whatever allies it can muster. This would be difficult for both superpowers but, perhaps, less so for Moscow than for Washington. Thus, if economic conditions should ordain a tapering off for the Soviet Union, and if security threats do not appear too harsh, the Kremlin will probably manage to resist major new military demands. This is less simple in the United States, where, under *current* circumstances, the administration and its congressional supporters would have to estimate the maximum arms limitation permissible in terms of domestic politics: the most likely case would involve a variety of "side payments" to the defense lobby, which could come close to neutralizing the initial accomplishment. In this vein, it can be argued that the need to acquiesce in calls for sustained future increases in military spending and in the development of the MX missile system had virtually offset, long before the invasion of Afghanistan, the import of the negotiated SALT II agreement.

But current circumstances need not endure and one of the most valuable potential effects of successfully breaking the link between defense and the economy is to weaken the basis for the military-industrial alliance. As the cost of cutbacks appeared less dire, there would be less cause for some major firms to lobby in Washington, or for subcontractors to mobilize support in congressmen's constituencies for military programs that are not necessitated by long-term security needs.

It should also be borne in mind that a major difference between conversion and direct challenges to the military is that one is seeking, in the first case, to replace one way of meeting an economic need with an alternative way of satisfying the same need. The economic need itself is not being challenged; one is merely changing instruments. In the second case, the organizational interests (expanded resources and missions) are being challenged. While this too must eventually be done, the outlook for success is improved if the basis for the support of the organizations' allies is weakened. It is this variable that has an attractive combination of impact and manipulability.

CONCLUSIONS

Lest the case should be overstated, a few final remarks are in order. The causal sequences in terms of which the arguments were made were of a logical rather than a chronological nature; thus some temporal overlap between cause and effect must be assumed. For example, conversion cannot get very far underway if there is no cutback in defense programs to stimulate it, but the extent to which cutbacks are acceptable will depend on the demonstrated promise of conversion. The problem is that there is some circularity here since most of the variables are endogenous to the causal system. Therefore, what effective arms limitation requires is some added, *exogenous*, impetus to help set the process in motion and to prompt it along when necessary. If this could be accomplished, then the problem of dampening the Richardsonian cycle of action, reaction, and overreaction could also be more confidently addressed. But this leads us away from the domestic economic and political context and back into the international system. It is the latter that the next chapter will investigate.

NOTES

1. Alva Myrdal does examine the question of sincerity at some length. See Alva Myrdal, The Game of Disarmament (New York: Pantheon Books, 1976).
2. For some of the problems involved in assigning numbers to Soviet economic performance, see Robert W. Campbell, *The Soviet-Type Economies* (Boston: Houghton-Mifflin, 1974), pp. 83-99.
3. A good description of Soviet planning mechanisms is provided in Paul Gregory and Robert C. Stuart, *Soviet Economic Structure and Performance* (New York: Harper & Row, 1974), chap. 5.
4. For a discussion of some of these problems see ibid., pp. 361-64.
5. Some consequences of relaxing these assumptions are analyzed in Heny W. Schaefer, "Soviet Power and Intentions: Military-Economic Choices," in Joint Economic Committee, Congress of the United States, *Soviet Economy in a Time of Change*, (Washington, D.C.: U.S. Government Printing Office, 1979), pp. 341-52.

6. Hedrick Smith, *The Russians* (New York: Ballantine Books, 1976), p. 667.
7. Nikolai V. Sivachev and Nikolai N. Yakovlev, *Russia and the United States: US-Soviet Relations from a Soviet Point of View* (Chicago: University of Chicago Press, 1979), p. 232.
8. See also M. Nincic and T. Cusack, "The Political Economy of U.S. Military Spending" *Journal of Peace Research* 10 (1979):101-15.
9. See also Murray Weidenbaum, "Defense Expenditures and the Domestic Economy," in Edwin Mansfield, ed., *Defense Science and Public Policy* (New York: Norton, 1968).
10. Roger H. Bezdek, "The 1980 Economic Impact—Regional and Occupational—of Compensated Shifts in Defense Spending," *Journal of Regional Science* 15 (1975):183-98.
11. This case is described in The President's Economic Adjustment Committee, *Economic Recovery: Community Response to Defense Decisions to Close Bases* (Washington, D. C.: Defense Office of Economic Adjustment, 1976), pp. 8-10.
12. Ibid., pp. 42-44.
13. Described in Thomas P. Ruane, *Federal Responses to Economic Crises: The Case of Defense Economic Adjustment* (Washington, D.C.: Department of Defense, 1977).
14. President's Economic Adjustment Committee, op.cit., p. 51.
15. According to one estimate, the average lag of time needed for successful conversion is five years. See B. G. Lall, *Prosperity Without Guns: The Economic Impact of Reductions in Defense Spending* (New York: Operation Turning Point, Institute for World Order, 1977).
16. A thorough analysis of the major difficulties is provided by Murray L. Weidenbaum, "Industrial Adjustments to Military Expenditures," in Bernard Udis, ed., *Adjustments of the US Economy to Reductions in Military Spending* (Washington, D.C.: U.S. Arms Control and Disarmament Agency, 1970). See also Lall, op.cit., pp. 13-21.
17. An example is provided by the Boeing Vertol installation near Philadelphia, which had been a major supplier of military helicopters. After the Vietnam involvement peaked, the firm began considering methods of conversion and diversification. In 1971 it decided to develop urban transit equipment on the model of successful European cities and has since built several hundred advanced trolley cars and stainless steel rapid transit cars. These vehicles possess innovations capable of significantly reducing the operating costs of public transportation and have been destined for the Boston-Massachusetts Bay Transit Authority, the San Francisco Municipal Railway, and the Chicago Transit Authority. The possibility that the skyrocketing price of gasoline may lead to an expansion of urban transportation in the near future makes this an attractive undertaking. The case is described in some detail by Seymour Melman, "Converting from Military to Civilian Industry: Conclusions from American Experiences," in Peter Wallensteen, ed., *Experiences in Disarmament: On Conversion of Military Industry and Closing of Military Bases* (Uppsala, Sweden: Uppsala University, Dept. of Peace and Conflict Research, Report No. 19, 1978) pp. 55-87.
18. One slight problem for the aerospace industry is that, because of the price-earning ratios of their stocks, financing for diversification must come from borrowing rather than the exchange of stock.

19. A brief survey of the OEA is provided in Milton Leitenberg, "Base Closing in the United States: A Note on the Office of Economic Adjustment," in Wallensteen op. cit., pp. 135-39. A more extensive treatment is contained in Ruane, op. cit.
20. This, of course, is a danger inherent in the economic sanctions imposed by the United States against the USSR in the wake of their invasion of Afghanistan. The problems involved are obvious.
21. William Taubman, "The Change to Change in Communist Systems: Modernization, Post-Modernization and Soviet Politics," in Henry W. Morton and Rudolf L. Tokes, eds., *Soviet Politics and Society in the 1970s* (New York: The Free Press, 1974).
22. Quoted in Marriner S. Eccles, *Beckoning Frontiers* (New York: Knopf, 1951), p. 336.
23. Adam Yarmolinsky, *The Military Establishment: Its Impact on American Society* (New York: Harper & Row, 1971), pp. 41-42.

8

ARMS LIMITATION:
THE BILATERAL DIMENSION

In the previous chapter, I outlined an approach for dealing with a major inducement to military growth in the United States and indicated some likely internal developments in the Soviet Union. Nevertheless, it bears reiterating that not all causes of the arms race are domestic and that *significant* initiatives (if not every movement) by one superpower will provide a sufficient, though unnecessary, condition for a corresponding move by the rival. The Soviets have equalled most U.S. spending increases and weapons innovations and, while U.S. economic and technological superiority have typically made it the leader rather than the follower, the United States has always responded vigorously and successfully where the Soviets did manage to acquire an edge. Such sensitivity flows from mutual hostility and distrust, and dealing with this is as much part of a viable strategy of arms limitation as is, for example, the promotion of economic conversion. One must ask, therefore, whether this hostility can be mitigated or failing that, whether its *link* to the arms race can be weakened.

Even if the issue of hostility could be dealt with in a satisfactory manner, another set of issues that would have to be settled concerns the choice of a direct object of arms-limitation negotiations. Most negotiations so far have focused on the *physical output* of the arms race, that is, on weapons and related equipment. While this seems like the obvious way of proceeding, it may actually be a relatively unpromising tack to adopt. These too are important issues and to complement the previous discussion of domestic political and economic conditions, the matters of bilateral hostility and an optimal direct object of negotiation will now be addressed.

ARMS, HOSTILITY, AND DISTRUST

Hostility affects arms-race behavior in two ways. In the first place, it furnishes convenient grounds for rationalizing military activity taken in response to essentially domestic needs. Secondly, it provides an *authentic justification* for interpreting such activity by the other side as a threat to national security. For example, even if the economic burden of defense became increasingly onerous for Moscow, a hostile climate may lead to a tighter squeeze on the civilian sector rather than to military restraint. Similarly, even if conversion is feasible and ultimately beneficial for the U.S. economy, it may never be given a chance if mutual tension and distrust cannot be dealt with. If domestic drives *could* be checked, a beneficial feedback loop would probably be established between the internal and external environments. Unfortunately, the process is unlikely to be initiated if a better climate cannot be established between the two nations even in the absence of prior achievements in arms limitation, or if the arms race cannot be at least partly insulated from tensions in other areas of superpower competition.

Both political scientists and a number of social psychologists have suggested that mutual perceptions are distorted between nations whose relations are characterized by tension and distrust.[1] This does not mean that hostility does not often derive from objective conflicts of interest—this is clearly so in the present case— but it does suggest that there are mechanisms that exacerbate hostility beyond the levels that these incompatibilities alone would suggest. It leads to an exaggerated view of the other side's capacities and degree of organizational regimentation, to an overstatement of the predatory and single-mindedly purposive nature of its behavior, and to a situation where "tough" solutions dominate official thinking to the exclusion of creative approaches to conflict resolution. Evidence is selectively interpreted by means of various "perceptual emphases" and dissonance-reducing mechanisms, causing such perceptions to be further reinforced. In such a context, military initiatives can be justified even in the face of very flimsy evidence of a real external threat.

Thus a comprehensive approach to arms limitation should deal with the problem of the circular traps that mutual hostility sets. Two strategies (which are not mutually exclusive) are suggested: one can try to *dissipate* hostility or one can seek to *circumvent* it. In the first case, one would reason that since superpower hostility is, at least partly, the result of mutually reinforcing attitudes, an attempt should be made to undo the harm by making the process operate in reverse. Underlying conflicts of interest would not be resolved merely by acting on perceptions, but this would, nevertheless, help place them in proper perspective. Alternatively (and perhaps temporarily) one could attempt to obviate the *effects* of existing hostility. Specifically, its presence would be recognized but made less relevant to the arms race (by increasing, for example, the costs of acting on this link between hostility and the arms race).

While neither of these two broad strategies has ever been effectively pursued, statesmen and scholars have not been oblivious to such possibilities. Let us begin with the first, and apparently more direct, of the two approaches.

DISSIPATING HOSTILITY

Generalizing from their observations of interpersonal conflicts, certain psychologists have suggested rather detailed methods for dealing with closed cycles of negative perceptions between nations.[2] The premise behind the proposals is that positive reinforcements are, as a rule, more effective instruments of behavior modification then are negative sanctions. Thus rewards for acts that dampen hostility are preferable to punishments for those that increase it. To set the reversal of the cycle on course, one-sided gestures are needed at first and definite, though not necessarily very large, conciliatory moves should be initiated. It should be made clear that reciprocation would be welcome but that the gesture is not contingent on this. The point is that immediate reciprocity is not the object but, rather, an unmistakable demonstration of sincerity; in fact, one or more *additional* concessions should be made even in the absence of corresponding gestures from the adversary. When a favorable response does occur, another step should immediately be initiated and, hopefully, a deescalating spiral would soon be set in motion. Initial gestures need not involve armaments but, once the parties set forth on their journey toward mutual understanding and tolerance, some action regarding armaments will become necessary to maintain the acquired momentum. Obviously, both sides should remain ready and willing to defend their fundamental interests; indeed, one author suggests that the most important weapons (those meant for nuclear retaliation) should not be relinquished until last.[3] Also, unilateral concessions are appropriate only as long as is reasonably necessary to establish one's sincerity.

While the line of reasoning underlying such proposals is appealing, there is a quality of political naiveté about them. The assumption that the amount of unilateralism needed to establish sincerity can be satisfactorily determined is highly debatable. One would think, at the very least, that the nation taking the initiative would have a more restricted idea of what is reasonably called for than the nation from which a helpful response is expected. The latter might regard the initial gestures as tricks designed to lull it into a misguided complacency and may take much longer to convince than the initiator's patience (and sense of insecurity) will bear. An even worse situation would arise if the second party interprets the gestures as signs of weakness and hastens to adopt a yet harder line of its own. Even if this were not the case, David Singer points out that when conciliatory moves are initiated by national decision makers, "the probabilities are all too high that the competence, courage or patriotism of one or both sets of elites will then be challenged by a 'hard-line' domestic opposition, be it a legitimate political party in a democratic system or a less institutionalized faction in a more autocratic system."[4]

This last point deserves to be dwelt on and, indeed, expanded since domestic resistance to conciliation need not originate from typical political opposition groups. Within both superpowers, the existence and growth of various national security bureaucracies depends on a measure of foreign hostility (whether or not there is an arms race); they are thus unlikely to accede to the other side's being portrayed in anything other than an unfavorable and predatory light. At times also, the very nature of the political system seems to benefit from hostility. Certainly a number of features of the Soviet system would be hard to justify in the absence of a plausible external threat. In another vein, a convenient plank for a political platform in the United States is often fashioned by appealing for vigilance against the external foe and reminding the public of its unsavory character.

The psychologically-based policy is therefore stymied by the presence of obdurate problems in the domestic realm that encourage bilateral hostility (and may or may not overlap with those that specifically call for military competition). It may then seem necessary to attack the problem at its source and, at this point, the emphasis might shift to the prior need to *restructure* these societies to get rid of the internal obstacles.

The idea of transforming societies to do away with the roots of international conflict has a long and distinguished pedigree. Rousseau saw the causes of clashes between countries in the existence of despotic monarchical rule and thought that peace could be ensured by eliminating absolute monarchies. Lenin, who attributed wars to the internal dynamics of capitalism (declining rates of profit and the ascendance of financial capital), thought the solution lay in transcending the system itself. Yet republics have not proven much less prone to war than absolute monarchies, and socialism has been no guarantor of peace (even between nominally Marxist nations). The fact that systems as divergent as those of the two superpowers should both find hostility useful for some internal purpose suggests that no obvious internal transformation would solve the problem. Moreover, even if a more promising domestic arrangement could be designed, the likelihood that it would actually be erected in the name of arms control is rather remote. The dissipation of hostility is a goal toward which we should strive, but it would be rash to allow arms limitation to await its realization.

CIRCUMVENTING HOSTILITY

If the endogenous roots of international tension cannot be eliminated, perhaps they can, at least, be balanced by some countervailing influence. Specifically, the cost of not achieving arms limitation could be aggravated, or the rewards for progress toward the goal increased, despite the existing hostility. Of course, ways of countering the effects of hostility may also, as a side effect, modify (in either direction) the level of underlying hostility and thus affect both sides of the balance; nevertheless, the emphasis is on counterpoise and the strategy designed to attain this usually involves some form of *linkage policy*.

When a nation pursues this brand of policy, it is making the other side's attainment on one (or several) goals contingent on progress toward the first nation's *own* goals. This strategy is never very far from the surface in East-West relations and has been particularly embraced by the United States in the Nixon-Kissinger period (and announced as a policy by the Reagan administration). It is, however, a complex strategy with several variants and any appreciation of its merits should begin with the understanding that it can take different forms.

To get a firmer grip on the matter, linkage policy will first be discussed from the perspective of U.S. foreign policy toward the Soviet Union, and the options available to U.S. decision makers will be surveyed.

Linkages can be established in two directions. To begin with, progress on arms limitation with Moscow can be made the *dependent* variable, that is, something that is contingent on USSR attitudes toward other U.S. foreign-policy objectives. Conversely, U.S. attitudes toward other Soviet interests can be made contingent on prior USSR gestures with regard to military matters (which makes arms limitation the *independent* variable). Thus two possibilities are available depending on the direction of the linkage.

Another useful distinction involves the *method* by which the policy is pursued. Regardless of its direction, the linkage can involve a threat of punishment or a promise of reward. In the first case, the United States would declare its readiness to make the Soviet Union weaker with respect to an initial baseline if Moscow did not display a cooperative attitude; in the second case, Washington would promise to ameliorate the Soviet position with respect to that same baseline in exchange for cooperative moves. Both methods can be used simultaneously, but their implications for arms limitation may be very different.

These possibilities can be illustrated with the following matrix (see Figure 8.1), which presents four "pure" brands of linkage policies that are theoretically available to U.S. decision makers.

The first row (Cell 1 and Cell 2) involves linkages by means of threatened sanctions. In the first instance, Washington might withdraw a concession which it had offered in earlier military negotiations or undertake, for example, the unilateral deployment of some new weapon, if the Kremlin behaved in a particularly provocative manner. In the second case, the terms of the linkage are reversed

FIGURE 8.1
Strategies of U.S. Linkage Politics

Arms Limitation

		Dependent variable	Independent variable
Forms of Linkage	Punishment	1.	2.
	Reward	4.	3.

and an uncooperative Soviet stance on matters of arms limitation are met by U.S. punishments (for example, curbing shipments of advanced technology). While we have more experience with the former sort of linkage than with the latter (for example, the U.S. decision to suspend the ratification process for SALT II following the invasion of Afghanistan) neither is truly desirable for our purposes. As I indicated at the beginning of this section, some policies designed to serve as a counterpoise to hostility's impact on arms limitation can actually increase the level of underlying tension; clearly, punishment would intensify the Soviet Union's perception of an external threat, which would thereby reduce the prospects for negotiated military restraint. Accordingly, the first two types of linkage will not be further entertained as policies that are conducive to arms limitation.

The second row (Cell 3 and Cell 4) is more promising since the linkages are not likely to backfire by increasing hostility levels) and thus neutralizing the initial attempt to balance it). There is no reason to think that this will help reduce existing hostility either: the expectation is simply that it should make it less *relevant*. In Cell 3, the U.S. ties military concessions to prior Soviet help with other issues. For example, a USSR withdrawal from Afghanistan might be rewarded by U.S. limits on the deployment of Pershing II missiles in Europe. In the Cell 4 approach, a cooperative stance by the Kremlin on questions of the arms race (for example, a willingness to restrict production of the Backfire bomber) would be greeted by rewards in nonmilitary areas (for example, by Export-Import Bank credits or by Most Favored Nation trading status).

Even when only reward-based strategies are considered, there is a difference in assumed context depending on the direction of the linkage. In the first case (Cell 3), success would imply that arms limitation is more important to the Soviet Union than to the United States, since it is the former that is assumed willing to make the initial concession toward this end. The converse assumption is implicit in the second case (Cell 4), since the United States is meant to provide inducements (at some cost) to the Soviets in order to check the military competition. Thus the value of a linkage of either sort for arms limitation might depend on the relative importance that the parties assign to it.

So far, I have been assuming that the United States would be the party pursuing the linkage policy, since the Soviets have traditionally preferred to discuss military matters independently of other issues. Nevertheless, two caveats are called for. In the first place, the Kremlin's unwillingness to jeopardize the pursuit of politically necessary interests has led it to object mainly to linkages involving punishments. For example, the goal of projecting Soviet power in the Third World has never been abandoned and, given the regime's legitimizing ideology, it is not obvious that it could be. Thus a tradeoff between two goals would be avoided if such linkages were never established. By the same token, Moscow has not sought to make its own attitudes on arms control contingent on U.S. restraint in other parts of the world. Thus Soviet willingness to sign the ABM treaty was not affected by Nixon's accelerated bombing of North Vietnamese cities nor by the mining of their harbors. In the second place, a Russian policy of linkages based on *inducements* to the United States has been of doubtful relevance given the meager store of rewards available to the Kremlin. Major *political* concessions are not usually considered and, unlike the United States (which has a similar attitude toward political interests), the USSR has little to offer as inducement in the *economic* sphere.

Thus, if the matrix of relevant Soviet linkages were presented, it might have just one nonempty cell (see Figure 8.2). In other words, the major (and perhaps sole) legitimate linkage from the point of view of USSR policy involves rewards granted in the military sphere in exchange for United States favors in other areas.

The fact that Cell 4 may not be relevant from the Soviet perspective implies, by the same token, that Cell 3 could be inapposite from the point of view of U.S. foreign policy (because

FIGURE 8.2
Strategies of Soviet Linkage Politics

Arms Limitation

		Dependent variable	Independent variable
Forms of Linkage	Punishment	1. empty	2. empty
	Reward	4.	3. empty

both involve the same expectations). As punishments are being excluded from our list of useful strategies, the remaining two policies (U.S. Cell 4 and Soviet Cell 3) both imply a strategy of *linking* Soviet concessions on arms limitation to U.S. inducements in other areas. Since, moreover, economic problems may make Moscow particularly eager to restrain military competition in the 1980s (assuming there is no significant increase in tension), this may indeed be the key to future progress. Of course, the Kremlin should not be expected to yield very much on arms-related matters without, eventually, a similar response. But it should be remembered that this is simply a way of making a needed initial cut into a vicious circle. It is not always easy to discern clearcut chronological sequences in the referent world, and one should not expect to see linkage strategies of an entirely pure type either; nevertheless, the following scenario might represent a promising set of steps.

In a first instance, the United States would offer the Soviets a significant concession in the economic realm (for example, import credits or an access to desired technology). The Soviets, recognizing the weight of their economic problems (and not experiencing intensified security fears), decide that this sort of assistance is worth a meaningful gesture in the military realm and consent to a reduction in their "heavy" missiles or armored units in Europe. Washington, in turn, reciprocates with an adequate curb on its own arms-race activity and blunts anticipated political opposition by pointing to the previous Soviet move. This could proceed through several iterations, with a concurrent U.S. policy for mitigating the temporary effects of economic dislocations through energetic support for conversion efforts. Eventually, the experience of the several steps taken jointly along the path of arms limitation might dissipate some portion of mutual hostility and distrust (at least that which does not serve an immediate bureaucratic or political purpose) making subsequent steps less and less painful.

This may not be the *only* scenario of a progression in the right direction, but it does flow most naturally from the major propositions and conclusions of this study. Still, one should guard against undue optimism. The initial step would involve a measure of political courage by decision makers on both sides—this may not be forthcoming. Even if this initial linkage (a Soviet military concession in exchange for a U.S. economic gesture) is established, domestic opposition may block the U.S. administration from responding with an instance of its own military restraint. Furthermore, conversion may take longer than expected and the economic dislocations could be more serious, in the short run, than anticipated. The composition of the Politburo might change in a decidedly hawkish direction as a result of the imminent generational turnover. Therefore, there is no reason to be smug about this approach, and all that might be said is that, under the circumstances, we may have more reason to be pessimistic about the chances of most other conceivable strategies.

THE ROLE OF FRIGHT

I have suggested two ways of dealing with the mutual hostility of the superpowers and, while the second approach appears more promising, efforts on both fronts are certainly desirable. Still, these do not exhaust the range of paths toward arms limitation and at least one more way of transcending the effects of this hostility must be recognized. Fear is a significant motivating force in the behavior of various social entities; often, in fact, dread acts more effectively than inducements do. Moreover, when applied to our current concerns, this is something that can theoretically permeate the domestic setting of both nations in a rather uniform manner. If the various bureaucratic, political, and economic interests that, on one side or the other, sustain the arms race were to be acted on directly, then virtually as many policies would be necessary as there are organized interests. Each group would clamor for alternative forms of satisfaction and very many would have to be indulged or, somehow, restrained. While interests are manifold, fear, for its part, operates rather uniformly—across the board so to speak. Of course, this proposition should not be pushed too far, since even death and destruction do not have a perfectly identical meaning for everyone. Also, different groups and individuals will, even at the very brink, assign different probabilities to the actual occurrence of disaster. Nevertheless, as long as a nuclear holocaust appeared imminent but not inevitable, one would anticipate a much intensified dread, a repugnance at the situation into which we have led ourselves, and a desperate resolve to do better if given the chance.

As an illustration, it seems evident that the Cuban missile crisis of 1962 had a salutary (though ephemeral) effect on both sides' determination to achieve a meaningful measure of arms control, a determination that appeared all but absent during the years immediately preceding the events. Although Cold War crises were not new (indeed the upheaval over Berlin had barely subsided), a direct threat of nuclear confrontation had not yet been experienced. But in October 1962, the discovery of Soviet missile emplacements in Cuba and the military action threatened by the United States led to a situation for which Chairman Khrushchev observed that "the smell of burning pervaded the air," and wherein President Kennedy estimated that the odds of a disaster claiming some 100 million lives on both sides were "between one out of three and even."[5] While it did bring the world to the brink of the precipice, the fright engendered by the crisis also jolted the superpowers out of their lethargy on matters of military restraint.

The need to limit nuclear tests had been a major issue in this area during the precrisis years but very little progress had been made. A major stumbling block had been the Soviet unwillingness to permit on-site inspections by the United States. By December of 1962, however, Khrushchev made a major concession by agreeing to permit two or three inspections on Soviet soil every year to determine compliance with the desired test ban.[6] By the following June, Kennedy delivered a major and unusual speech in which he emphasized the USSRs abhorrence toward war and recognized that nation's past sufferings and current achievements. On July 25, 1963, the Limited Test Ban Treaty, which prohibited the testing of nuclear weapons under water, in the atmosphere, and in outer space, was signed. There were other developments as well. Six months after the Cuban scare, the Hot Line was established between the White House and the Kremlin as a significant gesture at arms control and crisis management. Within the next few years, efforts were made at establishing a framework for limiting the spread of nuclear weapons (the Treaty on the Non-Proliferation of Nuclear Weapons was signed in 1968) and the first serious talks on limiting strategic missiles were undertaken in 1967. By the end of the decade, the momentum created by the Cuban crisis had been exhausted, but the institutions for arms limitation had been created and, even after the memories of the near-holocaust had dimmed, some halting progress was registered on the basis of the course it had charted.

Instructive though this example might be, it is hardly a guide to action. Although the impact of intense alarm may be considerable, and while crises can be provoked, no rational policy maker would opt for this path toward arms control or disarmament. War was averted in 1962—judicious decisions and self-restraint characterized both sides during the crucial hours—but we may not always be so fortunate. Nevertheless, if the arms race (and its strategic component in particular) is ever to be significantly curbed or reversed, this may well be because of the wisdom acquired through a brush with nuclear disaster.

NEGOTIATING ARMS CONTROL

This chapter (and the previous one) have focused on methods of countering or neutralizing the drives behind the arms race. Let us now assume that, despite the sheer magnitude of the task, the major internal and external issues had been dealt with successfully: arms limitation would still require that a number of "technical" (in the sense of not directly involving political or economic interests) problems be surmounted. A major decision at this stage would concern the object of the desired agreement—what, precisely, should be limited. At first sight, the answer seems obvious: what we wish to achieve is a reduction in military growth. Yet when we try to translate this into a direct object of negotiation, there are several possibilities.

In the first place, one could focus directly on the *physical output* of the arms race, on weapons and associated hardware that would be the object of comparable sacrifices on both sides. While physical output limitation (POL) has been the most frequently chosen approach, it is not the only possibility. A second strategy could involve a logically prior stage of the process by seeking to limit the *economic resources* available for the pursuit of the arms race. Military expenditure limitation (MEL) would be the goal and would take the form of curbs on the financial inputs on which military growth depends—nipping it in the bud so to speak. Finally, one could adopt a rather different tack by focusing on the *final* "good" that the arms race yields—in other words, one would be concerned with direct restraints on the capacity to destroy. While the limitation of destructive capacity (DCL) is implicit in the other two approaches, here it is the primary and explicit object of an agreement and the other limitations (on hardware and money) follow as a consequence of negotiated ceilings on this capacity. Finally, one could proceed in a rather indirect fashion by seeking to ban, not the purchase or production of weapons, but their testing.

Direct Limits on Physical Output:

The negotiation of quantitative limits on various items of military force is the most obvious approach to the task at hand and the one with which we have the most experience. SALT I, for example, placed a numerical ceiling on both Soviet and United States ICBM launchers. SALT II sought *overall* limits on each side's strategic arsenal with specific sublimits on different categories of weapons within the aggregate figure. The Mutual Force Reduction (MFR) talks in Vienna also bear on limits of men and military material, and so forth. While POL may be the intuitively obvious strategy, it does have its shortcomings: on the whole, this may be the approach that holds the best promise of producing *some* results in the area of arms limitation but provides the least promise of producing a substantial impact. A close scrutiny reveals the major problems and pitfalls and suggests that progress along this path may be quite arduous beyond the first several steps.

The major difficulty (but not the only one) involves the lack of a standard for comparing (and hence balancing) the limits imposed on the two sides. The military needs and productive capabilities of any two nations are never quite the same; thus they adopt different force postures and procure weaponry of different descriptions and composition. Were this not the case, *identical* limitations on physical output could be sought with neither party bearing a disproportionate sacrifice—the only question would be how far to go. As matters stand, one is faced with the difficult task of matching the reductions which, in turn, involves a series of comparisons of the "apples versus oranges" sort. Indeed, it is this problem that best explains the glacial progress of the negotiations leading to SALT II (which lasted seven years before an agreement was signed) and why the Interim Offensive Arms Agreement (the strategic-missile side of SALT I) left room for so much dissatisfaction.

SALT I set a ceiling of 1,054 launchers for the United States while permitting the Soviet Union a total of 1,618. This may seem, at first glance, to have conferred an unfair advantage to the Soviets, but the background of the negotiations suggests otherwise. Initially, Moscow felt that U.S. Forward-Based Systems (FBSs) should be included in the negotiations[7] since they are capable of hitting the Soviet homeland from their European deployment sites. The Soviet Union was also interested in curbs on the MIRVing of U.S. missiles since, even if the number of launchers was balanced,[8] the United States could still destroy a considerably larger number of USSR targets than vice versa. Since no limits were placed on FBSs, and the agreement did not seek limits on warheads, it was inevitable that the Soviet Union should have been allowed some edge in terms of overall missile launchers. Even so, the compromise could not be viewed as *demonstrably* fair toward either side, since the extent to which a certain number of single-warhead ICBMs could be considered the equivalent of some quantity of multiple-warhead vehicles and FBSs had not been established.

Nevertheless, the discrepancy in numbers of strategic-missile launchers was immediately seized upon by U.S. opponents of SALT as evidence of the treaty's inequitable nature. Prominent among the opponents was Senator Henry Jackson who insisted that *equal* ceilings be placed on intercontinental strategic forces in future negotiations. Ultimately, SALT II's limit on 2,250 strategic-delivery vehicles provided such equality, but Senator Jackson and his followers deemed this treaty also unfair since it did not, in their opinion, reduce the number of Soviet "heavy" missiles sufficiently.

The point is that a mutually acceptable standard of comparison is extremely difficult to achieve with POL. In both rounds of SALT, the extent to which the Soviet edge in "heavy" missiles was balanced by the U.S. lead in MIRVed missiles and long-range bombers was argued by the representatives of both countries. In any subsequent round of talks, a question that will surely be asked is what United States FBSs can appropriately be exchanged for; another problem will involve the terms of exchange between megatonnage and accuracy.

If the issues seem complex with respect to strategic weaponry, they must be even more formidable when conventional weapons, which are more various and numerous, are considered. Under the circumstances, the lack of discernible progress in the MFR talks should come as no surprise. The point is not that it is necessarily *impossible* to establish standards of equivalence between dissimilar force components; the point is that one-to-one comparisons are arduous, lack prominent solutions, and make negotiations extremely slow and frustrating for both parties. In fact, the development of new weapons often manages to outstrip the negotiated limits on earlier systems.

In addition to the problem of establishing standards of equivalence, there is another pitfall associated with the POL approach. It is not at all unusual that limits on certain types of systems should be compensated for, by both sides, with increases in weapons that have not been limited by mutual agreement. As a result, there may be little *aggregate* effect on the arms race despite the agreement. This is occasionally referred to as the "balloon" effect and is reflected, for example, in SALT II curbs, which are offset by the development of MX missiles or the planned deployment of the Pershing II system in Europe. In one variant of this problem, the signatories do not develop new weapons but simply introduce significant qualitative ameliorations to those that the agreement does not seek to eliminate. Unfortunately, constraints on *properties* are invariably harder to negotiate than on *numbers*; quantitative trade barriers between nations (tariffs, quotas), for example, are much easier to scale down than are those of a qualitative nature (for example, performance or safety requirements). One solution would be to settle on standards whereby a modified earlier system becomes an altogether new one, and to bar these completely (as SALT II attempted to do). Still, the definition on "newness" is elusive and may be blurred by a series of relatively imperceptible and incremental modifications. As a Soviet SALT II negotiator remarked when restraints on new missile guidance systems were being discussed, "If we change a steel screw for a brass screw, does that make an old system into a new one?"[9]

An important advantage of POL is that the verification of compliance with negotiated curbs is often feasible, as is currently the case with the strategic weaponry (although developments of new systems may, once again, outrun technical capacities for monitoring their characteristics and numbers). Despite its intuitively attractive nature, therefore, the approach has inherent and serious short-comings. It does have one advantage but, clearly, there is a need to expand the repertoire of available approaches.

The Limitation of Military Expenditures

Arms limitation via restrictions on defense budgets involves a focus on inputs rather than outputs and is interesting in a number of ways. One *apparent* advantage is that money is among the most general of metrics, providing a basis for the direct comparison of programs and equipment of different sorts. This, in turn, should facilitate the task of balancing sacrifices on both sides and obviate a major problem associated with POL.

Another facet of MEL is that, by stemming the overall flow of financial resources into the military sector, its restrictions may be more encompassing than those typically generated by POL. One result is that "balloon" effects are less likely to present a significant problem. Indeed, this may be the ideal way to deal with the difficult problem of *qualitative* improvement since spending limits will check the research and development on which ameliorations and modifications depend.

Most of the support for this approach has come from the Soviet Union,[10] which has made over 20 proposals in this area since 1948. A particularly explicit plan was submitted at the 1973 General Assembly of the United Nations by Andrei Gromyko, who suggested that permanent members of the Security Council reduce their military budgets by 10 percent (and apply the savings to foreign aid for developing nations). However, the United States and its allies have not embraced MEL with much enthusiasm and have indicated a number of major problems with this tactic. The principal issue, from their point of view, involves the difficulty of assessing actual Soviet defense spending, and this problem illustrates the strategy's pitfalls.

To begin with, there is a surprising amount of ambiguity and variance in the way military budgets are defined. For example, some nations include the cost of scientific research but others do not; while benefits for war veterans are considered relevant items by certain countries, they are excluded by others; some consider it appropriate to include outlays for paramilitary forces, while others think it inappropriate. In the United States, the costs of procuring atomic warheads had traditionally been part of the budget of the Atomic Energy Commission rather than the Department of Defense. A single figure for defense is published in the State Budget of the Soviet Union which, almost certainly, represents only a fraction of what is defined as defense spending in the United States and seems to include solely the costs of military procurement and maintenance.[11]

Mel would surely be a fruitless approach without some understanding of what should legitimately be included in a military budget. Achieving a consensus may not, however, be a prohibitive task. Following Gromyko's 1973 proposal, the Secretary General of the United Nations appointed a group of experts to deal with the problem. A major contribution of the ensuing study was the design of a standard accounting model for reporting national defense spending which included a comprehensive list of military categories and expenditure across three time horizons.[12] The definitional problems are thus not insurmountable and should not be viewed as a major obstacle to the implementation of this particular strategy.

There are other problems. Since the aim of MEL is to curb actual military growth, the effect of price increases for weapons should be taken into account. The deflators habitually used for intertemporal comparisons of various spending categories under inflationary conditions do not necessarily provide an adequate index of changing *military* costs—a deflator for this specific task should therefore be devised. However, this too is a feasible task that pales when compared with the related issue of *international* comparisons of military costs. The dilemma, known by economists as the index-number problem, derives in this case from the existense of two different, but equally valid, measures of comparative military spending: one expressed in U.S. prices (and dollars), the other expressed in Soviet prices (and rubles). Each yields a different picture of the respective magnitudes of the superpowers' military efforts and thus, a different statement of the gap between the two. Unfortunately, exchange rates are virtually meaningless where the price of military goods is concerned (since these rates are determined by the relative prices of goods that are *habitually* traded) and are particularly meaningless where one set of prices is administratively set.

The essence of the matter is that both nations seek to acquire those goods and services that correspond not only to their respective strategic inclinations but also to their different resource endowments and advantages. Thus U.S. military activity and production relies comparatively more on capital and technology (which is more readily available and cheaper in the United States than in the Soviet Union) while the Soviet Union's involves more manpower (which is much less costly in the latter country). However, if Soviet military costs were to be estimated in U.S. prices, they would appear significantly greater than if this were done on the basis of USSR prices. Likewise, the valuation of the U.S. defense effort in ruble prices would produce precisely the same effect. While neither solution is intrinsically more valid, the choice of one over the other could have substantial political consequences.

It is noteworthy, for example, that the estimates of Soviet military outlays most often used in the United States are based on U.S. prices and expressed in dollars. These figures are regularly generated and updated by the CIA,[13] which uses an indirect approach: in the first stage, intelligence estimates on Soviet weapons, programs, and missions are collected, in the second stage, the dollar-cost of producing the same level of defense output in the United States is computed, and the aggregate figure is taken as a measure of USSR defense spending.

The bias inheres in the attribution of U.S. prices to a force composed according to Soviet comparative advantage. Military manpower, which is inexpensive in the Soviet Union, amounts to about 4.5 million men and is a major component of that nation's force posture. When it is prices according to pay scales applicable to the U.S. volunteer army, the defense budget is overstated. There may be other upward biases that would affect dollar *or* ruble estimates but, these figures should be interpreted with the necessary caveats, even assuming that the CIA does not err upward in its intelligence estimates and that the generally superior quality of U.S. equipment and training are adequately controlled for when prices are assigned. That the decision to use the dollar estimates produces significant political effects is evidenced by the fact that one of the major justifications for the current (and projected) swell in rates of U.S. military spending is, precisely, the Soviet spending lead that these figures portray. In a critical analysis of these estimates, an U.S. specialist on USSR economic and fiscal policy has concluded that:

> There would appear to be little basis, at present, for claiming that either nation is currently outspending the other on defense. Since the USSR spends more in a dollar comparison and we spend more in a ruble comparison—and dollar and ruble comparisons are equally valid—who outspends whom is indeterminate. [14]

Nevertheless, *some* common standard for the valuation of military spending will certainly be needed if a negotiated reduction, either by an absolute amount or as a percentage from an initial base, is to be achieved. An intuitively appealing rule (and one that has been used in other contexts) would be to rely on the *geometric mean* of the dollar and ruble figures. [15] More complex metrics could be devised if necessary, but the main point is that this problem is difficult but not *irresolvable*. A first step in the right direction might be to rely on an independent international body (similar to the United Nations Group of Experts) on the Reduction of Military Budgets, which devised the common definition and standard reporting instrument for military budgets) that, immune from immediate political pressures, could suggest a reasonable technical solution to the parties.

The major stumbling block associated with MEL is that of *verifying compliance*. Even with a standard definition of relevant items of expenditure, there is a real possibility that portions of actual defense spending would be hidden within the budgets of civilian bodies. This would appear to be a particular problem with respect to USSR outlays where much of this spending is even now camouflaged in other budgetary categories. In addition to a common definition of relevant expenditure types and a common metric for comparing them, verification requires supporting data on financial and physical flows. This, in turn, would imply significantly expanded United States access, not only to Soviet budgetary information but also to information concerning possible nonbudgetary sources of defense financing (such as the retained profits of state enterprises, the records of the State Bank or Gosbank, etc.). In short, this would involve a level of intrusiveness that Moscow would probably not consider compatible with its security but that Washington would, in all likelihood, consider essential.

Another possible problem should be mentioned. While a tendency for limitations in one area to be offset by expansion in another may be obviated with this approach, it would still be possible to reallocate *existing* resources toward particularly deadly existing systems without violating the spending ceiling or introducing qualitatively new weapons. This may be a lesser problem than are "balloon" effects, but it is a problem nevertheless.

The Limitation of Destructive Capacity

If enhanced destructive capacity is the ultimate "good" sought through defense activity, then spending and physical output are its first and second components. Therefore, might not a common denominator for the superpowers' military power best be sought here (rather than at the level of money or weapons)? With this approach, final military capacity, expressed in terms of an index, would be the explicit object of negotiation. In what follows, I will limit the discussion to the strategic realm and try to highlight some attributes of this approach.

Assuming that the superpowers could, somehow, settle on a mutually acceptable index of overall strategic capcity, and if limitations were negotiated on this basis, the problem of comparing reductions would automatically be resolved. Since strategic nuclear destructiveness would be limited, "balloon" effects (at least within this realm) would be avoided and even reallocations of limited resources to particularly deadly weapons would have no point. As the index would be functionally related to items of physical output, verification would pose no greater a problem than it does with POL. Finally, this tack would allow political authorities on both sides some flexibility in choosing the items of force posture that would bear the brunt of the restrictions; this would enable them to adjust the specifics of implementation to their domestic economic and political situation.

The major intellectual challenge would involve the actual measure of strategic capacity and the task would be twofold. To begin with, the index would have to be devised. Secondly, it would have to be functionally related to specific strategic systems (missiles, bombers, etc.) so that limits on its value could, in turn, be translated into items of physical output and financial outlays. However, since there is a logical sequence here, and since the second task is considerably more straightforward, I will confine myself to outlining some preliminary thoughts on the steps involved in constructing an index of overall strategic capacity (ISC). The purpose is essentially illustrative and I certainly do not presume to provide the last word on this matter. A number of possible directions are suggested. For example, one could define strategic capacity in terms of the ability to destroy objects over a given *area*, which, in turn, depends on the total number of megatons delivered. With area of likely destruction as an indicator of capacity, and deliverable megatonnage as its operational approximation, direct limitations could be discussed by the superpowers. A problem, however, inheres in the fact that the destructive power of nuclear weapons is not a linear combination of their yield (since a few large bombs will usually create less damage than a larger number of small bombs). The usual solution to this is to think in terms of "equivalent megatons" (EMTs), each of which has the destructive potential of a single one-megaton bomb. This, in turn, is calculated as the two-thirds power of a weapon's total yield ($EMT=Y^{2/3}$). Taking the individual nuclear weapon as the building block of our index, EMTs could be summed across all weapons to provide a measure of overall strategic power.

The major disadvantage of a measure based exclusively on equivalent megatons is that the area of destruction to which it applies involves only large unprotected objects such as cities or industrial parks. In other words, the military potential thus described concerns mainly what are known as "soft-area" targets. Obviously, this is the sort of capacity associated with a retaliatory (deterrent) strategy rather than with one based on a first-strike potential against specific (and highly protected) military targets. These include missiles in thick concrete silos, protected command structures (usually underground), and the like, and may be referred to as "hard-point targets." Their destruction calls for considerable *accuracy* rather than brute megatonnage, which is usually measured in terms of Circular Error Probable (CEP), that is the radius within which at least half of the incoming warheads are expected to fall. If this were the only additional variable, yield and accuracy could be combined into a measure of countermilitary potential. Another consideration, however, is the degree of resistance to blast, or "hardness," of the targets and, in fact, major efforts to harden targets have been made by both sides. With this variable (H) included in the calculations, an index of the probability that a given weapon will destroy a "hard-area" target can be expressed as a joint function of $Y^{2/3}$, CEP, and H.

In addition to these two categories of targets, there is an intermediate class of "soft-point" targets: discrete but unprotected objects, such as an enemy radar station or a submarine in port. These are targets that are extremely vulnerable to an atomic blast in the general vicinity and can confidently be destroyed with virtually any of the attained levels of accuracy.

A fourth and, for present purposes, final category involves mobile targets and, principally, missile-armed submarines on patrol (which are very nearly invulnerable). These may be designated "mobile-point" targets for which the probability of destruction in a nuclear attack is virtually nil.

Thus there are four basic sets of targets at which a nuclear bomb could be directed and, clearly, the strategic capacity of any weapon will depend on the enemy's target structure as well as on the weapon's own properties. In other words, even if the weapon could destroy one of the four kinds of targets with near certainty, effective capacity would be little enhanced if the enemy did not possess that type of target. The fraction of the total target structure that each of the four sorts represents is, therefore, an important aspect of military potential.

With these thoughts in mind, strategic capacity per weapon (SC_w) can be represented by an equation of the following form:

$$SC_w = (P_{sa} * F_{sa}) + (P_{hp} * F_{hp}) + (P_{sp} * F_{sp}) + (P_{mp} * F_{mp})$$

where, P refers to the probability of destroying a given type of target, F represents its fraction of the total target structure of the enemy, the subscripts refer to the specific type of target in question and, obviously, $F_{sa} + F_{hp} + F_{sp} + F_{mp} = 1$.

Several reasonable assumptions could be introduced at this point. As "mobile-point" targets are virtually invulnerable, we can set $P_{mp} = 0$. Also, since just about any nuclear weapon delivered within the general vicinity would destroy a "soft-point" target, it can also be assumed the $P_{sp} = 1$. Furthermore, since the area within which soft targets will be destroyed is determined by the number of equivalent megatons that the weapon can deliver to the area, we will have $P_{sa} = f(Y^{2/3})$. This probability function, in turn, should have two properties: it should be positive and it should have zero and unity as its range of variation. A function that satisfies these requirements is $P_{sa} = 1 - (1[Y^{2/3} + 1])$.

Things are somewhat more complicated where P_{hp} is concerned, since this involves three independent variables and complex functional forms. There are several formulas that are potential candidates and, while additional work would be needed to sort out their respective merits, two seem especially promising. The first is based on analytic work done at the Heavy Military Electronics Systems division of General Electric and is reported by Davis and Schilling[16] as:

$$P_{hp} = 1 - \{EXP - 5.83 \ Y^{2/3} \ [H^{2/3} \ (CEP)^2]\}$$

The second formula has been proposed by Kosta Tsipis,[17] an MIT physicist:

$$P_{hp} = 1 - \{EXP - Y^{2/3} \ /[0.22 * H^{2/3} * (CEP)^2]\}$$

Using, for the moment, the first of the two formulas, a general index for strategic capacity for each weapon can be derived as:

$$SC_W = F_{sp} + \{1 - [1/(Y^{2/3} + 1)]\} \ (F_{sa})$$
$$+ \ [1 - (EXP - 5.83 \ \{Y^{2/3} \ [H^{2/3} \ (CEP)^2]\})] \ (F_{hp})$$

To obtain an index of *overall* national strategic capacity, the per-weapon index could be summed across all nuclear weapons within each side's arsenal (ISC = $\Sigma_w SC_x$). Agreements could then directly address the question of balanced ceilings on ISC. With a formula of this (or a similar) kind, general curbs could be translated into specific restraints on items of physical output by each side. The countries would decide, partly on the basis of domestic economic and political considerations, which combinations of weapons would bear the brunt of the limitations.

The formula was provided for essentially illustrative purposes— to outline the logic behind nuclear potential—and a more complex and polished variant would probably be needed. As with the issue of measuring military spending, it may be wise to have an independent international body of experts work out most of the technical aspects of computation. At the moment, the task does not seem too formidable as far as *strategic* capacity goes. However, it may become more and more forbidding if the arms race progresses to new heights. For example, an MX system, or even a moderately effective ABM system, would complicate the task considerably as would, for example, significant advances in antisubmarine warfare. Plainly, the costs of waiting are considerable.

This approach, moreover, may not be applicable to other spheres of military competition. In particular, the far greater diversity and more various nature of conventional weapons, and of their target structures and missions, would seem to make this task inappropriate in that area.

The limitation of destructive capacity is not a definitive solution to the problems that hobble arms limitation negotiations; it may, nevertheless, be less inadequate than others in the strategic realm and should, in any case, be viewed as one more avenue along which solutions could be sought. At this point, the reader may be far more impressed with the difficulties that must face any efforts at controlling the arms race than with the chances that they will be successful. Even if far more political will had been mustered than has ever been the case so far, progress would seem sure to be slow and arduous. But we have not yet quite exhausted the list of possibilities.

The Test Ban Approach

While it may seem a circuitous way of going about things, the idea of checking military growth by prohibiting the testing of new weapons is not altogether new and is best known in the form of endeavours at achieving a nuclear test ban. The initial agreement to forbid all but underground nuclear explosions was guided at least as much by the fear of fallout as by the desire for arms limitation; nevertheless, it did set the superpowers on a path that they could have benefited from by pursuing it more zealously.

The basic notion here is that, given the greater technological complexity of each new generation of strategic weapons, their ultimate characteristics can only be known, and their performance levels honed, with extensive testing. If both sides agreed to forego such testing, fewer new weapons would be developed and the qualitative arms race at least could be substantially dampened. But this may not be the only, and perhaps not even the major, benefit that such an agreement would provide. Another important and immediate boon could be a reduction in crisis instability, that is, in the temptation for both sides to be the first to use their nuclear weapons in situations of exceptional tension. Thus, independently even of the issue of limiting arms, it should be useful to diminish the probability that they would be used.

Bombs, for example, are subject to storage-induced deterioration over time, and occasional tests are necessary to determine the nature and extent of such damage as well as the best means of remedying it. If such "proof testing" could not be undertaken, neither side might have sufficient confidence in its ability to launch a successful preemptive strike and would impute a similar lack of assurance to its adversary. As a result, the likelihood of an acute crisis producing an all-out nuclear war would be significantly diminished.

Nor is a ban on detonations the only relevant tack within this general approach. Another possibility would be to prohibit, or seriously limit, test-flights of nuclear missiles (ground-based missiles, SLBMs, and cruise missiles). Two sources of uncertainty might then confront the strategic planner: one concerning the reliability of the propulsion system, the other involving the performance of the guidance system. In the first case, the probability of a successful launch would decrease; in the second case, faith in the weapon's accuracy would be weakened. Not only would a full-scale pre-emptive strike be less likely, but the precision required for a controlled nuclear exchange could not be assumed under the circumstances. Both paths to a holocaust would thus be partially barred, to the benefit of not only the superpowers but of virtually every other nation as well.

There are problems however, and very much progress may be unlikely in the near future. To begin with, there is scant reason to believe that the strategic doctrines that so emphatically call for high levels of reliability and accuracy would abruptly be reversed to accomodate the imperatives of crisis stability. If the major benefit of a test ban is not recognized, it is not obvious why it should be sought. Even assuming that political authorities did experience a sudden enlightment on this score, domestic opposition to an arrangement that could virtually preclude the development of new types of strategic systems would certainly be formidable in both nations, and the fact that all problems of verification have not yet been completely resolved would provide valuable ammunition to such opposition. A final problem should also be understood. If the confidence of strategic planners in the performance of each individual weapon were to diminish sufficiently, there could be an incentive to compensate by increasing the *number* of weapons that could be directed each individual target. Thus the quantitative arms race could actually be accelerated by the expanded deployment of systems that had already been developed.

None of this suggests that the idea of a broad test ban should not be vigorously pursued; the issue is simply that not all eggs should be placed in this particular basket.

TOWARD AN ECLECTIC APPROACH

While each of the strategies concerning a direct object of negotiation had some attractive feature, none was appealing in every respect. Because of this, they should probably be used in a complementary and selective fashion to counter the shortcomings of one by the advantages of another.

Although the third approach seemed to be the best response to the problem of strategic arms limitation, it could, under certain circumstances, benefit from the availability of POL. For instance, it may be that the overall level of strategic capacity could be reduced, but both sides would, nevertheless, retain some weapons that were, for psychological reasons perhaps particularly *destabilizing*. It might then be useful to negotiate a separate reduction for that particular category of arms or to prohibit its further testing.[18] Another example in this general vein should be mentioned; if an acceptable formuls for ISC were achievable only if one type of weapon (e.g., the MX missile) were abandoned, separate negotiations on this weapon would be a necessary prerequisite to an agreement in terms of overall strategic capacity.

If physical output limitations provided the basis for arms-limitation talks, MEL might also be necessary to control some obvious forms of "balloon" effects. If MEL provided the context for negotiations, but there was a belief that reduced budgets would leave the most *deadly* systems intact, then a ceiling on permissible SC_W could also be sought. Or if one feared that a quantitative proliferation of certain weapons would follow a test ban, POL may be invoked to obviate this damage.

Various choices are possible but one thing is certainly clear: a disregard for the gamut of available opportunities has penalized virtually all arms-limitation talks to date. In any case, a willingness to attempt novel approaches will be likely to benefit from simultaneous efforts to deal with the circumstances surrounding mutual hotility. It may be here that political will and foresight shall be most severely tested.

NOTES

1. For example, see Dean G. Pruitt, "Definition of the Situation as a Determinant of International Action," in Herbert C. Kelman, ed., *International Behavior: A Social Psychological Analysis* (New York: Holt, Rinehart and Winston, 1966), pp. 391-432; Robert Jervis, "Hypotheses on Misperception," *World Politics* 20 (1968):454-79.
2. Notably, Charles E. Osgood, *An Alternative to War or Surrender* (Urbana: University of Illinois Press), especially chap. 5. Morton Deutsch, "A Psychological Basis for Peace," in Quincy Wright, et al., eds., *Preventing World War III* (New York: Simon and Schuster, 1962) is in a similar vein, as is Jerome Frank, *Sanity and Survival* (New York: Random House, 1967).
3. Osgood, op.cit., pp. 91-92.
4. David Singer, "Disarmament: The Domestic and Global Context," in John H. Gilbert, ed., *The New Era in American Foreign Policy* (New York: St.

Martin's Press, 1973) pp. 179-80.

5. Quoted in Graham T. Allison, *The Essence of Decision* (Boston: Little, Brown, 1971), p. 1.

6. Eventually, this offer fell through.

7. For the evolution of the Soviet position on this, see John H. Barton and Lawrence D. Weiler, *International Arms Control: Issues and Agreements* (Stanford, Calif.: Stanford University Press, 1976), chap. 9.

8. The SALT decision to place curbs on launchers rather than on the projectiles themselves was dictated by the issue of verification.

9. Quoted by Strobe Talbott, *Endgame: The Inside Story of SALT II* (New York: Harper & Row, 1979), p. 162.

10. Apparently, the first initiative aimed at arms control via restrictions on military spending was made by Imperial Russia at the Hague Peace Conference in 1899.

11. There is, however, no way of verifying this.

12. See *Reduction of Military Budgets: Measurement and Reporting of Military Expenditures*, Report of the Secretary General, A/31/222, United Nations, New York, 1977. A detailed description of the rationale behind the proposal is provided by Abraham S. Becker, *Military Expenditure Limitation for Arms Control: Problems and Prospects* (Cambridge, Mass.: Ballinger, 1977).

13. For example, Central Intelligence Agency, *A Dollar Cost Comparison of Soviet and U.S. Defense Activities, 1966-76*, Washington, D.C., January 1978.

14. Franklyn D. Holzman, "Are the Soviets Really Outspending the U.S. on Defense?" *International Security* 4 (1980):99-100.

15. In this case, this would amount to the square root of the product of the dollar and ruble figures.

16. Lynn E. Davis and Warner R. Schilling, "All You Ever Wanted to Know About MIRV and ICBM Calculations But Were Not Cleared to Ask," *Journal of Conflict Resolution* 17 (1972):217-43.

17. Kosta Tsipis, "Minuteman Invulnerability," *Science*, November 2, 1979, p. 510.

9

A FINAL VIEW

We have covered a fair amount of ground and are approaching the end of this study. Its goal, as stated in the introductory chapter, has been to: examine the principal causal processes behind the arms race; place some of our beliefs in sharper perspective; and suggest certain steps that might stem the headlong accumulation of an increasingly awesome destructive capacity, which is acquired at an ever-greater price and yields no evident gains to security. It is particularly necessary to confront the problem at a time when it seems more acute than it has been for some years. During much of the 1970s, we were led to entertain overly ambitious expectations about the future. History has whisked us too fast through a period that seemed to presage a willingness to embark on new paths. Hopes were understandably raised only to be swiftly dashed. SALT I and the Vladivostok Accord, while unimpressive in themselves, were assumed to be the first steps along a road to much better things. U.S.-Soviet relations displayed an altogether novel quality of maturity and vision. The trauma of Vietnam created a virtually unprecedented skepticism in the United States concerning the value of military force and lavish defense budgets as solutions to international problems.[1] This brief era seems to have ended and, for the time being at least, we must recognize the reversion to an earlier and less auspicious state of affairs. As before, national security is being reduced to its military dimension, and the accepted solution to external challenges is to produce more weapons, develop more thorough techniques of mass destruction, and increase outlays on the armed forces. Yet it is unlikely that future problems will be any more amenable to coercive solutions than were those of the past or that security will not depend on circumstances of a different nature. At the very least, national security depends as much on the relative absence of the potential for conflict as on an assumed ability to prevail in conflict. This is particularly true since the notion of prevailing is meaningless in a nuclear context. Moreover, since a trained predilection to think in military terms impairs nations' ability to transcend (or even to substantially mitigate) antagonisms through creative solutions, security may actually suffer as a result. Furthermore, it should be realized that the national interest is also a matter of satisfying the tangible needs of one's citizenry and that few normative orders manage to escape unscathed when serious economic deterioration sets in. The Soviet Union will soon have to face up to the obvious costs with which the arms race is burdening its economy; in the United States, these costs may have been obscured by short-term gains but, here too, they may become increasingly apparent (and the recent stress on "supply-side" economics, with its concern for the effects of excessive fiscal burdens on investment and productivity, may hasten the process).

The dangers of the arms race are substantial, and an awareness of this fact should provide the motivation to do something about it; a grasp of its fundamental causes, however, should guide the choice of methods. If its sources remain a mystery, policy will be misdirected and an unfortunate impression of inevitability may come to dominate our perceptions.

To fully understand the problem, it must be realized that social structures and processes often have functions that are distinct from those with which popular beliefs and official pronouncements endow them. Thus, if one were to think of the arms race exclusively in terms of responses to mutual challenges, some of the most pertinent requirements of remedial policy might be missed, and the wrong questions would often be formulated. For example, it is often asked whether peace must precede disarmament or vice versa and, prima facia, this may seem like the crucial question. However, if defense programs serve powerful endogenous needs, a mellowing of international relations may produce a rather slight effect on military growth. Thus policies should be aimed at both the internal and the external front if they are to be more than mere rituals. Social science too will make a useful contribution only if it applies its tools to both areas.

Accordingly, this book has sought to point out that, within both superpowers, there are groups for which the arms race is, by virtue of their interests, a solution rather than a problem. It has attempted to identify these groups, to compare them where appropriate, and to discuss their implications for efforts at achieving military restraint. Two sets of internal pressures seemed especially prominent on the United States side: those that stem from the pursuit of short-term macroeconomic benefits related to defense activities and those that flow from the claims of organizations whose status, responsibilities, and influence depend on the magnitude of the nation's military programs. For the Soviets, this latter sort of pressure is equally relevant, but economic circumstances are far more likely to play an inhibiting than a stimulating role. Therefore, in addition to whatever else one may attempt, effective policy should contain measures relevant to the domestic arena.

It is not being asserted that these propositions are necessarily novel, and the aim in the early chapters was not so much to discover that which had eluded others as to sift through extant beliefs, bring the more plausible hypotheses together in a distilled form, and erect an analytical framework that could shed a more focused light on the arms race, and thus suggest the strategies for restraining it. For example, if economic needs lie beneath the surface of certain forms of military activity, an important component of effective policy would be to facilitate a smooth conversion of military-industrial facilities to civilian production. If vested bureaucratic interests challenge governments' arms limitation efforts, then this obstacle too should be addressed as a matter of explicit policy. These are substantial tasks and national leaders who seek to restrain the arms race will need the support of domestic allies whose own influence might help counteract the power of promilitary interests. While the top leadership's control may be tighter in the Soviet Union, such help would surely facilitate things and would probably be sought from the ranks of those who bear the brunt of the defense burden: most notably the branches of industry that lose most from the military's privileged claim on financial, scientific, and managerial resources, as well as the "modernists" who consider access to Western technology and credits a matter of higher priority than Cold War rhetoric. These are the most likely sources of support for the moderates in the Kremlin who think it possible to cooperate with the "realists" in the capitalist world and who do not tend to view the international "correlation of forces" exclusively in military terms. The situation is somewhat different in the United States where the opportunity costs of defense are more muted and are visible mainly in the long run. Under these circumstances, it is harder to identify groups whose self-interest disposes them to lobby against expanded defense programs and procurement.

Certain organizations, such as the Center for Defense Information, the Arms Control Association, and the National Committee for a Sane Nuclear Policy (SANE), actively support arms control and engage in very useful informational work, but they are formed on the basis of a shared awareness of the deleterious consequences of the arms race rather than on the basis of direct self-interest. Despite considerable dedication, their effectiveness is limited by modest organizational and financial resources relative to those of groups on the other side.

It should once again be stressed at this point that it would be unwise to slight the role of the mutual hostility that links the superpowers by placing too exclusive an emphasis on internal dynamics. The resulting fear and distrust force each side to be attentive to movements by the other; they provide an authentically perceived need for increased military capacity as well as a convenient justification for indulging domestic interests. In this fashion, moreover, the external and internal context of the arms race is connected by an obvious feedback loop. Thus a material decline in bilateral hostility would strengthen the position of leaders committed to military restraint by depriving their opponents of the source of the rationalizations with which they cloak the pursuit of their own zeal. It may, nevertheless, be very hard to eliminate this hostility to the point where such rationalizations can be completely discredited. There are objective conflicts of interest between the superpowers and, in any case, these very groups also have the ability to impede détente. While I discussed these matters in Chapter 8, it could still be argued that the conclusion is too bleak. After all, few would have predicted several decades ago that France and Germany would soon enjoy the intimate relationship that they now do. In the 1960s, it would have seemed inconceivable that the United States and the People's Republic of China would be the quasi-allies that, in certain respects, they now are. While it is true that nations that had once been considered irreconcilable have experienced a radical reversal in their relationship, this seems to have been dependent on two crucial conditions. In the first place, they may have discovered a common enemy more threatening to both than they are to each other and decided to cooperate in confronting the common threat. Secondly, at least one side may have undergone fundamental internal changes, making the parties less alien to each other (and possibly weakening the domestic influence of those most opposed to a rapprochement). In the example of France and Germany, both circumstances have been amply present since World War II; in the case of the United States and China, a common fear of the Soviet Union has satisfied the first condition and the reforms of the post-Mao era have substantially mitigated political extremism in China. As for the United States and the Soviet Union, it is not likely that either will experience much internal restructuring in the near future. Moreover, the only remotely conceivable scenario that could provide them with a common enemy would involve a serious deterioration of United States relations with China—a contingency that should be neither expected nor desired.

The long run may yet bring surprises but it would be hard, in the near future, to completely purge superpower relations of the hostility that has characterized them for so long. Fear and distrust will surely experience ebbs and flows occasioned by changes of political incumbents as well as other circumstances, and arms control will feel the influence of such fluctuations. Even at the trough of these cyclical movements, however, there is likely to be enough underlying hostility to give *some* modicum of plausibility to the eloquently formulated arguments of those most strongly endowed with a martial spirit. These arguments may not stand up to a thorough appraisal of their merits but, as we are aware, their effectiveness is not always contingent on this ability. Arms limitation would have to countenance a measure of tension and incompatibility between the two nations; however, this problem may not be insurmountable. For example, U.S. economic inducements may be used to obtain some Soviet military restraint, which might relieve (though certainly not eliminate) arms-race pressures within the United States. The inducements would be offered in a purely pragmatic spirit, and the economic benefits would have to confer roughly symmetrical absolute economic advantages of the two nations (to make this politically palatable). But the marginal utility of any economic gain would almost surely be greater for the Soviets, making the exercise of military circumspection worthwhile.

While helpful policies may be available, past achievements have been extremely disappointing. Habitually, such paltry accomplishments as the Vladivostok Accord or the Threshold Test Ban have been justified as merely the first steps toward much more ambitious goals. But by choosing to accomplish only that which encounters minimal resistance, the causal circumstances behind military growth have remained unchallenged and unaltered. Subsequent efforts to go to meaningful lengths then founder on the unsolved problems and the illusion of progress that had been previously created yields to disillusioned cynicism. The idea of progressive motion toward continuously bigger achievements is, nevertheless, quite sound:

arms limitation should not be viewed as an end-state but as a process involving successive steps, each of which represents a meaningful advance. For this to occur, however, some portion of the drives behind the arms race must be neutralized each time. Furthermore, success should be gauged with respect to the overall prior situation rather than with respect to the specific arms-control accomplishment of the previous step. For example, it may be possible, in the next decade or so, to agree on significant cuts in fixed-site ICBMs (say by decreasing their number by 30 percent) and the superpowers might congratulate themselves on doing that which had previously seemed unattainable. Still, it is very likely that these missiles would have lost most of their strategic importance by that time because of the deployment of MX systems, cruise missiles, improved SLBMs, and so forth. Despite the cutbacks, the situation could actually be much worse than it had previously been, and claims of progress would be vacuous and misleading.

While progress will imply a readiness to address fundamental problems, it will also be necessary to be more innovative with respect to such issues as the selection of a direct object of negotiation. A broad and flexible grasp of all possibilities will certainly be needed, but a number of problems may be resolved by focusing the talks on an index of overall destructive capacity (which can accommodate a wide range of weapons). If the idea seems unrealistic, I suspect that this is partly because it does not have much of a history. Given the record of the more traditional approaches, however, it would be foolish to count this as an argument in its disfavor. Nor is the direct and bilateral approach to arms limitation the only acceptable strategy.

One piece of news that provided some recent ground for optimism was the report that the United States, Soviet Union, and United Kingdom in 1980 were rapidly approaching an agreement on a Comprehensive Test Ban (CTB), which would have prohibited all tests of nuclear explosives and thus eliminated the current exception (which is sufficient for most military purposes). While such a ban is usually discussed in terms of its restraining effect on nuclear proliferation, it may also have helped curb the Soviet-United States arms race by placing an effective obstacle to new types of warheads (since their development would require prior testing). It would not necessarily have discouraged the further multiplication of existing weapons (an agreement on the basis of an ISC would probably be needed for this) nor would it have precluded the development of new vehicles with existing warheads (for example, an MX system with a Mark 12a warhead). Nevertheless, it would have constrained the development of untested nuclear weapons and thus placed a type of qualitative ceiling on the arms race. In addition, existing weapons must be occasionally tested since they are vulnerable to storage-induced damage. Without adequate proof testing, their reliability would decrease which would, in turn, lessen the likelihood that either side would hazard a first strike directed against the other's arsenal. Enhanced strategic stability and a diminished probability of warfare would thus have been the payoff. A comprehensive test ban had, in one form or another, been under discussion for over 30 years, and it was encouraging to hear that an agreement seemed at hand. Subsequent political developments have more or less destroyed hopes for an agreement of this sort and, indeed, the outlook for arms limitation is more discouraging now than it had been for many years. The ascent of military interests, the dramatic increase in superpower tension and Cold War invective, and the increasing willingness to consider nuclear war as an instrument of foreign policy do not encourage optimism. Under these circumstances, and before the consequences of irresponsibility become irreversible, we should try to understand the nature of the predicament into which we have been led.

NOTES

1. See Bruce M. Russett, "The Americans' Retreat from World Power," *Political Science Quarterly* 1 (Spring 1975): 1-21; and Bruce M. Russett and Miroslav Nincic, "American Opinion on the Use of Military Force Abroad," *Political Science Quarterly* 91 (1976): 411-31.

NAME INDEX

SUBJECT INDEX

Accuracy of nuclear weapons: 95, 97; Counterforce doctrine and, 97; MAD doctrine and, 95

Anti-ballistic missile systems (ABMs), 188; Soviet as justification for U.S. MIRVs, 15, 17, 19, 95 (*see also* Strategic weapons)

Arms Control Association, 196

Arms Control Treaties and Talks, 8; ABM treaty, 3, 19; Comprehensive Test Ban, 4, 137, 177, 198; Limited Test Ban Treaty, 3, 177; Mutual Force Reduction Talks, 4, 178; Non-Proliferation Treaty, 5, 137, 177; SALT I, 178-179; SALT II, 4, 137, 178-79; Threshold Test Ban Treaty, 3, 197; Vladivostok Accord, 197

Arms Exports: balance of payment and (American) 125, 127-128; (Soviet) 124-126; dependence of recipient and, 118; domestic military costs and, 123-124; East-West rivalry and, 117-120; effectiveness as instrument of foreign policy, 120-122; exporters other than superpowers, 112; extent of sales by superpowers, 112-13; ideological compatability and, 119-120; regional power balances and, 119, 134; sophisticated weaponry and, 115; spare military-industrial capacity and, 122-123, 124-125; terms of superpower transfers, 112-114, 124-125

Arms Imports: changing composition of importers, 115-116; military regime and, 118-119, 128-130; multinational corporations and, 132-133; political stability of recipient and, 118, 120-121, 134-136; recipient foreign-exchange shortages and, 132, 133; recipient hostility to U.S. and, 120, 121; recipient infrastructural development and, 131; regional arms races and, 134; social costs to developing nations, 133; stimulant to industrial activity, 131-132

Arms Races: as action-reaction process (from American side) 10-14, 33, (from Soviet side) 59-60; 71-73; American public and, 5-6, 27, 55; bureaucratic momentum and (on American side) 19-21, 33, 159-161; (on Soviet side) 53, 60-63; interests of political authorities and, 25-26, 34, 69; inter-service military and, 21-22, 33; Keynes-

ABOUT THE AUTHOR

MIROSLAV NINCIC is assistant professor of Political Science at the University of Michigan in Ann Arbor. He publishes in the areas of international relations and peace research. His articles have appeared in a number of journals including the *Journal of Conflict Resolution* and the *Journal of Peace Research*. Professor Nincic holds an M.A. in International Relations and a Ph.D. in Political Science from Yale University.